Love and Trade War

Li Sheng • Dmitri Felix do Nascimento

Love and Trade War

China and the U. S. in Historical Context

palgrave
macmillan

Li Sheng
Faculty of Social Sciences
University of Macau
Macau, China

Dmitri Felix do Nascimento
Faculty of Social Sciences
University of Macau
Macau, China

ISBN 978-981-33-4896-7 ISBN 978-981-33-4897-4 (eBook)
https://doi.org/10.1007/978-981-33-4897-4

This Palgrave Macmillan imprint is published by the registered company Springer Nature Singapore Pte Ltd.
The registered company address is: 152 Beach Road, #21-01/04 Gateway East, Singapore 189721, Singapore

Preface

The aim of this book lies in various dimensions surrounding the conflicts that emerged from the trade war between the United States and China after the victory of Donald Trump (Republicans) in the 2016 American elections. Despite having a history of cooperation since the visit of Former Richard Nixon in the 1970s, the United States (U.S.) and the People's Republic of China (PRC) experienced different phases of the relationship until the second decade of the twenty-first century. Our focus is on finding elements that can explain the trade war, which started in the historical and dialectical perspective as a reaction process of U.S. trade and foreign policy that has China as the main actor in this confrontation.

The continuous process of the changing status of China's political and economic power, which accelerates after the rise of Xi Jinping in 2013, has led the country as a major international player, whether in international trade, finance, multilateral institutions, technological innovation, and military issues. The rise of China caused a change in posture in the bases of relations with the United States. In 2017, U.S. President Donald Trump instructed the U.S. Trade Representative (USTR) to investigate Chinese intellectual property rights violations, invoking Section 301 of the 1974 Trade Law. In 2018, the United States triggered the device of increasing tariffs on almost 50% of China's imports. The reasons, perspectives, reactions, and influence of the trade war on American domestic and foreign policy are part of our main concerns in writing this book.

In Chap. 1, "A Brief History of Trade Wars," this is an introduction to the history of trade wars. We will touch on the trade war that may have led to the Great Depression in the 1930s and the many trade wars since 1945. The interest in the subject of this introduction is derived from the ongoing trade wars between the United States and its important trading partners, such as China, the European Union (EU), and Japan, that started in 2018. As U.S. relations with these partners constitute the bedrock of global prosperity and stability, these trade wars will likely have a great impact on both the present and the future. Therefore, it is meaningful and important to begin with an introduction on this topic, which will act as the starting point for the whole line of logic in the book.

Additionally, some countries that are currently against globalization were pro-globalization in the past, so they have experienced a transition. In this process, changes in the society of these countries cannot be ignored. This section of the book will elaborate on how the seemingly insignificant complaints of blue-collar workers in the United States in the 1970s converged into the elective power of anti-globalization, which smoothed the way for the Trump presidency. Under the mantle of misrule, deindustrialization, surging inequality, and other ongoing politics and policies that foster misrule, U.S. citizens cannot evade their responsibility in the surging trade deficit of the United States. As the misrule is caused by the many politics and policies mentioned above, is it possible for one U.S. presidency to solve these problems in a short time through reindustrialization, even though this solution also feeds a self-damaging trade war? If the results are negative, what can a country such as the United States do?

In addition to establishing globalization as the reason for the current dilemma, this book will show how trade wars start and end, how states bargaining with each other over their interests can collaborate for better results, and how wise concessions can be made among smart politicians in the resolution processes. These three "how's" will be discussed, and then, in a discussion on the past experiences of ending trade wars, the question of whether the U.S. trade wars benefit or hamper the United States in resolving these problems is raised. If these trade wars do not help but instead hamper, why does the United States engage in them? Can the United States only give up on the trade war or take another action at the same time as giving up on the war? This topic will be discussed in the following chapters.

In Chap. 2, "On Sino-U.S. Trade Wars: A Dialectical Consideration," we wonder why Donald Trump starts a trade war with China knowing that this country is one of the United States' largest economic partners, as well as a recipient of foreign direct investment (FDI). We argue that there are two directions a country can choose to take when faces with a dilemma. One direction a country can take is blaming others for its own misrule; the country resorts to conflicting diplomacy to force others to accept its demands. This has been the technique of the Trump administration. In taking this direction, the accusing country may have a poor understanding of itself, and its misrule may deepen as it wastes time on blaming others rather than determining how to start domestic reform. The other direction a country can take is establishing its culpability in the dilemma. In this case, a country chooses to exert itself in reforming domestic affairs. This is the path that China has taken since its reform and opening up in 1978. In taking this direction, diplomacy and other countries are used as supplemental supports to help the country's reform.

We point out the problem of deindustrialization that both the United States and developed countries are going through. And the reasons Trump administration has given to pursue an economic policy with a protectionist bias, using economic barriers to preserve the interests of American companies and to consequently boost job creation, found support in domestic politics and received recognition from the electorate during the election. The ideological political composition of the Trump administration's first echelon influences the trade war with China, in the central ideas in *Scoring the Trump Economic Plan* of Peter Navarro and Wilbur Ross. Also, the role of the Office of the U.S. Trade Representative (*USTR*) with Robert Lighthizer, the characteristics of FDI in U.S.-China relations, the measurable impacts during the trade war on American agriculture, and some observations on the signing of Phase One of the trade agreement between the countries are discussed deeply in this part.

We end the chapter with the idea of *the Globalization Paradox*, that globalization has strengthened the links between countries, as trade has changed in a new way that connects various national economies together at a deeper level than in the past,[1] enabling capital and talent to flow at the global scale and creating a large amount of wealth. However, deeper globalization, which follows market-oriented fundamentalism and has been promoted by the United States, has also brought special fragility in pursuing sustainable development for some other countries, especially for developing countries.

In Chap. 3, "Geopolitics in the Trade War," we explain that a new global phase of conflicts from the perspective of geopolitics starts to be projected in U.S.-China relations. This is stated by the military escalation, with the increased reach of the U.S. Indo-Pacific Command, in the context of the South China Sea and in the U.S. military and intelligence documents in affirming China as a "strategic competitor," along with Russia. This is resulting in the elaboration of a great strategy toward China.

In Chap. 4, "The G-2 (the United States-China)," we work from the perspective of the possibility of building a G-2. As they are the two largest economies in the world, this conflict also highlights the spread of a "Trump Doctrine," focused on the conflict as well as the result of American socio-economic inequality. The trade war now has a direct impact beyond economic matters and branches to multilateral institutions like the UN.

To conclude, in Chap. 5, we try to demonstrate that the meanings of the trade war go far beyond market disputes, the impacts of COVID-19 after the signing of Phase One Economic and Trade Agreement and the creations of a new consensus in the case of American trade policy. We aim to bring general elements of this conflict between two great titans of the global economy in this book.

Li Sheng
Dmitri Felix do Nascimento

[1] David Held, Anthony McGrew, David Goldblatt and Jonathan Perraton, Globalization, Global Governance, Vol. 5, No. 4 (Oct.–Dec. 1999), pp. 483–496.

Contents

List of Figures

List of Tables

1

A Brief History of Trade Wars

Introduction

As the future is unpredictable, humans in contemporary states facing dilemmas can only do their best to prepare themselves for the possibilities stemming from such dilemmas. In this endeavor, there is no more valuable asset than history: On the one side, we can use it to examine how our forebears navigated similar dilemmas, such as trade wars. Learning from history, countries deeply involved in trade frictions need to consider how to address the challenges wisely and whether and how the slide in the wrong direction can be halted. On the other hand, it is of vital importance to note that today by no means exists in isolation but arises from the past. Looking back at history, directional change is not made in a particular moment or through a single event but rather the accumulation of many small adjustments to specific problems. The big picture only reveals itself later. In this light, good knowledge of the history course is helpful to understand the ins and outs of the current situation. And what's more, as Winston Churchill said, "The farther backward you can look, the farther forward you will see." Comparisons can be made between historical incidents and current events, which benefit us in forecasting

L. Sheng, D. Felix do Nascimento, *Love and Trade War*,
https://doi.org/10.1007/978-981-33-4897-4_1

future trends and then making the right moves. To be more specific, comparing historical incidents with the current events will enable us to define the central challenge of the global age—rethinking our values, in situations as well as identities so that politics can remain an effective vehicle for human aspirations and needs.[1]

Distinct from constant even prodigious changes of the present, historic events and the lessons learned from them, which have already been stored as a collective memory, are real, accessible, and enlightening. Making reasonable use of these lessons will save the countries haunted by trade war a great deal of attention, energy, and strength in coping with current affairs. Countries must understand the reasons for the war to avoid future trade wars. Studying what had happened in the history and the related economic consequences is even more important for people including businessmen and government policymakers to prepare for them and make corresponding decisions. This is also the significance of this book: drawing some lessons, giving advice, and establishing two circles of domestic and foreign affairs. For this purpose, this chapter firstly presents a retrospect of trade wars between the United States and its important trading partners in history, serving as the logical starting point of the whole book.

When it comes to the history of trade wars, globalization has to be mentioned due to its inextricable link with trade wars. Actually, the history of trade wars could be deemed as a history of fight between countries for competitive advantages or national interests in the context of globalization. As the economy-induced globalization interconnects the whole world economy,[2] globalization first makes states interconnected, then forms a structure of international division, which eventually boosts international trade activities. In essence, trade wars are governmental reactions to globalization. For example, some government might be tempted to respond to the economic crisis by means of adopting trade-impairing policies, imposing rules that inhibit global financial integration,[3] that is,

[1] Held, D., McGrew, A., Goldblatt, D., & Perraton, J. (1999). Globalization. *Global Governance*, 5(4), 483–496.

[2] Pooch, M. U. (2016). *DiverCity–Global Cities as a Literary Phenomenon: Toronto, New York, and Los Angeles in a Globalizing Age*. transcript Verlag.

[3] Moisés Naím (2009). Globalization. *Foreign Policy*, No. 171, 28–30, 32, 34.

an attempt of taking tariff imposition as an effective measure to influence the distribution of interests derived from globalization. However, if trade war has to happen, it would probably involve a protracted and painful process, and the extent of the damage to each country and its people's well-being is hard to predict, as well as the damage to the world economy in the context of globalization. In this sense, it is globalization that has made trade wars possible, as without globalization there will be no trade wars.

The first high wave of economic globalization has been known to take place from the late nineteenth century until the early twentieth century, when the second industrial revolution brought about enormous changes in every aspect of social life. The extensive application of internal combustion engine and electric power created new transportation facilities as well as communication means, such as automobiles, railways, telephones, radios, and telegraphs, so that ideas, goods, information, capital, and people can move much more quickly,[4] helping to reduce the information cost and strengthen the contacts among countries,[5] which dramatically shortened the time and distance of the world and greatly promoted the growth of international trade. In addition to technological progress, Adam Smith's free-trade thought,[6] along with the prevalence of comparative advantage theory proposed by David Ricardo,[7] further accelerated the development of international

[4] Held, D., McGrew, A., Goldblatt, D., & Perraton, J. (1999). Globalization. *Global Governance*, 5(4), 483–496.

[5] Li, Q., & Reuveny, R. (2003). Economic globalization and democracy: An empirical analysis. *British journal of political science*, 33(1), 29–54.

[6] Adam Smith's free-trade thought includes free trade in land through the repeal of laws establishing entails, primogenitures, and other restrictions on the free transfer of land by gift, devise, or sale; internal free trade by abolition of local customs taxes; and most important of all, free trade in foreign commerce through the abolition of the duties, bounties, and prohibitions of the merchantilistic regime and trading monopolies of the chartered companies.

Quoted in Naggar, T. (1977). Adam Smith's laissez faire. *The American Economist*, 21(2), 35–39.

[7] David Ricardo (1817) provided a mathematical example for this theory, showing that countries could gain from trade by exploiting innate differences in their ability to make different goods. In the basic Ricardian example, comparative advantage theory refers to the situation that two countries do better by specializing in different goods and exchanging them for each other, even when one country is better at making both.

Quoted in Eaton, J., & Kortum, S. (2012). Putting Ricardo to work. *Journal of Economic Perspectives*, 26(2), 65–90.

business around the world. In the world of David Ricardo, who assumes that market is efficient and that comparative advantages are the main drivers for international trade, free trade indeed benefits each country by expanding the production possibility frontier (PPF). When each country can concentrate on producing the product in which the country has a comparative advantage and then trade it for the other product that is produced by the other country with corresponding comparative advantage around the world, the global welfare is maximized without trade barrier. In this situation, many countries came to realize that international trade was not a zero-sum exchange, but a win-win deal. Many countries such as Britain, the United States, and France not only exported goods in large volume but also made overseas investment. Consequently, the expansion of foreign investment gradually transformed the relation of countries from the external connection in the form of commodity exchange to the internal integration in the form of production division. Such transformation led to a greater interdependence among nations, in addition, apart from an increase in interdependency across space, an increase in speed with which this relationship also occur,[8] thus marking a new stage of globalization. At that time, a variety of products from all over the world were available in New York or London market. And it was easy for international capital to flow from one country to another, since domestic currencies were allowed to trade freely with gold at a fixed price under the gold standard. However, the distribution of gains from the trade in the process of globalization is highly uneven,[9] as some countries and some groups are able to get access to large amounts of capital while others are shut out. In addition, the increased inequality, in turn, not only leads to wasted resources but is also likely to increase instability and thus further the gap between

[8] Jwala, K. (2009). Globalization and the dalits. *The Indian Journal of Political Science*, 70(3), 919–924.

[9] Held, D., McGrew, A., Goldblatt, D., & Perraton, J. (1999). Globalization. *Global Governance*, 5(4), 483–496.

those who are considered good and poor credit risks.[10] Therefore, it was inevitable that the foregoing globalization led to the imbalance of wealth allocation among nations, although it improved the total welfare of society.

Regrettably, the process of the first wave of globalization was interrupted by World War I and the Great Depression of 1930s. Global markets were disrupted and disconnected during that period, first by economic warfare, then by postwar protectionism. Prices went haywire: a number of major economies suffered from both hyperinflation and steep deflation in the space of a decade, and national price levels moved unpredictably over short horizons. Several countries attempted to aid the reconstruction process through public expenditures and financed their purchase simply by printing the money they need, thus resulting a sharp rise in money supplies and price level, such as the German hyperinflation of the 1920s. At the same time, the technological advances of the 1900s petered out: innovation hit a plateau, and stagnating consumption discouraged the development of even existing technologies such as the automobile.[11] As a result, international commodity markets did not make further development but suffered a serious setback during the conflict, largely because the cost of shipping goods between countries and continents increased dramatically. Figure 1.1 demonstrates the level of world exports and world production during this period. The outbreak of World War I in 1914 interrupted expanding world trade supported by the gold standard and then economic integration, but the spread of postwar trade restrictions was more especially damaging. Specifically, although world trade tended to increase more rapidly than production before World War I and in the first half of 1920s, it collapsed to a much greater extent in the early 1930s. What's worse, having been saddled with a new and heavy layer of trade restrictions, world trade failed to rebound significantly after the recovery had begun. Even by 1938, world trade was still far below its

[10] Stallings, B. (2007). The globalization of capital flows: Who benefits?. *The ANNALS of the American Academy of Political and Social Science*, 610(1), 201–216.

[11] Ferguson, N. (2005). Sinking globalization. *Foreign Aff.*, 84(2), 64–77.

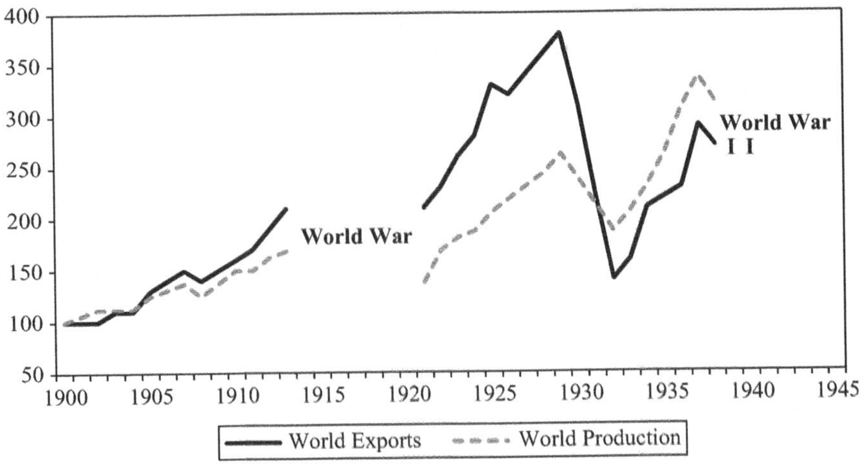

Fig. 1.1 The value of world trade and production from 1900 to 1945 (*Source: Gu, X.H. and Sheng, L. (2011) A Sensible Policy Tool for Pareto Improvement: Capital Controls. Journal of World Trade, 44(3), 567–589.)*

peak. As described in Irwin D.'s book (2008), the growth of protectionist measures had stifled world trade severely and thereby hindered a full and complete recovery from the depression.[12] What's worse, when the world economic recovery was coming in fits and starts, the outbreak of World War II once again destroyed the effort.

The Smoot-Hawley Tariff Act: The Shield of American Protectionism

The infamous trade protectionist law Smoot-Hawley Tariff Act was born in this background and bore large responsibility for this situation. In October of 1929, the New York stock market fell sharply, which was followed by a severe worldwide economic depression subsequently—between 1929 and 1932, the volume of world trade fell by one quarter; even five years later, the 1929 peak had still not been recovered. What's

[12] Irwin, D. A., Mavroidis, P. C., & Sykes, A. O. (2008). The Genesis of the GATT.

more, it is found that most of the trade contraction during the Great Depression could be attributed to the trade restrictions, as were falls of several percent in international output and investment.

Meanwhile, it was estimated that 8% of the fall in world trade volumes was due to discretionary increases in tariffs, 5% to deflation-induced tariff increases, and 6% to non-tariff barriers. The trigger for much of the restrictive trade policy at first sight was American protectionism.[13] By then the reality of the United States was that productivity gains from technology advance had resulted in agricultural commodity overproduction, but the demand had been growing slowly, as the consumption of agricultural products was price- and income-inelastic, and the European population was increasing much more slowly,[14] which cannot be absorbed by the post-war Europe as before. The supply surplus, combined with fierce competition from foreign agricultural imports, depressed the prices of agricultural products, putting American farmers under massive pressure. In that case, republican candidate Hoover was naturally elected president in 1928 for his promise to deal with the farm crisis. After taking office, he proposed tariffs on agricultural imports to bail domestic agriculture out.

As a consequence, it is no doubt that the increases in tariff are largely directed to the interest of the farmer. Of the increases, it is stated by the Tariff Commission that 93.73% are upon products of agricultural origin measured in value, as distinguished from 6.25% upon commodities of strictly nonagricultural origin.[15] However, manufactural interests lobbied congressmen to demand an equal protection on grounds of stimulating job creation and economic growth. Senators Reed Smoot and Willis Hawley hence offered their own legislation and added a slew of industrial tariffs for their interests. Despite a petition signed by 1000 U.S.

---

[13] Foreman-Peck, J., Hughes Hallett, A., & Ma, Y. (2007). Trade wars and the Slump. *European Review of Economic History*, 11(1), 73–98.

[14] Federico, G. (2005). Not guilty? Agriculture in the 1920s and the Great Depression. *Journal of Economic History*, 65(4), 949–976.

[15] PRESIDENT HOOVER ON THE HAWLEY-SMOOT TARIFF ACT OF 1930, Advocate of Peace through Justice, 93(3), 191–193, Sage Publications, Inc.

economists calling for Hoover to veto the plan,[16] bowing to the pressure from interest groups, Hoover's administration finally passed Smoot-Hawley Tariffs Act to raise tariffs sharply on thousands of imports including both agricultural and industrial goods in 1930. The House passed the Hawley bill on May 28, 1929, by a vote of 264 (244 Republicans and 20 Democrats) to 147 (12 Republicans, 134 Democrats, and 1 Farmer Labor). Figure 1.1 shows that the bill passed with a great advantage. Immediately after, on March 24, 1930, the Senate passed the Hawley bill by a vote of 53 (46 Republicans and 7 Democrats) to 31 (5 Republicans and 26 Democrats). As Fig. 1.2 shows that Republicans from the Northeast, industrial Midwest, and the far West supported the bill. Beaudreau, B. C. (2017) also emphasizes that the importance of political parties and interest group in making the Tariff Act of 1930 to protect their interests cannot be neglected.[17] Obviously, the Smoot-Hawley Tariff Act of 1930 can be viewed as being the Republican Party's policy response to placate agricultural interests and electoral commitment in the 1928 general election to a certain extent (Table 1.1).

However, it was pointed out that this trade policy imparted a contractionary shock to the United States through a number of channels. Directly, without any retaliation, the resulting increase in the imports and close substitutes altered the division of the nominal income decline between output and prices in 1930–1932, so output fell more than otherwise and prices fell less. Retaliation could also lower aggregate demand through the trade multiplier. Lastly, foreign against U.S. food exports could have aggravated the decline in farm prices, worsening the banking crisis and in turn the decline in the supply of money due to currency

[16] A thousand economists warn: On May 5, 1930, there was published throughout the country a message to Congress and the president signed by 1028 economists, members of the American Economic Association. This plea from the bulk of the nation's students of economics urged that any general upward revision of tariff rates be rejected by Congress, or if passed, vetoed by the president. They warned that "increased restrictive duties would not only increase prices but encourage concerns with higher costs to undertake production, thus causing the community to subsidize waste and inefficiency in industry and force it to pay higher rates of profit to established firms."

Quoted in FLEMING, D. (1936). How the Smoot-Hawley Tariff Was Made. *Proceedings of the Annual Session (Southern Political Science Association)*, 9, pp. 14–19, The University of Chicago Press on behalf of the Southern Political Science Association.

[17] Beaudreau, B. C. (2017). Reexamining the Origins of the Smoot–Hawley Tariff Act. In *Research in Economic History*. Emerald Publishing Limited.

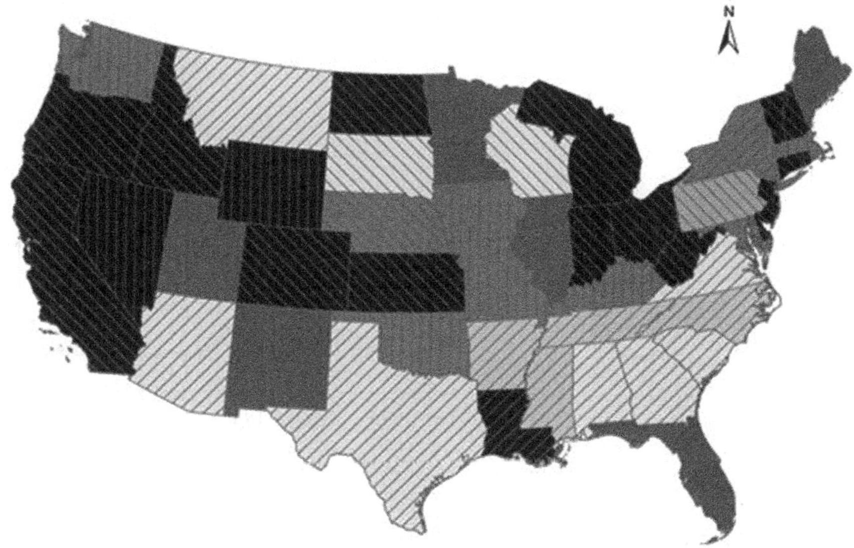

Fig. 1.2 Senate voting on the Hawley tariff bill, March 24, 1930. (*Note: The votes are taken from the GovTrack.us, Senate Vote on March 24, 1930, 71st Congress [*https://www.govtrack.us/congress/votes/71-2/s295*]. "Two Yeas" refers to the state with all senators voting in favor, "One Yea One Not Voting" to the state with one senator voting yes and the other abstention, "One Yea One Nay" to the state with one senator voting yes and the other voting no, "Two Not Voting" to the state with all senators abstaining from voting, "One Nay One Not Voting" to the state with one senator voting no and the other abstention, and "Two Nays" to the state with all senators voting against the bill. Hence, the darker the state in* Fig. 1.2*, the more the state supports the passage of the bill. Similarly, "Two Republicans" represents the state with two Republican senators, and "Two Democrats" demonstrates the state with two Democratic senators. From this classification, we can identify the influence of political parties and interest group on the bill*)

Table 1.1 House voting on the Hawley tariff bill, May 28, 1929

House voting on the Hawley tariff bill				
	Republicans	Democrats	In total	Ratio
Voting Yea	244	20	264	64%
Voting Nay	12	134	147	36%

Note: The votes are taken from the GovTrack.us, House Vote on May 28, 1929, *71st Congress (https://www.govtrack.us/congress/votes/71-1/h7)*

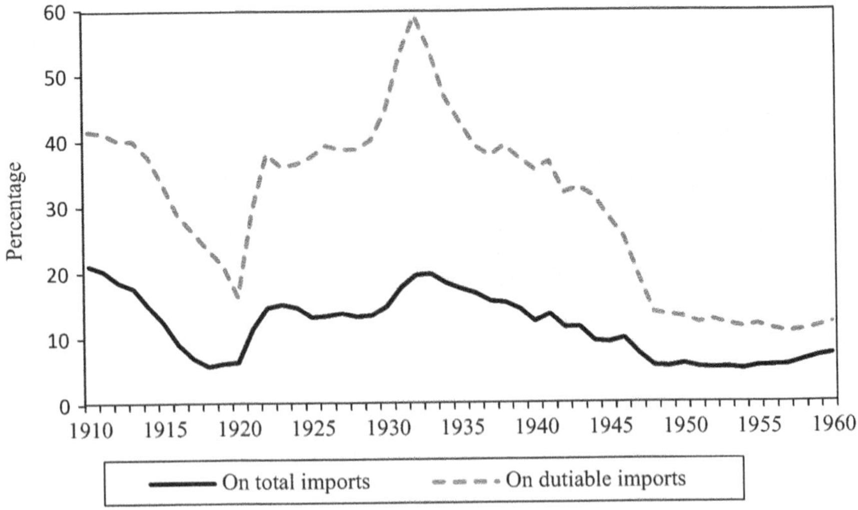

Fig. 1.3 Average U.S. tariff on imports from 1910 to 1960. (*Source: United States Census, Historical Statistics of the United States, Colonial Times to 1970, Series U207–212: Value of Merchandise Imports and Duties: 1821 to 1970*)

hoarding.[18] In fact, the Hawley-Smoot tariff pushed already high protective tariffs much higher, and the tariff did not simply jump in 1930 and stop. Figure 1.3 shows the average tariff on dutiable and total imports during this period. The average tariff on dutiable imports increased in 1930, but then rose further in 1931 and again in 1932, when it peaked at 59.1%, the second highest recorded value in the U.S. history.[19]

However, most noticeably, this initiative immediately resulted in vigorous protestation and tariff retaliation from 35 other nations eager to shield their economies. Between 1930 and 1934, as a result of retaliation against the Smoot-Hawley Act, the depression, and motivations internal to various countries, the level of protection within the international

[18] Archibald, R. B., & Feldman, D. H. (1998). Investment during the great depression: uncertainty and the role of the Smoot-Hawley tariff. *Southern Economic Journal*, 64(4), 857–879.

[19] The average tariff on dutiable imports reached 61.7% in 1830, shortly after the enactment of the Tariff of Abominations in 1828.

Irwin, Douglas A. (2017). *Peddling protectionism: Smoot-Hawley and the great depression.* Princeton University Press.

economy rose precipitously.[20] For instance, Canada, the largest trading partner of the United States, heavily dependent on the U.S. market (in 1929, 18% of U.S. merchandise exports went to Canada and 11% of U.S. merchandise imports came from Canada),[21] took the lead in responding with retaliatory tariffs on 16 American-made products that accounted altogether for around 30% of U.S. exports to Canada and swiftly turned to Commonwealth countries for trade cooperation. Italy levied double tariffs on American automobiles in return, which dramatically cut its sales in Italy by 90%. Higher duties were imposed on radios and radio equipment, products that also came largely from the United States. In addition, the Italian government had some control over the country's purchase of bulk commodities and used its influence to shift its source of cotton, wheat, copper, and other goods from the United States. Worse still, in Spain, a new tariff schedule published on July 23 of 1930 directly increased such typically American products as automobiles, motorcycles, pneumatic tires, safety-razor blades, and sewing machines[22] to such an extent that no consumers would pay the high prices. Spain also withdrew most-favored nation treatment from the United States so that Spain was free to discriminate against American commerce. The Canadian tariff, Italian automobile tariff, and Spanish tariff were direct retaliations against Smoot-Hawley that seriously reduced world trade. France and Britain also began to exploit the new market while Germany reacted with becoming more self-sufficient. Some American agriculture officials once believed that the absence of American wheat in world market would necessarily give rise to a worldwide shortage of wheat supply and thus the trade war could end with concessions of other countries. But the fact was U.S. wheat producers gradually lost their market share and competitiveness to those from Canada and Argentina.

Despite implementation for only four years, this act and retaliatory measures that followed not only destroyed U.S. domestic economy but

[20] Lake, D. A. (1988). Protection, retaliation, and response, 1930–1939, in Lake, D. A. (1988). *Power, protection, and free trade: International sources of US commercial strategy, 1887–1939*. Cornell University Press.

[21] McDonald, J. A., O'Brien, A. P., & Callahan, C. M. (1997). Trade wars: Canada's reaction to the Smoot-Hawley Tariff. *The Journal of Economic History*, 57(4), 802–826.

[22] Bidwell, P. W. (1930). The new American tariff: Europe's answer. *Foreign Affairs*, 9(1), 13–26.

also deepened the depression around the world. The commercial policies of 1930s became characterized as "beggar-thy-neighbour" policies, and reducing imports proved to be a futile method of combating the economic downturn because one country's imports were another country's exports. Between 1929 and 1933, U.S. imports decreased by 66% and exports dropped by 61%. U.S. Gross National Products fell by almost half from $103.1 billion to $55.6 billion. The unemployment rate jumped from 8% to 25%. Overall, the world trade reduced by over 65%. Specifically, the book *Power and Plenty: Trade, War, and the World Economy in the Second Millennium* (2009)[23] demonstrates that export revenues fell by over 60% in Latin America and Asia between 1929 and 1932, by over 50% in Australasia, and by over 40% in Africa. There was a particularly spectacular decline in world. Another more serious consequence was that the act intensified nationalism all over the world, which unintentionally provided the soil for the rise of fascism and brought fascism to power. Specifically, the economic distress of the decade undermined faith in democratic governments to manage their economies and hence abet a turn to more authoritarian regimes in Germany and elsewhere. As the implication is clear, if only the United States had adopted the free trade, there would have been no depression, the Weimar Republic would have evolved into today's Federal Republic, and a second Russo-German War, as well as the first Japanese-American War, could have been averted.[24]

As a result of the failure of Smoot-Hawley, Hoover lost the next election to Franklin Roosevelt, who campaigned on the slogan "New Deal."[25] In the election of 1932, Roosevelt charged Hoover with complete responsibility for the depression. Among its domestic cause, he argued, was the new tariff regime that inhibited foreign debt repayment and elicited

---

[23] Findlay, R., & O'rourke, K. H. (2009). *Power and plenty: trade, war, and the world economy in the second millennium*. Princeton University Press, 450.

[24] Lind, M. (1994). The op-ed history of America. *The National Interest*, (37), 16–28.

[25] Eight months earlier than Franklin Roosevelt's March 1933 inauguration, he had confidently promised the American people a "New Deal" to fight the Great Depression, which made a respond to needs for relief, reform, and recovery from the Great Depression. In addition, his "Brains Trust" advisers had been hard at work on a program ever since.

Quoted in Lee, B. A. (1982). The new deal reconsidered. *The Wilson Quarterly* (1976-), 6(2), 62–76.

strong trade retaliation.[26] As a result, the Roosevelt administration believed that it was high tariffs that largely contributed to the collapse in world trade and the recession in global economy. In line with this idea, Smoot-Hawley was replaced soon with Roosevelt's Reciprocal Trade Agreements Act of 1934, which allowed the president to negotiate tariff reductions. The enforcement of this trade agreements act could be regarded as a turning point in American commercial policy, which played a significant role in curbing global trade protectionism, as the average tariff level fell 80%, effectively opening the U.S. market to international competition and helping to erase the merchandise surplus that had embarrassed U.S. officials during the 1930s.[27] What is more, its unconditional most-favor-nation treatment which afterwards became the cornerstone and nucleus of General Agreement on Tariff and Trade (GATT), namely the predecessor of the World Trade Organization (WTO).

Liberal But Not So Much: The Emergence of the Multilateral Order and the New Trade Battles

After the Great Depression, World War II and the Cold War changed the entire course of human history and hindered the process of globalization as well. Still, the step of globalization has never ceased to advance. Actually, it has been clearly realized through this history that the war or confrontation itself contributed nothing to the progress of human society but devastated the fruits of human development, such as economic growth. In terms of economic convergence and divergence, the "dark middle years" can only be calculated as a period of overall divergence by including the sudden and brief divergence of the years immediately after World War II.[28] At the same time, the GATT-based regime for the gover-

[26] Archibald, R. B., & Feldman, D. H. (1998). Investment during the Great Depression: uncertainty and the Role of the Smoot-Hawley tariff. *Southern Economic Journal*, 64(4), 857–879.

[27] Schwob, C. (2009). Did the Reciprocal Trade Agreements Act of 1934 initiate a revolution in the American trade policy?. *Historical Social Research/Historische Sozialforschung*, 34(4), 130 in Halling, T., Fehlemann, S., & Voegele, J. (2009). Premature death and patterns of identity and meaning from a historical perspective, 377–379.

[28] McKeown, A. (2007, March). Periodizing globalization. *In History Workshop Journal* (Vol. 63, No. 1, pp. 218–230). Oxford University Press.

nance of international trade relations sought to ensure that domestic intervention did not reproduce the mutually destructive consequences of the interwar period and that it be constrained by multilateral norms. From those twin concerns emerged a historic institutional compromise called "embedded liberalism,"[29] which implies a combination of free trade with the freedom for domestic intervention. The searing experience of the Great Depression in the 1930s provided the impetus for establishing a formal system of world trade rules (GATT).[30] Hence, it was hardly surprising that three major international economic organizations, that is, the GATT, the World Bank, and the International Monetary Fund, committed to establish and maintain international economic order came into being at the end of World War II, aiming at creating a national monetary and trading environment for the world economy, accelerating growth in developing nations and harmonizing growth in the more advanced nations.[31] It was these international economic organizations, coupled with the third technology revolution rising since the early 1950s, that pushed globalization to advance amid the twists and turns. Increasing international interdependence has been accompanied by heightened commercial rivalry among nations. To some extent, as the integration of economy will introduce even greater leverage and flexibility for countries,[32] the development of globalization means increasingly fierce competition for the global market, which was inevitably accompanied by trade frictions. Trade conflicts between advanced industrial countries have intensified as these states have competed to maintain a vibrant domestic

---

[29] Mainstream scholars generally describe embedded liberalism as involving a compromise between two desirable but partially conflicting objectives. The first objective was to revive free trade. The second objective was to allow national governments the freedom to provide generous welfare programs and to intervene in their economies to maintain full employment. The term was first used by John Ruggie in 1982.

Ruggie, J. G. (1982). International regimes, transactions, and change: embedded liberalism in the postwar economic order. *International organization*, 36(2), 379–415.

Ruggie, J. (1994). Trade, protectionism and the future of welfare capitalism. *Journal of International Affairs*, 48(1), 1–11.

[30] Irwin, D. A. (2015). *Free trade under fire*. Princeton University Press.

[31] Rostow, W. W. (1970). The Past Quarter-Century as Economic History and the Tasks of International Economic Organization. *The Journal of Economic History*, 30(1), 150–187.

[32] Gartzke, E., & Li, Q. (2003). War, peace, and the invisible hand: Positive political externalities of economic globalization. *International Studies Quarterly*, 47(4), 561–586.

production base. During this period, trade wars of massive influence occurring between the United States and its trading partners involved the Chicken Tariff War of the 1960s with the European Union (EU) and the 1987 Trade War with Japan.

With the rise of mass-produced, factory chicken farming in the United States, cheaper U.S. poultry gained great popularity in the European market, particularly West Germany. In the latter 1950s, the American poultry industry discovered and began exploiting a thriving outlet in Germany.[33] By 1962, U.S. poultry had accounted for nearly 25% of West Germany's poultry imports, which was only approximately 1.1% in 1956. In that same year, to cope with their poultry industry crisis, European Economic Community countries tripled tariffs on U.S. chicken from 4.5 cents per pound to 13.5 cents per pound. The curbing of this poultry trade was understandably quite objectionable to the United States—the high tariff policy immediately led to a sharp decline in U.S. chicken exports, and American shipments fell off sharply to a level of about $20 million annually, prompting poultry farmers' complaints within the United States.[34] For U.S. poultry growers, the increased common market tariffs on table poultry meant virtual elimination of their rich export market in West Germany and other European areas.

Despite an appeal to GATT (the General Agreement on Tariffs and Trade), a law named the Trade Expansion Act was still promulgated in 1962 to authorize the president to fight against unfair trade practices, through tariffs or other means such as to negotiate with the European Community for a progressive, but extensive, lowering of trade barriers (not only against American exports to them, but against the exports of the underdeveloped nations of the world as well)[35] if necessary, under which the following year President Lyndon Johnson levied retaliatory tariffs on a great number of commodities mainly from Europe including

[33] Walker, H. (1964). Dispute Settlement: The Chicken War. *The American Journal of International Law*, 58(3), 671–685.

[34] Sheng, L. (2011). A Political Economy Approach to Foreign Investment and Local Welfare. *The Social Sciences Journal*, 48(1), 52–71.

[35] Metzger, S. D. (1962). Trade Expansion Act of 1962, The. Geo. LJ, 51(3), 425.

trucks and other products.[36] The U.S. government even threatened to reduce NATO troops in Europe in an attempt to persuade Europe to abolish its protectionist chicken policy.

It was a pity that the United States failed in its attempt eventually. This chicken war ended up with the U.S. concession. However, there were no winners in this war, although European countries appeared to be. Actually, owing to retaliatory tariffs on trucks, West Germany exports of automobile trucks to the United States declined to a value of $5.7 million, only one-third of the value exported in the previous year. Shortly after, Volkswagen cargo vans and pickup trucks also lost the U.S. market. European countries paid a heavy price for their win: not only can their consumers not access to less-costly chicken, but also auto industries suffered great losses. The situation in the United States was surely worse. Since truck tariff has remained in place until now, U.S. auto industry was completely cut off from the world market, thus was deprived of the precious opportunity to upgrade itself through the participation in competition, which was directly responsible for decades of U.S. auto industry recession. Forty years later, the truck tariff still stands at a whopping 25%. Until now, the "chicken tax" has effectively insulated U.S. truck manufacturers from competition for five long decades. That's kept prices high and created so huge profit centers at Chrysler, Ford, and General Motors that the Big Three have slacked off in developing innovative cars because they've become addicted to the easy money offered by pickups.

As the Chinese idiom goes, "a fire on the city gate brings disaster to the fish in the moat." What calls for special attention was some Japanese auto manufacturers, such as Toyota and Isuzu, also took a big hit from the tariff war, though they were not the intended targets. To remain viable after truck tariff imposition, they had to build assembly plants on U.S. territory. Not even U.S. producers themselves can be insulated from impacts of the high truck tariff, the U.S. auto industry has been insulated from international competition by catering to the demand for larger and more

[36] On December 4, 1963, President Johnson issued Presidential Proclamation No. 3564 which suspended the trade agreement concessions on potato starch, soluble and chemically treated starches, dextrin, trucks over 1000 dollars, and brandy over $9 per gallon.

Galloway, L. T. (1972). Star Industries, Inc. v. United States: Sequel to The Chicken War. *The International Lawyer*, 6(1), 48–63.

luxurious cars than those made elsewhere.[37] To that point, some U.S. producers had built auto plants overseas because of their inexperience in the design and production. Nonetheless, higher per capita incomes, lower gasoline prices, longer driving distances, wider roads, and other factors accounted for the larger autos purchased in the United States. As a consequence, given substantial economies of scale in vehicle manufacturing, a foreign manufacturer would be reluctant to produce a U.S.-style automobile that it could not sell in significant numbers in its home market.[38] The introduction of these trucks into the domestic market was affected so that the United States had to cut these overseas plants out of the loop. What happened in this chicken war has fully demonstrated the fact that in an era of globalization no country can isolate itself from the rest of the world and be absolutely immune to the results of an economic crisis in other nations. This is the lesson which should not be forgotten even now.

In the same period, the Japanese manufacturing industry, on the other side of the Pacific Ocean, was growing fast under the export-oriented policy. In 1968, postwar Japan became the world's second-largest economy behind the United States after 23 years of reconstruction.[39] The post-World War II prosperity enjoyed in Japan has been made possible, in part, because Japanese products have found a market in the United States. Further, U.S. companies have been willing to license technology to Japanese companies. Above all, Japanese security and political stability have been ensured by the Security Treaty between the two countries. However, the growth of export trade led to not only a huge favorable trade balance but also frequent trade conflicts between Japan and its trading partners such as the United States. Early in 1950s, textile trade conflict occurred between Japan and the United States, after which there

[37] Gomez-Ibanez, J. A., & Harrison, D. (1982). Imports and the Future of the US Automobile Industry. *The American Economic Review*, 72(2), 319–323.

[38] Sheng, L. (2013). Free Capital Mobility and Sustainable Community Development: A Theoretical Framework. Habitat International, 40(4), 278–284.

[39] An essential ingredient in this amazing reconstruction was the strong protectionism fostered by the Ministry of International Trade and Industry. A series of tariff and non-tariff barriers kept more competitive American and other foreign goods out. The man in the street was indoctrinated with the view that selling to foreigners and buying Japanese produced good was a civic responsibility.

Quoted in Schulze, D. L. (1985). US-Japan Trade Relations. *Economic and Political Weekly*, 20(28), 1176.

were another two serious trade conflicts arising from their bilateral trade from the 1960s to 1970s, involving iron, steel, and home appliances (color television).[40] The time period surrounding the conclusion of the Kennedy Round[41] in 1967 signaled the start of trade problems between the United States and Japan, though trade problems had occurred as early as 1950 in areas such as textiles and toys. Following the Kennedy Round, trade problems spread from light industries to heavier, more sophisticated industries such as electronics, steel, automobiles and, more recently, to high-technology areas such as semiconductor chips. Generally, it can be said that the trade problems in the 1960s and 1970s were mostly concentrated in conventional industries, but the problems in the late 1970s and 1980s have continued in those industries and have spread to high-technology and other sophisticated areas.[42] In fact, these trade frictions occurred in the context of globalization and Japan's industrial transformation, mainly from the light (labor-intensive) industry in mid-late 1950s to the heavy chemical industry in 1960s and 1970s. For example, by the late 1950s, Japan had surpassed Britain and became the United States' and even world's largest exporter of textile. The market share of Japan's cotton textiles in the United States rose from about 17% in 1951 to more than 60% in 1955. By the end of the 1960s, Japan's exports of wool products accounted for 30% of the U.S. market, and synthetic fiber products accounted for as much as 25%, heavily affecting the interests of the U.S. textile industry. In 1960, Kennedy won the votes of the southern states during the campaign because of his commitment to protect the textile industry. After he became president, he quickly established the Textile Industry Ministers Committee to study the policy of supporting the textile industry. Under pressure the Japanese-American textile friction finally ended with United States-Japanese Textile Agreement. Fortunately, all of these trade conflicts were kept from escalation into a trade war for Japan ended them with a series of trade agreements that agreed to take voluntary export restraints, such as Steel Voluntary Export Restraint

[40] Shank, G. (1994). Japan—US Trade War?. *Social Justice*, 212(56), 20–23.

[41] The Kennedy Round was the sixth session of General Agreement on Tariffs and Trade (GATT) multilateral trade negotiations held between 1964 and 1967 in Geneva, Switzerland, aiming to global tariff cuts.

[42] Matsushita, M. (1987). A Japanese View of United States Trade Laws. *Nw. J. Int'l L. & Bus.*, 8, 29.

Agreement of 1969 and the 1983 Specialty Steel Voluntary Export Restraint.

When coming into the 1980s, this was no longer the case. Half of all U.S. exports to Japan are foodstuffs and raw materials; the United States imports mainly machinery and vehicle parts from Japan. This pattern is typical of trade between developing and core economies, with the United States playing the role of the periphery.[43] In addition, a variety of technological products from Japan, such as semiconductor, chips, and automobiles, had dominated the U.S. as well as the global markets, which was considered as a serious threat to the status and power of the United States. Especially, U.S. automobile manufacturing as the pillar industry was at risk. By 1980, sales of American-made cars reached a 19-year low, the year's losses for the three major manufacturers totaled an unprecedented $4.2 billion, and approximately one quarter of all auto workers were on indefinite layoff.[44] It was exactly the moment when the U.S. economy was stuck in the quagmire of stagflation after the two petroleum crisis of the 1970s. However, automobiles from Japan were favored with their fuel efficiency performance, with the result that Japanese automobiles accounted for 80% of total automobile imports, achieving 20% share in the U.S. market. As a contrast, the demand for domestic automobiles shrunk enough to bring 60,000 of auto workers out of work. Actually, U.S. traditional manufacturing sectors, not merely automobile industry, became vulnerable to attack from rising Japanese manufacturing. A large number of factories which specialized in the manufacture of steel and steel-derived products such as automobiles and industrial equipment shut down, thus creating the severely depressed area, namely Rust Belt.

Until 1985, the U.S. trade deficit had surged to $148.5 billion, triple the level of 1980, one-third of which stemmed from the bilateral trade with Japan. The size of the deficit as well as its rapid growth has created a situation that threatens good relations between the United States and Japan. Both countries feel wronged by the other. The United States blames the deficit on Japanese barriers to its domestic markets. The

[43] Li, S. (2014). Economic structure, cost outsourcing and global imbalances. *Journal of Australian Political Economy*, The, (74), 81.

[44] Gomez-Ibanez, J. A., & Harrison, D. (1982). Imports and the Future of the US Automobile Industry. *The American Economic Review*, 72(2), 319–323.

Japanese blame the deficit on American mismanagement of its economy—huge budget deficits and high domestic interest rates result in a grossly overvalued American dollar (makes American imports relatively inexpensive, while American exports find themselves priced out of many overseas markets).[45] In addition, the soaring trade deficit not only intensified the existing internal contradictions but also expanded its own opposite, which made the United States gradually turn toward protectionism. Confronted with the possibility of eroding economic competitiveness and challenged by other developed nations, the United States has engaged in a never-ending series of trade conflicts with its Japanese competitors, particularly in those high-technology industries such as semiconductors and automobile that directly affect the national economic and security interests.

In 1979, the United States had already imposed a set of requirements directly upon Japan to reduce the huge trade imbalance between them, relating to opening up Japanese auto market, establishing plants in the United States, and adopting voluntary restriction on auto exports, and so on, which didn't fundamentally reverse the U.S. trade deficit in spite of wholesale acceptance by Japan. But at the same time, these restrictions acted as a catalyst for Japan's development of global production and industrial upgrade. A key adjustment deployed by Japanese auto companies was to move up the value chain to manufacture high-end luxury cars. It was first implemented by three major auto companies: Toyota, Nissan and Honda, which launched luxury brands: Lexus, Infiniti and Acura, respectively. After six to seven years of research and development, these products were listed in the late 1980s and were well received by U.S. consumers. Hence, although limitation is put on the number of cars exported, higher-priced cars increased the value of Japanese car exports in 1981 considerably above the larger number of units exported. In 1980, Japanese sales accounted for 21.4% of all new car purchases. While domestic production in the United States dropped 16.0%, Japanese sales rose by 7.8% in the United States. In 1981 and 1982, Japanese sales still accounted for

[45] Schulze, D. L. (1985). US-Japan Trade Relations. *Economic and Political Weekly*, 20(28), 1176.

over 20% of the American market.[46] In 1984, the market-oriented sector selective talks (MOSS) were held between the United States and Japan to eliminate all overt and informal barriers to imports in forest products, telecommunications equipment and services, electronics, and pharmaceuticals and medical equipment, especially on the Japanese side. In 1985, the trade war reached a new high when Japan was compelled to sign the Plaza Accord under U.S. pressure, which allowed yen to appreciate against the U.S. dollar for undermining the competitiveness of Japanese products. But no one emerged as a winner in the trade war. Both Japanese car producers and American consumers suffered substantially from the trade conflict. On the one hand, car producers from Japan experienced a sharp decrease in revenue, and on the other hand, consumers in the United States faced a sharp jump in automobile prices. Specifically, in the United States, the average prices of imported and domestic cars increased by US$900 and US$400, respectively, resulting in a remarkable decline in car sales. More importantly, more than 60,000 jobs in the automobile industry were lost, and the unemployment rate peaked at the height of the trade war under the Reagan presidency.[47] In the following years, the U.S. government had been increasingly pressuring Japan to improve the imbalance of trade in various ways. President Reagan further doubled the import prices on $300 million worth of Japanese computers, power tools, and TVs in 1987. Later Japanese autos were also subject to high tariffs. In 1989, based on the perception that it was the oligopolistic industrial sector in which large companies linked together that caused the trade imbalance, President Bush initiated talks on Structural Impediments Initiative (SII) aiming to eliminate these structural impediments through Japanese reform, which was concluded by two countries in June 1990.

Accepting all, the Japanese government didn't take any retaliatory measures. Nevertheless, the Plaza Accord was totally disastrous for Japan, which caused a miserable decade of economic stagflation in the 1990s. The appreciation of the Japanese yen resulted in a sharp slowdown in

[46] Langdon, F. (1983). Japan–United States Trade Friction: The Reciprocity Issue. *Asian Survey*, 23(5), 653–666.

[47] Chong, T. T. L., & Li, X. (2019). Understanding the China–US trade war: causes, economic impact, and the worst-case scenario. *Economic and Political Studies*, 7(2), 185–202.

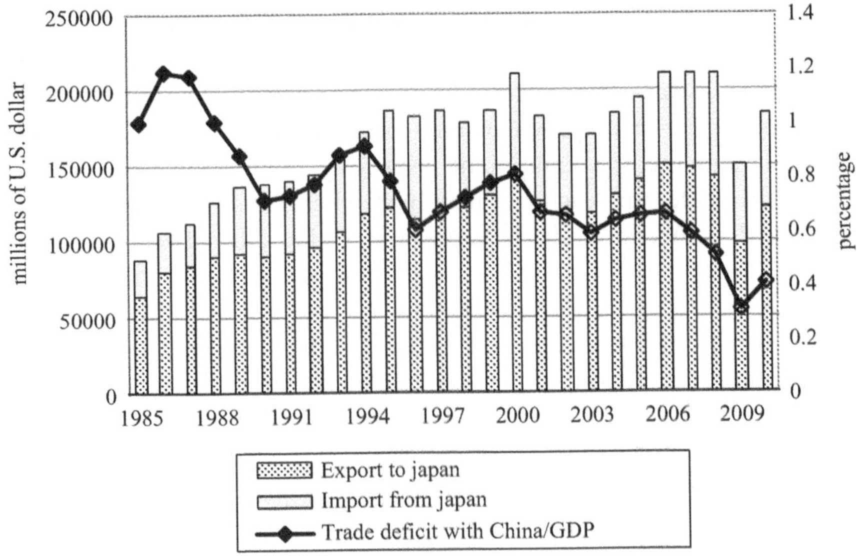

Fig. 1.4 The Yen-U.S. dollar exchange rate and the bilateral U.S.-Japan merchandise trade deficits (1980–2010). (*Data Source: U.S. Government Publishing Office, The Economic Report of the President [1985–2012]; U.S. Bureau of Economic Analysis,* https://www.bea.gov)

exports growth. As Fig. 1.4 shows, the average Yen-U.S. dollar exchange rate appreciated the most, going from 238 Yen per U.S. dollar in 1985 to 144 in 1987, almost a doubling in value for the yen and then staying at around 128 in 1988. The U.S. merchandise trade deficit to Japan did not decline until 1986 from 1.18% of GDP to 0.71% in 1990, a drop of 0.04 percentage points. This change had the desired effect, bringing down the dollar and reducing the trade deficit.[48] However, for defusing the negative effect of yen appreciation on its economy, the Japanese government took loose monetary policies along with expansionary fiscal policies as a stimulus to domestic demand. It was unexpected that loose monetary and fiscal policies combined with the influx of hot money induced by the yen appreciation sent asset prices soaring, plunging the country into illusive prosperity, which ultimately triggered the Japanese

[48] Frankel, J. (2015). *The Plaza Accord, 30 Years Later* (No. w21813). National Bureau of Economic Research.

economic crisis of the 1990s. Not until the middle of the 1990s when there was a declining trend in the proportion of GDP in the U.S. trade deficit had the trade relationship of the United States and Japan gradually improved. It can only be hoped that the positive side of the relationship with the United States will inspire Japan to take the initiative in proposing some temporary compromises to ease the pressure of its highly competitive exports and to make some magnanimous gesture on market entry that would make its enthusiasm for free trade seem less self-serving. It is unfortunate and dangerous to rely too much on threats and criticism in a relationship with much common benefit.[49] After the year 2000, most of the trade conflicts between both countries were solved under the WTO framework.

The historical U.S.-Japan trade war displayed a possibility of development of trade war. That is, if the situation cannot be properly controlled, it is probable that the trade war would extend to all aspects of social life, including finance, economy, ideology, and military, which will inevitably plunge two countries into the "Thucydides's trap"[50] with devastating results. At that moment it will be not easy for two countries to get back to the previous relationship in which two countries not only seek common development hand in hand but also deal with the challenge the human being faces together. Actually, so-called Thucydides's trap does not necessarily exist, especially at present when countries have a strong complementarity to each other. Any country will not go far without others' cooperation and support. Another lesson is that the appropriate

[49] Langdon, F. (1983). Japan–United States Trade Friction: The Reciprocity Issue. *Asian Survey*, 23(5), 653–666.

[50] Thucydides was a political pathologist, a student of political disease, especially as it occurs during war. This is most evident from his account of the plague in Athens. He describes the physical symptoms of the disease first, but then turns to its political effects, including the breakdown of the Athenian political order. Thucydides's self-understanding as a political pathologist is also evident in his account of the civil war in Corcyra. He begins with just the facts: the Corinthians inserted a fifth column into Corcyra to incite a revolution, in which the oligarchic faction would overthrow the democracy. The quarrel polarized the community and escalated to a struggle of extermination—while the Athenians watched, callously, from their ships at the port in Corcyra. War is a harsh teacher that reduces most of us to the necessities that war imposes on us, Thucydides said, so no means, fair or foul, were off-limits during this civil war.

Walling, K. F. (2018). The United States, China, and Thucydides's many, many traps. *Naval War College Review*, 17(1), 152–158. Reviewed Naval War College Review Allison, G. (2017). *Destined for war: Can America and China escape Thucydides's trap?*. Houghton Mifflin Harcourt.

response of the government plays a significant role in coping with the external challenges. If Japan chooses to focus on its internal reform at its own pace, the story may be completely different. As to domestic reform, a stable environment is of great importance. Maintaining a bad relationship with other countries will harm its internal reform when facing a trade war as well as domestic misrule.

The Post-Cold War and the Trade Wars

In the post-Cold War era, the collapse of the Soviet Union in 1991, along with advancements in computer technology, fueled the second major wave of modern globalization. The expansion of trade organizations like WTO helps to shorten the international trade disputes lifespans effectively, which encouraged nations worldwide to enter into free-trade agreements, greatly enhanced the efficiency of cross-border trade.[51]

Then the development of information technology from the Third Industrial Revolution, especially the emergence of network, connected people all over the world (with the click of the mouse, digitized information—the essence of knowledge-based output could be made available instantaneously anywhere in the world)[52] and strengthened the economic interaction among countries, which allowed for a further global integration of value chains. Specifically, such cheap, efficient, instantaneous computer-based communication is an even more important technological development because it has transformed the nature of trade while expanding its volume. It has spurred corporations to plan globally by organizing geographically dispersed operational units into a single production and trade network. Each stage of production is shifted to the region where it can be performed most cheaply, with trade in raw materials, parts, and intermediate products linking the stages into an integrated commodity chain. The result is a finely calibrated and very efficient

[51] Grinols, E. L., & Perrelli, R. (2006). The WTO impact on international trade disputes: An event history analysis. *The Review of Economics and Statistics*, 88(4), 613–624.

[52] Roach, S., & Roach, S. S. (2014). *Unbalanced: The Codependency of America and China.* Yale University Press.

division of labor.[53] In addition, this globalization was also achieved by the development of multinational corporations, as they extend the geographic sphere of their activities across nations and continents,[54] which have increasingly become the main carriers and beneficiaries in the economic globalization. Consequently, production processes by multinational corporations are becoming geographically fragmented to an unprecedented degree. Development and application of high-techs has enabled companies in developed countries not only to move the production of manufacturing industries overseas but to outsource certain service sectors to developing countries so as to cut management costs.[55] This production sharing enlarges considerably upon the gains from trade envisioned by Ricardo, who defined comparative advantage in terms of the production costs of final goods rather than their various components. In one sense, the global production chain of the multinational corporation represents the logical extension of comparative advantage, but in other senses it completely recasts its basic logic. Ricardo—and later Heckscher-Ohlin—conceived of trade as a means to take advantage of the different factor endowments inherent in the basic geographic, economic, technological, and human attributes of national units. By contrast, this new pattern of global production requires extensive cross-national movements of the factor endowments themselves, especially capital and technology. These flows also transform fundamental aspects of national economies in order to create the comparative advantages.[52] For these reasons, global trade reached a milestone in the 2000s as evidenced by that the sum of imports and exports rose to about half of world GDP. In this process, U.S. multinationals have earned huge profits, and the United States has been the main long-term beneficiary of globalization. As before, the United States set the tone and led the way to maintain its prosperity and high living standards helped by low-cost overseas manufacturing, low-priced imports, and the global circulation of dollars, but many other countries benefited in their slipstream in that more population of these countries achieved their middle-class status by participating in the global

[53] Moon, B. E. (2010). *Dilemmas of international trade* (second edition). Routledge.

[54] Mandle, J. (2001). Reforming globalization. *Challenge*, 44(2), 24–38.

[55] Bingxi, Z. (2007). Rethinking Economic Globalization. *China Int'l Stud.*, 8, 86.

economy. Additionally, during this period, the trend toward a multipolar world has gained strong momentum. In this context, as was reflected in the flowing "Banana Trade War" and "Steel Trade War," which were the most two remarkable trade wars in this period, international trade regulations have been applied more by many countries to deal with trade conflicts.

In 1993, to restrict the import of Bananas to its colonies in Africa and Caribbean, Europe imposed heavy tariffs on the import of Latin American bananas. Since the U.S. companies owned most of the banana farms in Latin America, European high tariff policy also caused great damages to the U.S. farming. In retaliation, the United States placed punitive tariffs up to 100% on $520 million worth of items from the EU such as French handbags, British linens, and Danish hams in March of 1999. This retaliatory move was taken in accordance with "Section 301" of U.S. Trade Law.

When the United States filed eight separate complaints to the WTO, the EU made a request to review the legality of "Section 301" as a response. After one month's investigation, the WTO concluded that the EU had amended the banana import deal and thus the United States was entitled to impose sanctions on $191.4 million of EU products. The EU has also formally filed a complaint in the WTO against Section 301 of the U.S. Trade Act, which is often arbitrarily used by the United States.[56] Nevertheless, at last, the EU had to agree to gradually reduce tariffs on bananas from Latin America. However, it was only in 2012 that the EU and ten Latin American countries signed an agreement to formally end all the eight WTO cases, ending the 20-year long banana war.

At the beginning of this century, the vast overcapacity in global steel market impelled the U.S. steelmakers to seek the protection of the government against foreign rivals. In an effort to help domestic steel companies restructure the industry, President Bush imposed temporary tariffs on steel imports in 2002. These tariffs ranged from 8% to 30% for ten categories of imported products such as flat rolled steel, machine wire, and welded pipe. In addition to tariffs, import licenses and quotas, which can be amended by Bush if the industry's financial crisis worsens or eases

[56] Satapathy, C. (1998). US-EU Trade War over Bananas. *Economic and Political Weekly*, 33(52), 3303–3304.

in the next three years, were also applied. Canada and Mexico were exempt from this tariff because of penalties the United States would face under a free-trade accord. Developing countries such as Argentina, Thailand, and Turkey were also exempt for the backlash from U.S. manufacturers relying on cheap steel, while the EU was not so lucky. This move drew instant criticism from the European Union, which estimates that it will suffer a loss of up to $2.5 billion in annual steel exports and worries that third countries, such as Korea, Russia, and Ukraine, will divert their steel exports to Europe. Among its remedies, the European Union bring a WTO challenge against U.S. safeguard provisions and impose its own restrictions to prevent a surge in redirected steel imports.

Soon the EU retaliated with tariffs on Florida oranges, U.S. autos and more, an attempt to inflict significant damage on Bush's campaign for re-election. A complaint against the United States was also filed by the EU as well as seven other nations with the WTO. The economic retaliation by the EU was detrimental to the American manufacturing industry and economy as a whole. Being regarded as a violation of tariff rate commitments, Bush had to bring the tariffs to an end in 18 months, earlier than the planned three-year period. However, the tariffs, combined with other challenges present in the marketplace at the time and in the months that followed, boosted steel costs to the detriment of American companies that use steel to produce goods in the United States. Within months of the tariff, the World Trade Organization had deemed Bush's tariffs to be illegal, permitting the EU to set $1 to $4 billion worth of its own tariffs and sanctions in response. This sparked an international trade war leading to major steel shortages within America, which, according to Trade Partnership Worldwide, increased steel prices up to 38% within eight months. These volatile price hikes had collateral effects on the manufacturing industry: automobile and appliance companies now faced rising production costs along with shortages on steel. In addition, the tariffs led to higher steel prices and, according to the Institute for International Economics, the loss of up to 26,000 jobs in steel-using industries. This figure was estimated to be even more than all the jobs in the steel industry itself at that time due to rising steel prices.[57] Worse still, companies across most American industries needed to cut down on costs and did so largely at the expense of their workers, leading to a roughly $4 billion decrease in wages by March of 2002.[58]

As the United States was forced to adopt an increasingly aggressive trade strategy in dealing with its competitors in the industrialized world, it also had to cope with growing trade challenges from developing countries.

A New Competitor in Asia: U.S.-China Trade War

More recently, China's remarkable economic growth has begun to pose another major challenge to American trade policy in the twenty-first century. By dint of the successful export-oriented strategy, China has enjoyed impressive economic growth over the past few decades at an annual growth rate over 6% and has overtaken Japan to become the world's second-largest economy in 2010. Consequently, China and the United States have become the two largest economies in terms of GDP and the largest trading countries in the world.

As shown in Fig. 1.5, since China's accession to the WTO, bilateral trade between China and the United States has been increasing over time. In 2000, China for the first time surpassed Japan as the country with the largest trade surplus with the United States. The bilateral trade volume in goods and services between China and the United States has rapidly surged, from $101.8 billion in 1999 to $736.7 billion in 2018, showing the increasingly important trade partnership between China and the United States. Meanwhile, the trade imbalance between China and the United States has also grown, resulting in a deficit of $380.8 billion in 2018. The rapid pace of economic integration between China and the United States, while benefiting both sides overall, has made the trade relationship increasingly complex. On the one hand, China's large

[57] Francois, J., & Baughman, L. M. (2003). The unintended consequences of US steel import tariffs: A quantification of the impact during 2002. *Washington DC: CITAC Foundation.*

[58] John Kahn. (2018). Comparing the Bush and Trump Tariffs, Dartmouth Business Journal, http://dartmouthbusinessjournal.com/2018/09/04/comparing-bush-trump-tariffs/

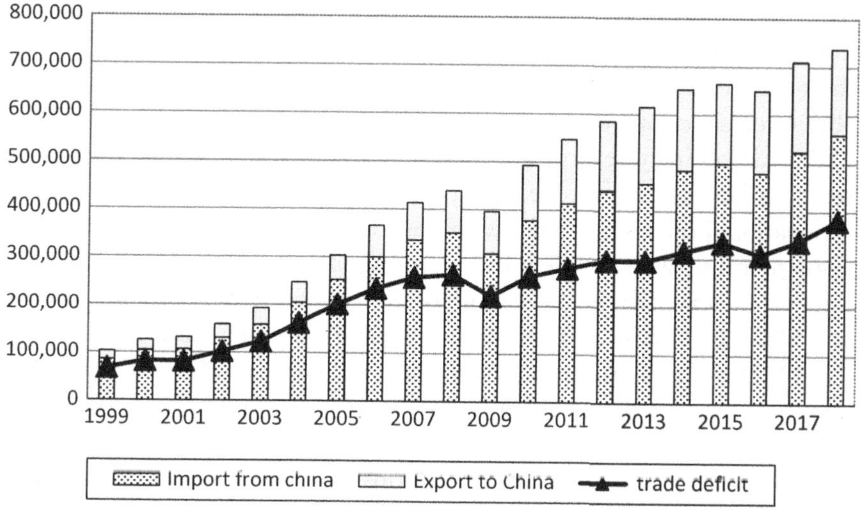

Fig. 1.5 Sino-U.S. bilateral trade in goods and services, 1999–2018 (millions of U.S. dollars). (*Data Source: U.S. Bureau of Economic Analysis*, https://www.bea.gov)

population and booming economy have made it a large and growing market for U.S. exporters. Over the past decade, China has been the fastest-growing market for U.S. exports. U.S. imports of low-cost goods from China greatly benefit U.S. consumers by increasing their purchasing power. U.S. firms that use China as the final point of assembly for their products, or use Chinese-made inputs for production in the United States, are able to lower costs and become more globally competitive. In addition, China's purchases of U.S. Treasury securities help keep U.S. interest rates relatively low. On the other hand, many analysts argue that growing economic ties with China have exposed U.S. manufacturing firms to greater, and what is often perceived to be "unfair" competition from low-cost Chinese firms. They argue that this has induced many U.S. production facilities to relocate to China, resulting in the loss of thousands of U.S. manufacturing jobs.[59] As a result, despite growing economic relations and mutual dependence, China and the United States

[59] Morrison, W. M. (2010, July). China-US trade issues. LIBRARY OF CONGRESS WASHINGTON DC CONGRESSIONAL RESEARCH SERVICE.

bilateral disputes have become increasingly intensive. China criticizes the United States of their export restrictions on high-technology products, their unfair treatments of China's market economy status, and unreasonable trade sanctions on China. Major areas of concern expressed by the United States include large numbers of trade surplus, relatively ineffective record of enforcing intellectual property rights (IPR), discriminatory innovation policies, forced technology transfer, and mixed record on implementing WTO obligations. Although faced with gradually increasing commercial disputes, the China-U.S. economic relations are positive and develop fast in general with agreement in the framework of the WTO. But the harmonious situation seems to change after Donald Trump was elected to be the president of the United States. In 2017, U.S. President Donald Trump instructed the U.S. Trade Representative (USTR) to investigate Chinese violations of intellectual property rights, invoking Section 301 of the Trade Act of 1974.[60] Until this period, China was willing to compromise up to a point to avoid its escalation of trade frictions.

Unfortunately, a trade war is happening between these two countries, which started in early 2018. In 2018, the United States increased tariffs on nearly 50% of its imports from China, raising the average U.S. tariff on imports from China from 3% to over 12%, while China immediately responded with tariff retaliation covering more than 70% of imports from the United States, increasing the average tariff applied to U.S. exports from less than 10% to over 18%.[61] Specifically, it started first by the United States imposing an additional 25% of tariffs on around US$34 billion worth of Chinese mechanical and technological products, including cars, aircraft parts, and computer hard drives, and then China immediately retaliated with tariffs on US$34 billion of U.S. goods, largely agricultural products. The first round of tariffs also on US$16 billion of Chinese goods including iron or steel products, electrical machinery, railway products, instruments, and apparatus quickly triggered China; it

[60] Li, C., He, C., & Lin, C. (2018). Economic impacts of the possible China–US trade war. *Emerging Markets Finance and Trade*, 54(7), 1557–1577.

[61] Bown, C. P. (2019). The 2018 US-China trade conflict after forty years of special protection. *China Economic Journal*, 12(2), 109–136.

responds by applying 25% tariffs on US$16 billion of U.S. goods, including motorcycles, bourbon, and orange juice. By the end of this year, the leaders of the two countries, Xi Jinping and Donald Trump, reached a consensus at the G20 Buenos Aires Summit, agreed to hold a 90-day negotiation, and suspended new trade measures during the negotiation period. At the meantime, the United States announced significant progress and extended the time limit for suspending new trade measures. Nevertheless, in May 2019, the United States further placed 10% taxes on US$200 billion of Chinese imports in the its second round of trade war, and then China responded by placing customs duties on US$60 billion of U.S. goods and filing additional charges against the U.S. trade measures on Chinese goods at the World Trade Organization (WTO). Then in June 2019, President Xi Jinping and President Trump held talks at the G20 Osaka Summit and agreed to restart economic and trade consultations. In which, President Trump promised that the United States would no longer impose new tariffs on Chinese products. Ironically, the same thing happened again. Just a month after the summit, due to Trump administration was dissatisfied with the Chinese government's purchase of American agricultural products, President Trump announced on Twitter that an additional 10% tariff would be imposed to US$300 billion goods from September 1. Immediately, the exchange rate of yuan sunk to 7 against the U.S. dollar—its lowest level in 11 years. After that, the U.S. Treasury declared China to be a currency manipulator, accusing China of manipulating its currency "to gain unfair competitive advantage in international trade." However, the People's Bank of China has refuted these claims in a strongly worded statement, maintaining that "China has never used and will not use the RMB exchange rate as a tool to deal with the trade frictions" and that "changes to the RMB exchange rate is determined by market supply and demand." Subsequently, the Chinese government announced a moratorium on the purchase of U.S. agricultural products. It seems that trade wars could become full economic wars, precisely as what happened under similar international conditions in Japan during 1980s. There can be no doubt that this trade war will not end easily so soon but reverberate for a long time to come. But the ever-increasing trade war seemed to turn around in September, when China and the United States agreed on September 5 to hold a new round of consultations in Washington in early October. The Chinese Ministry of Commerce said that the two countries would conduct serious consultations in mid-September to fully prepare for the substantive progress of the high-level consultations. And the U.S. Trade Representative Office confirmed that U.S. Trade Representative Wright Heze and Finance Minister Nuchin had spoken with Chinese Vice Premier Liu He and agreed to hold ministerial trade consultations in Washington in the coming weeks. In general, the trade war between China and the United States has always been twists and turns; it is still too early to predict its ending. The prospects for Sino-U.S. trade remain unclear.

Ostensibly, the existing explanations for President Trump's decision to trigger this trade war are the rapidly widening trade gap between the two countries. Figure 1.6 depicts an overview of the U.S. merchandise trade deficit with several important trading partners, including China, the European Union (EU), Mexico, Canada, and Japan. The merchandise trade deficit with China had become a major source of net imports of the United States since 2009, even larger than the sum of other four

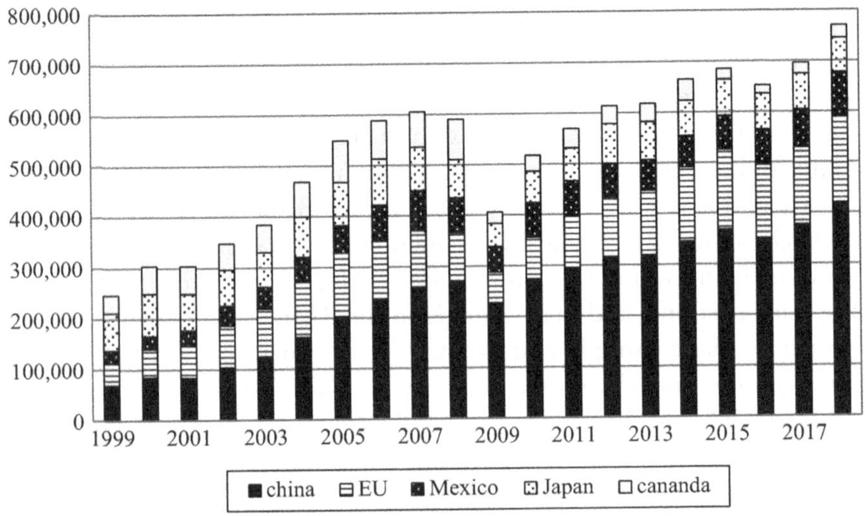

Fig. 1.6 The U.S. merchandise trade deficit with several important trading partners, 1999–2018 (millions of U.S. dollars). (*Data Source: U.S. Bureau of Economic Analysis,* https://www.bea.gov)

countries, reaching US$349 billion in 2018. The Trump administration holds the view that the "unfair" trade policies in China made the U.S. firms and products uncompetitive, thus resulting huge trade deficits to depress job creation in the U.S. economy.[62] The United States also accuses China of using policies to force American companies to transfer technology to their Chinese partners. In many sectors, American companies are required to engage in joint venture with Chinese companies in order to invest directly in China by setting up production facilities there. The United States also accuses China of failing to enforce intellectual property rights protection for American firms. Therefore, to "Make America Great Again," adopting trade protectionism policies is necessary before the United States re-negotiate a better deal with other countries on trade policies for president's "America First" agenda. However, the Chinese government considers that the deficit is an inevitable result brought about by the U.S. economic structure featured by insufficient domestic saving, high consumption level, and high labor costs. China also argues that the deficit is intrinsically determined by the comparative advantages and the international labor divisions of the two countries. Consequently, the slow growth and high unemployment of the U.S. economy could not be primarily attributed to China's WTO entry and industrial policies. In addition to the above-mentioned economic forces, political concerns are also important drivers for trade policies. Given that one of Trump's main promises during his election campaign was to solve the trade deficit problem, the China-U.S. trade war appears to be a timely and logical move to secure votes for his political party in the midterm elections.

While there are economic factors and political motives at play, at the crux of the China-U.S. trade war lies, in fact, a battle for global economic dominance. The wide array of strategic plans China announced lately, from the Belt and Road Initiative, Asian Infrastructure Investment Bank, to "Made in China 2025," have reinforced the image of China as a threat

[62] Sheng, L. (2015). Theorizing global imbalances: a perspective on savings and inequality. *Cambridge Review of International Affairs*, 28(2), 191–204.

to U.S. dominance.[63] "Made in China 2025" aims to build up and strengthen China's capacity as a global trade power, including information technology, high-end machinery and robotics, aerospace, marine equipment and ships, advanced rail transport, new-energy vehicles, electric power, agricultural machinery, new materials, and biomedical products. Looking at the actions that Trump administration has taken, it is urged that keeping China from achieving this goal has become the main motivation for the United States' continued expansion of the trade conflict. This is the most important view of the Trump administration, which believes that doing so can prevent the Chinese economy from catching up with the U.S. economy.[64] Moreover, real economic competition between the United States and China is in industries of the future—robotics, artificial intelligence, biotech, and more.[65] For example, the U.S. President has personally accused the Chinese telecommunications equipment and mobile phone maker, Huawei, of posing national security threats to Western countries without providing any evidence to support his claim. Moreover, the U.S. Department of Commerce announces the addition of Huawei to its "entity list," which effectively bans U.S. companies from selling to the Chinese telecommunications company without approval. Huawei is widely recognized as the company that could become the world leader in providing 5G technology to mobile devices in the future and is competing keenly with U.S. firms and others for the next generation of services. The fact that the president of the United States badmouths a rival without providing solid evidence was very unusual. It has gone beyond self-defense. All these actions of the United States taken together reveal how an incumbent economic, political, and military power tries to suppress the rise of an emerging rival.[66] Therefore, it is a reasonable motive for Trump to contain China's technological

[63] Chong, T. T. L., & Li, X. (2019). Understanding the China–US trade war: causes, economic impact, and the worst-case scenario. *Economic and Political Studies*, 7(2), 185–202.

[64] Yu, M., & Zhang, R. (2019). Understanding the recent Sino-US trade conflict. *China Economic Journal*, 12(2), 160–174.

[65] Lake, David A., and Jessica Chen Weiss. (2018, September 24). The Trump Administration Wrongly Assumed China Would Capitulate in a Trade War. What Happens Now? The Washington Post.

[66] Edwin L. C. Lai. (2019). The US–China trade war, the American public opinions and its effects on China. *Economic and Political Studies*, 7(2), 169–184.

upgrades, derail the "Made in China 2025" plan, and maintain U.S. dominance in the high-tech field through the trade war.[67]

Although it is too early to look for definitive results in the data and reliance should never be placed on short-term outcomes, the trade war has already caused damage to both sides and even the world. The aim of trade war is to push other countries to buy more U.S. industrial goods, energy products, and farm produce. However, U.S. exports have instead become one of the chief victims of the president's trade conflicts when export growth has plummeted in 2018. According to the OECD, the growth rate of exports in goods and services of the United States is 3.016% in 2018, lower than 2017's. What's more, in the same year, its imports by China still go upward, while exports by China slightly decrease.[68] That is to say, what President Trump has done even makes the situation worse—Trump's import barriers triggered foreign retaliation that cuts U.S. exports directly, and agricultural sales have been hit particularly hard. For example, China's retaliatory tariffs will hurt U.S. suppliers directly when the tariffs on soybeans will finally fall on U.S. farmers. The certain upshot of Trump's tariff war is that soybean exports from Brazil and other suppliers will enjoy higher prices, as China shifts its purchases away from the United States, while soybean exports from the United States will suffer lower prices. According to the U.S. Census, China is the world's largest consumer of soybeans and accounted for 60% of U.S. soybean exports before the trade dispute pulled shipment levels down. However, due to the recent trade conflict, American soybean exports to China has fallen sharply, with total shipment to the Asian economic giant expected to end this marketing year some two-thirds lower. In this case, American farmers are expected to be left with a record high level of ending stocks of over 1 billion bushels in this marketing year, as estimated by the U.S. Department of Agriculture.[69] There is no doubt, American farmers are forced to suffer a lot in the trade war. Worse still,

---

[67] Di, D., Luft, G., & Zhong, D. (2019). Why did Trump launch a trade war? A political economy explanation from the perspective of financial constraints. *Economic and Political Studies*, 7(2), 203–216.

[68] OECD Quarterly International Trade Statistics, Volume 2018 Issue 4.

[69] Tan, H. (2019, August 9). US Soybean Farmers are Working New Markets Now that Exports to China have Tanked, CNBC.

considering that international trade flows depend on confidence in future stability, the huge uncertainties surrounding Trump's trade policies and foreign reactions to them discourage exporters from making the investments needed to improve their competitiveness and expand their markets. The trade war also created financial turbulence, resulting in sharp decrease in the U.S. Dow Jones Industrial Average (DJI) and NASDAQ Index in 2018.[70] Besides, numerous studies have shown that American consumers are bearing much of the cost of the tariffs. It is found that the U.S. tariffs were almost completely passed through into U.S. domestic prices so that the entire incidence of the tariffs fell on domestic consumers and importers up to now, with no impact so far on the prices received by foreign exporters, and that U.S. producers responded to reduced import competition by raising their prices.[71] The damage is concentrated, as a percentage of income, among the lowest earners, who spend a larger share of their pay on imports than the upper middle class and the rich. On the other side, the reliance on U.S. trade leads to concerns that China might suffer substantial losses from the trade war. This uncertainty weighs on market sentiments and results in capital flowing out of China, which in turn suppresses its asset prices. For instance, over the past year, the Shanghai Securities Composite Index has decreased by 26% and reached 2493 in the end of 2018, which is even lower than the trough seen during the Chinese stock market turbulence from 2015 to 2016. Rapid capital outflows put strong depreciation pressure on the Renminbi (RMB). The RMB has depreciated past 7% against the U.S. dollar since August 2019. There is little sign, though, that China's loss is America's gain. Much of the business activity is shifting to other low-cost countries, like Vietnam, with a transition cost attached for American companies that depend on them. U.S. trade protectionist moves are seriously undermining international trade and the world economy, and disrupting the global supply and industrial value chains, destabilizing the global resource distribution system and harming multinational companies' productivity. Unless the

---

[70] Sheng, L., Zhao, H., & Zhao, J. (2019). Why will Trump lose the trade war?. *China Economic Journal*, 12(2), 137–159.

[71] Redding, S., Amiti, M., & Weinstein, D. (2019). The impact of the 2018 trade war on US prices and welfare. CEP Discussion Papers (1603). Centre for Economic Performance, LSE, London, UK., http://eprints.lse.ac.uk/102619/

president reverses course, his trade policy will continue to weaken rather than strengthen the U.S. economy as well as undermine the global trading system.

Undisputedly, as the two largest economies in the world, the relationship between the two countries will have huge impacts on not only their economies but also the global economy. These negative effects will be magnified by the global supply chains of production, ultimately hurting international trade and then globalization.[72] Since the second half of the twentieth century, the world economy has been focused on integration of production processes and globalization of cooperation institutions, the active opening of borders to facilitate the movement of capital, technology, and economic resources between countries.[73] In today's world, it is misleading that products sold to consumers are marked "made in XX," since the final product bought by consumer may have been assembled in country XX, but would normally have components from a large number of countries.[74] That is to say, in the context of globalization, a product which "made in China" also made in other countries, especially developing countries. In this case, a trade war between the two giants is also a trade war which could influence the whole world.

In Asia, a strong supply chain has been built with China importing intermediate goods to be assembled into final products for export to the United States.[75] According to China Semiconductor Industry Association, China is the world's largest semiconductor consumer market. In 2017, China imported US$260 billion in semiconductors, with a self-made rate of less than 20%. Of which, most of semiconductors China have imported comes from South Korea and Japan, as well as Taiwan. Besides, Vietnam and Malaysia also supply China with machine parts and components for communications equipment. In a word,

[72] Qiu, L. D., & Wei, X. (2019). China–US trade: implications on conflicts. *China Economic Journal*, 12(2), 175–194.

[73] Semin, A. N., Kostyaev, A. I., Truba, A. S., Ponkratov, V. V., & Gagarina, M. V. (2019). Economic ramifications of China–United States trade war for the Russian Federation. *China Economic Journal*, 12(3), 316–335, DOI: https://doi.org/10.1080/17538963.2019.1591573.

[74] Moeller, J. O. (2018). U.S.–China Trade War: Opportunities & Risks for Southeast Asia. © ISEAS Yusof Ishak Institute. http://hdl.handle.net/11540/8906.

[75] Moeller, J. O. (2018). U.S.–China Trade War: Opportunities & Risks for Southeast Asia. © ISEAS Yusof Ishak Institute. http://hdl.handle.net/11540/8906.

every electronic product that China sells to the United States has close ties with other Asian countries. In a short term, tariffs on Chinese goods would cause its price to rise and market competitiveness to decline, which would further lead to a decline in demand for the commodity market. In this case, due to the export-oriented structure, China's demand of importing semiconductors would decrease, which could directly influence those semiconductor exporters. In a long term, however, the trade war may cause several positive impacts for them. First of all, on the American market, the decline of demand toward Chinese goods means an opportunity for other Asian countries, since tariffs lead to trade diversion. If the U.S. imports switch from coming from China to having Southeast Asia as the source, it is an excellent trading opportunity for these developing countries. Secondly, the same situation also exists on the Chinese market, when U.S. products are no longer popular with Chinese consumers. What's more, trade war could lead to relocation of investments. According to a survey conducted by American Chamber of Commerce in China, around 19% of respondents consider moving capacity outside of China, the majority of which attributes such consideration on U.S. tariffs on China. About 40% of the respondents that consider relocating their production capacities consider developing Asia as their main destination for relocation.[76] Hence, Southeast Asian countries with cheap and abundant labor are good places to invest. Some even say that Southeast Asia is about to replace China and become a new world factory.

The Sino-U.S. trade war also affects other continents. Affected by the trade war, the economic growth of both the United States and China will slow down. According to the World Growth Forecast, the International Monetary Fund cut its 2019 U.S. growth forecast to 2.5% from 2.7% previously, while it cuts China's 2019 growth forecast to 6.2% from 6.4%.[77] A slowdown in the Chinese economy because of the duties imposed on the Chinese exports of goods and services to the United States can prompt a reduced demand for oil and a decrease in its prices

[76] AMCHARM.

[77] Lawder, D. (2018, October 9). IMF Cuts World Economic Growth Forecasts on Tariff War, Emerging Market Strains. *Reuters*.

on the global energy market.[78] For example, in August 2019, President Trump tweeted that he was applying 10% tariffs on an additional $300 billion of Chinese goods. Subsequently, oil prices sank by 8% with the stocks of oil producers also plummeting, some by more than 10%.[79] This fluctuation of oil prices has a conspicuous impact toward those oil exporting countries, for instance, Russia. Eighty percent of Russian exports to the PRC are energy sources, primarily oil and coal as well as wood.[80] Consequently, a reduction in Chinese procurement and an inevitable downturn in international energy prices have made the Russian economy at risk. But, at the same time, Sino-U.S. trade war also offers Russia an opportunity to enhance cooperation with China. In June 2019, President Xi and President Putin announced in Moscow that the two countries would strengthen the comprehensive strategic cooperation. According to the statement, the PRC and Russian Federation would strengthen cooperation in areas of aerospace technology, information and communication technology, digital economy, and agriculture.[81] It is worth mentioning that the cooperation agreement signed by the two sides also included the 5G contract signed by Russia's largest operator, Russia Mobile Telecommunications System Corporation (MTS), and China's telecom giant Huawei. Alexey Kornya, president and CEO of Russia Mobile Telecommunications Systems, said in a statement that the agreement with Huawei would not only develop commercial 5G networks in Russia in the near future but also contribute to the development of closer economic relations for China and Russia.[82] As the United States is currently trying to prevent other countries from using Huawei's equipment on the grounds of security, as well as suppress the development of China's high technology, the Sino-Russian cooperation statement seems to be a counterbalance to the Trump administration.

---

[78] Semin, A. N., Kostyaev, A. I., Truba, A. S., Ponkratov, V. V., & Gagarina, M. V. (2019). Economic ramifications of China–United States trade war for the Russian Federation. China Economic Journal, 12(3), 316–335, DOI: https://doi.org/10.1080/17538963.2019.1591573.

[79] Cohen, A. (2019, August, 6). Trump's China Trade War Hamming Oil Markets, *Forbes*.

[80] Russian Trade with China in 2018, Russian Foreign Trade, Feb 10th, 2019.

[81] Liangyu. (2019, June 6). Joint Statement between China and Russia on the Development of a Comprehensive Strategic and Cooperative Partnership in the New Era, *Xinhua News Agency*.

[82] The strenghening of China-Russia comprehensive strategic cooperation arouses concern in the United States, Voice of America, April 1, 2019.

As the third-largest trading partner of the United States, as well as its neighbor country, Canada is inevitably affected by the Sino-U.S. trade war. On the one hand, as the price of Chinese electronics, clothing, and other consumer goods rises in the United States, the decline demand for Chinese products has helped Canadian retailers to seek better market in the United States. However, the close relationship with its neighbor has also made Canada a sandwich between China and the United States. In December 2018, while Meng Wanzhou, CEO of Huawei, was transiting through Vancouver, she was arrested by the Canadian police at the request of the U.S. government without any conclusive evidence. This action subsequently caused strong dissatisfaction from the PRC government. The Ministry of Foreign Affairs has repeatedly made solemn representations and strong protests against Canada's detention of Meng Wanzhou, and demanded Canada to release Meng. At the meantime, since Meng Wanzhou was arrested, Sino-Canadian relations also fell into a freezing point. In March 2019, the PRC government announced to restrict import of rapeseed from two Canadian agribusinesses, Viterra and Richardson International, on the grounds of pests.[83] Therefore, it is widely believed that this action is China's retaliation against Canada for detaining Meng Wanzhou. According to the data of Canada, about 40% of Canadian rapeseed production is exported to China every year, which is worth $2 billion.[84] The prohibition of import announced by the PRC could cause a huge negative impact for the Canadian rapeseed products. What's more, in June, China alleged that the banned feed additive, clenbuterol, was found in a batch of pork products imported from Canada. China also found that as many as 188 health certificates related to pork exported to China were counterfeit. Therefore, the Canadian government is expected to suspend the export of meat to China. This action has affected nearly $500 million in trade in meat products.[85] Of course, there is no valid evidence which could illustrate

[83] Canola is banned by China, Canada has limited options, *Voice of America*, April 3, 2019.

[84] Canada claims to have a third rapeseed exportter's Chinese business in trouble, *Reuters*, April 3, 2019.

[85] Canada suspends all meat exports to China at China's request, *Wall Street Journal*, June 27, 2019.

that these are China's retaliation against Canada, but it is certain that Canada is playing an embarrassing role in the Sino-U.S. trade war.

There is a similar situation in the Britain too. First of all, as Britain's second-largest trading partner, which just ranks only second to the European Union, the slowdown of U.S. economy has a significant negative impact on the Britain. At the same time, its open economy is vulnerable to the global economic downturn. Besides, Britain is also puzzled by the Huawei issue. In May 2019, the United States stepped up pressure on Britain, warning that American intelligence sharing could be risked by the involvement of a Chinese company in a new British telecommunications network. The Secretary of State, Mike Pompeo, argues that China posed a range of economic and security threats that the world now faced "a new kind of challenge, an authoritarian regime that's integrated economically into the West."[86] Obviously, the Trump administration is trying to suppress Huawei's 5G technology by exerting pressure on its allies. Now the question on the table in Britain is whether the government should allow Huawei to help build some of the next generation, 5G cellular network in the country. On the one hand, Huawei is the leader of 5G technology nowadays. On the other hand, if Britain does cooperation with Huawei, this action must lead to the dissatisfaction of President Trump. In this case, Britain is forced to catch up in the diplomatic row between Washington and Beijing—the 5G issue becomes more complex. Although the former Prime Minister Theresa May had agreed to allow Huawei "restricted access to non-core parts of the 5G network," the decision has been put on hold following the U.S. intervention.[87] As new Prime Minister Boris Johnson takes office, there must be more uncertainties of Huawei issue.

Other European countries are also affected by the trade war, Germany, for example. As the biggest economy and the industrial powerhouse of Europe, Germany, its economy heavily, depends on exports. Germany has a degree of openness in trade (exports plus imports in relation to the GDP) of 85%, which is one of the highest numbers for developed

---

[86] Castle, S. (2019, May 8). Pompeo Attacks China and Warns Britain Over Huawei Security Risks. *The New York Times*.

[87] Holton, K. (2019, June, 13). UK Tells Telecom Firms to be Cautious over Huawei after U.S. Warnings. *Reuters*.

countries.[88] According to the World Bank, exports amount to almost half the German economy—47%—as its companies play a dominant role in global markets for luxury autos and complex industrial machinery.[89] Of which, the United States and China are Germany's largest and third-largest export markets respectively. That is to say, the external conditions, especially the U.S. and Chinese factors, make German economy extremely vulnerable. Since the types of products taxed by both China and the United States are different from the types of goods exported by Germany, it is nearly impossible for Germany to make profit within the Sino--U.S. trade war. This makes the impacts of the trade war on Germany almost entirely negative—a huge change in the flow of export commodities and the fluctuation of prices. It is said that Germany's industrial output dropped 1.5% in June and is now down 5.2% year-on-year, which prompting warnings from economists that President Trump's trade war with China and threatened tariffs on car imports from Germany could potentially push the country toward a recession.[90] In sum, the unilateralism and protectionism that insisted by Trump administration, as well as the trade uncertainty which is caused by those ideas, will affect every corner of the world.

History also reveals that trade barriers are easy to impose and hard to remove. And it can take decades to repair the damage. Lessons from the past, such as the trade disaster of the 1930s, suggest that protectionism begets protectionism. Although Trump wants to use tariffs to protect certain manufacturing sectors of the United States so as to bring manufacturing jobs back to the United States, this is going against economic forces, as the United States does not have comparative advantage in many manufacturing sectors anymore. It can only lead to lower economic

[88] Schmucker, C. (2018). US-China Trade War: Why Germany Should Support EU? Itituto Per Gli Studi Di Politica internazionale.

[89] LeRoy, W. (2019, August, 12). New Figures Show U.S.-China Trade War is Hurting Germany—Europe Economic Motor. *Global News*.

[90] Noack, R. (2019, August 7). Germany was Europe's Economic Growth Engine, Trade War could Drive it to Recession. *The Washington Post*.

growth and lower living standard for the American people.[91] The current account deficits are also less likely to be reduced by simply increasing tariffs on imports from China, because trade deficits are mainly driven by the low household saving rates, high government deficits, and the demand for U.S. dollars.[92] Trade imbalances are rooted in savings disparities between some OECD and East Asian countries and particularly between China and the United States.[93] Besides, at the international level, U.S. trade policy in the Trump administration is protectionist, raising tariffs outside of WTO rules, threatening trade wars, withdrawing from existing trade agreements, and negotiating new bilateral trade deals rather than free-trade agreements. The reaction of the rest of the world has been to support the WTO rules-based trading system and to pursue new and expanded regional trade agreements that do not include the United States. The result may be U.S. disengagement from the world trading system, with countries diverting trade around the United States.[94] In fact, U.S. attempts to address problems through the WTO mostly ground to a halt.[95] And the United States put fewer and fewer of its grievances forward to formal WTO dispute settlement, the mechanism tasked with preventing bilateral trade spats from escalating into trade wars. The U.S. actions in 2018 not only brought trade frictions with China to a head, but its strategy also deliberately pushed the multilateral trading system to its breaking point. As a result, the global trading system, including the World Trade Organization, has been put at risk, and it is unclear whether markets will remain open in the future. Meanwhile, globalism and multilateralism are under attack, and the resurgence of geopolitical and power competition, mixed with populism and protectionism, is weakening the bonds built among countries in recent decades. These

[91] Irwin, D. A. (2017). The false promise of protectionism: Why trump's trade policy could backfire. *Foreign Affairs*, 96(3), 45–56.

[92] Sheng, L., Zhao, H., & Zhao, J. (2019). Why will Trump lose the trade war?. *China Economic Journal*, 12(2), 137–159.

[93] Sheng, L. (2014). Income inequality, financial systems, and global imbalances: a theoretical consideration. *Global Policy*, 5(3), 311–320.

[94] Robinson, S., & Thierfelder, K. (2019). Global adjustment to US disengagement from the world trading system. *Journal of Policy Modeling*, 41(3), 522–536.

[95] Bown, C. P. (2019). The 2018 US-China trade conflict after forty years of special protection. *China Economic Journal*, 12(2), 109–136.

uncertainties seem poised to drag the world back to the turbulent years of the early twentieth century.

Free Trade and Globalization Under Fire

One thing that is worth noting in this period is that with globalization advances, active economy interactions have transformed some countries or people from globalization proponents to anti-globalization protesters, triggering increasingly heating anti-globalization movements, typical as 1999 Seattle WTO protests.[96] Because most of the benefits from globalization are concentrated in a tiny number of hands, some people who are hurt by globalization become a critical anti-globalization power.

Expressions of anti-globalization revolts spread throughout the world. One of the most striking emerged in response to U.S.-led free-trade agreements. The NAFTA (North American Free Trade Agreement) between the United States, Canada, and Mexico made competition unfair for countries in the face of the superiority of the American economy: making the departure of U.S. factories to Mexico quite advantageous for multinational companies, taking advantage of the wage labor well below that of the Americans, in addition to putting Mexican agriculture at risk in the face of corn production. It was with the outbreak of the Zapatista Liberation Army (EZL) movement in the Chiapas region, in impoverished southern Mexico. In 1994, the world saw a strong-armed reaction led by indigenous people that opposed the pretensions of a globalization that only served the market interests.

The anti-globalization movements were gathering in a new context after previous decades marked by the polarization between two blocs (capitalist-socialist). The deepening of liberal reforms based on the Washington Consensus brought about a new dynamic of conflicts of

[96] On the World Trade Organization meeting in December 1999, there were significant numbers of international participants in Seattle, which exhibited labor, environmentalist, feminist, anticapitalist, animal rights, anarchist, and other groups organized to protest aspects of globalization and form new alliances and solidarities for future struggles. In addition, protests occurred throughout the world.

Quoted in Kellner, D. (2002). Theorizing globalization. *Sociological theory*, 20(3), 285–305.

multiple class nature, precarious work, territorial disputes, ethnic and environmental issues and on the external debts of underdeveloped countries. In 2001, the initiative of the World Social Forum in Brazil, as opposed to the Davos Forum in Switzerland, takes place in this context. This was an attempt to articulate the synthesis of the various social movements in the countryside and the city, environmentalists, women, indigenous, gender and ethnic groups, social organizations, NGOs, unions, and left parties that had the flag in common: "Another Globalization is Possible." Other forums were created by all the continents in an attempt to oppose neoliberal measures in full progress on what remained of the welfare state.

Specific to the United States, the globalization makes many manufacturing industries shift out of United States into developing countries including China and India, causing the United States to lose about a fifth of its share in global manufacturing output. Besides the stagnation of manufacturing industry, a huge trade deficit with others concerns U.S. society. The disadvantaged position transforms U.S. society. Blue collars have to work harder because of greater competition from cheaper labor markets, aided by a drive for productivity gains. Despite that, their pay only keeps at the same level as before, even lower. Laid-off workers attribute their misfortunes, job losses, and economic stagnation to globalization. Some politicians magnify the adverse effects of globalization to serve their political interests, which further misleads common people into changing their view. Finally, these sentiments converge to become an anti-globalization power spreading in today's American society. By contrast, those groups benefited most from the globalization process, including consumers who pay lower prices, managers who earn higher salaries, and shareholders enriched by dividends and equity growth, are more firmly supportive of globalization. However, for all the focus on globalization, in the long run, the most important force shaping the labor market and income inequality will be not trade or politics but technological change. Automation has already transformed the economies of the developed world and the nature of employment there, and almost all experts believe that the scope for expanding automation is enormous.

As costs fall and the pace of innovation accelerates, the impact of automation will spread to middle-income countries and, eventually, to lower-income ones, as well. Of course, no one knows with certainty how quickly such changes will occur, and every country should invest in education, technology, and infrastructure so that it can anticipate them better.[97]

Trade war, a product of the conflict between national interests and globalization, can also be regarded as a manifestation of anti-globalization. But anyway, no forces can hold back the progress of globalization; globalization has become the dominant political and economic discourse of the developed world—"a grand narrative of our time."[98] Trade and financial integration in the context of globalization tends to pacify relations between states, creating stakes that prefer peace to trade war, and the rise of global supply and production networks only enhances these tendencies. To some extent, anti-globalization itself is a kind of "globalization" phenomenon in that it is the globalization that brings anti-globalization protesters from all over the world, different industries, and different backgrounds with different political opinions together. The existence of these anti-globalization protesters reminds us of looking at the globalization dialectically. Then the aforementioned trade wars in history provide us with a chance of rethinking globalization profoundly. In fact, they reflect some problems arising from the process of globalization. What we should do is to learn about these problems and then to explore an appropriate global governance way to avoid them.[99]

---

[97] Hu, F., & Spence, M. (2017). Why Globalization Stalled: An How to Restart It. *Foreign Aff.*, 96, 54.

[98] Barber, P. G., & Lem, W. (2004). Commodities, Capitalism and Globalization: Introduction. *Anthropologica*, 46(2), 123–129.

[99] Sheng, L. (2010). Growth–volatility tradeoff in the face of financial openness: a perspective of developing economies. *Cambridge Review of International Affairs*, 23(4), 609–622.

2

On Sino-U.S. Trade Wars: A Dialectical Consideration

Why Did Trump Start the Trade War with China?

Historically, concerns about the health of the global economy often lead to collaboration, cooperation, and engagement among the world's largest countries. Hence, the positive relationship between the two largest countries in the world—China and the United States—can be viewed as a key element for global stability, development, and prosperity.[1] However, the situation is now different. The growing conflict between the United States and China, the first- and second-largest economies on Earth, has become the greatest threat to the global economy. While the global economy is far more integrated now, improvements in communications and technology have both accelerated the spread of information and increased its volume.[2] Consequently, as the leaders of these two countries openly exert

[1] Center for China & Globalization Report (2018). Understanding the US-China Trade War: Analyses and CCG Recommendations. http://en.ccg.org.cn/html/publications/2362.html

[2] Dobbins, J., Solomon, R. H., Chase, M. S., Henry, R., Larrabee, F. S., Lempert, R. J., ... & Shatz, H. J. (2015). *Choices for America in a Turbulent World: Strategic Rethink*. Rand Corporation.

L. Sheng, D. Felix do Nascimento, *Love and Trade War*,
https://doi.org/10.1007/978-981-33-4897-4_2

pressure on the other side, other countries in the world are now worried that they will suffer collateral damage in an escalating trade war. In fact, since the initiation of tariffs on Chinese imports by the United States and the tariff retaliation by China on U.S. imports, the impacts have started to show on global sales and purchases of products as well as commodities across the world.[3] Nonetheless, after rounds of consultations, the trade war between China and the United States has not been eased but has become even tenser.[4]

President Trump has made a strong domestic economy a core selling point for his presidency since taking office in 2016, and his campaign advisers also believe that this is the key to his re-election. During these years, Trump adhered to the principle of America First, using the tool of tariffs to make a big commotion in global trade and to take back the lost manufacturing interests of the United States. Meanwhile, China, which has the greatest trade surplus with the United States, bears the brunt of the tariffs.[5] Basically, the Trump administration that holds four views on the growing trade imbalance between China and the United States. (1) In bilateral trade between China and the United States, surplus benefits China, while deficit hurts the U.S. economy enormously. (2) The main causes of the Sino-U.S. trade imbalance are the Chinese government's subsidies for Chinese exporters and unfair tariff policies. (3) To tackle the problem of the trade imbalance between China and the United States,

[3] Iqbal, B. A., Rahman, N., & Elimimian, J. (2019). The future of global trade in the presence of the Sino-US trade war. *Economic and Political Studies*, 7(2), 217–231.

[4] On September 5, 2019, China and the United States agree to start the 13th round of trade talks. China and the United States have agreed to hold high-level trade talks in Washington, DC in early October, announced China's Ministry of Commerce. Trade teams from both countries will begin consultations in mid-September in preparation for these high-level talks. "The two sides agreed that they should work together and take practical actions to create favorable conditions for consultations," the announcement stated. Wong, D., & Koty, A, C. (2020, August 25). The US-China Trade War: A Timeline, China Briefing. https://www.china-briefing.com/news/the-us-china-trade-war-a-timeline/

[5] The U.S. trade deficit with China has been growing in both absolute and relative terms. By 2017, the trade deficit with China had become a major source of net imports of the United States, accounting for approximately 46% of the total deficit. Trade imbalances have long been the root of U.S. national debt crises as well as a source of public discontent in the United States, motivating the U.S. government to wage a trade war against China.

Chong, T. T. L., & Li, X. (2019). Understanding the China–US trade war: causes, economic impact, and the worst-case scenario. *Economic and Political Studies*, 7(2), 185–202.

the only solution is to suppress China's exports by imposing high tariffs on Chinese exports to the United States. (4) The Sino-U.S. economic and trade imbalances will be resolved by forcing China to continue specializing in the low-value-added segments of the global value chain (GVC), which will enable the United States to maintain its monopoly market power in the high-value-added segments of the global value chain.[6]

Americans were not in a particularly good mood during the 2016 presidential campaign. Indeed, one could scarcely read a newspaper or watch television without hearing that Americans were angry about something. Some were angry about the persistently weak economic recovery. Some complained about the escalating cost of healthcare. Some were upset about trade and the loss of American jobs. Still others were angry about their perception of a rigged system in which the interests of privileged elites receive greater consideration than the interests of ordinary Americans. As a consequence, Americans chose to direct their anger toward the federal government. Meanwhile, the anger expressed by the American electorate displayed a decidedly populist tone.[7] Trump's success in the presidential election can be considered the result of populism.[8] Like many populists, he was an outsider without support from the organizational structure of the Republican Party and had little in the way of a traditional campaign organization but was able to mobilize popular support by means of claiming the media spotlight as well as exploiting social media, particularly Twitter.[9] Today, the United States is still the country with the strongest comprehensive national power on this planet, where the wave of populism was considered unimaginable. In fact, the rise of populism in the United States stems from the setbacks suffered by its

[6] Yu, M., & Zhang, R. (2019). Understanding the recent Sino-US trade conflict. *China Economic Journal*, 12(2), 160–174.

[7] Rudolph, T. (2019). Populist anger, Donald Trump, and the 2016 election. Journal of Elections, *Public Opinion and Parties*, 1–26.

[8] Populism in America has been defined as the constellation of three interrelated dimensions: anti-elitism, mistrust of experts, and nationalism. The primary dimension of populism, anti-elite sentiment, is closely associated with anger toward the government.

Rudolph, T. (2019). Populist anger, Donald Trump, and the 2016 election. Journal of Elections, *Public Opinion and Parties*, 1–26.

[9] Hallin, D. C. (2019). Mediatisation, neoliberalism and populisms: the case of Trump. *Contemporary Social Science*, 14(1), 14–25.

domestic system, which is directly reflected in the increase in inequality in the United States. Therefore, the economic capability of the middle and lower classes continues to fall. After Trump's unexpected success in his election in 2016, the American business elites, who were not truly concerned about the middle or lower classes, began to pay attention to the research results of globalization over the past decade and began to reflect on the U.S. domestic system and the existing global trading system.

According to the research findings of Thomas Piketty, a professor of Paris School of Economics, the richest 10% of the population in the United States today holds 70% of the total capital, while 50% of the poorest population shares only 5% of the total capital, which shows the wide gap between the rich and the poor in the United States. In addition, increased international trade due to globalization, especially the import of manufactured goods by developed countries from developing countries, greatly alters the pattern of income distribution in wealthy nations. As developed countries import more labor-intensive manufactured goods from low labor-cost countries, downward pressure is exerted on the wages of less-educated and/or lower-skilled workers, thus further aggravating inequality.[10] According to statistics, the U.S. labor market lost approximately 4.4 million manufacturing jobs between 1990 and 2008.[11] Judging from the current existing public information, the consensus of academic, political, and public opinion in the United States, regardless of party and political views, is that the massive loss of manufacturing jobs is a key factor in making the middle and lower classes economically worse off in the United States.

Based on the above facts, it is not difficult to understand why mainstream American public opinion believes that the Chinese have taken advantage of globalization by stealing American people's jobs and why Trump's trade strategy with China has gained more recognition from the middle and lower classes in the United States. Trump was elected as president partly because of the support of these middle- and lower-class

[10] Brennan, J. (2016). United States income inequality: The concept of countervailing power revisited. *Journal of Post Keynesian Economics*, 39(1), 72–92.

[11] Spence, M., Katz, R., & Lawrence, R. Z. (2011). Manufacturing globalization: The real sources of US inequality and unemployment. *Foreign Affairs*, 90(6), 166–171.

people living in rural areas of the United States. Furthermore, many of these people are manufacturing workers who were affected negatively by imports from China, especially after China obtained access to the World Trade Organization (WTO) in 2001. In a paper titled "The China Syndrome: Local Labor Market Effects of Import Competition in the United States" published in the *American Economic Review*, Autor, Dorn, and Hanson (2013) show evidence that Chinese exports to the United States resulted in great job losses and hardship for manufacturing workers in regions of the United States, many of which were rural areas. According to their finding, "the increasing imports leads to increasing unemployment, lower labour force participation, and shrinking wages in local labour markets that house import competing manufacturing industries."[12] It is clear that public opinion on the economy and trade policies played an extremely crucial role in Trump's success in both the Republican primary and the general election. Jobs and the economy were the top issues for many voters, and Trump attached great significance to these issues—especially the association between unemployment and international trade throughout his campaign. During the campaign period, Trump responded to these concerns and repeatedly emphasized economic issues. As a result, Americans who negatively evaluated the economy or their individual financial situation were more likely to vote for Trump than those who expressed positive evaluations.[13] In the eyes of many Americans, China has adopted a series of unfair trade policies for a long time, which not only harm the national interests of the United States but also exacerbate the economic difficulties of the middle and lower classes.

Deindustrialization as a Concrete Problem

The rhetoric of Trump's political speeches and that of his economic staff, advisers, and secretaries in the trade war revolve around justifications for protecting the industrial, mining (steel and iron), intellectual property

[12] Lai, E. L. C. (2019). The US–China trade war, the American public opinions and its effects on China. *Economic and Political Studies*, 7(2), 169–184.

[13] Blendon, R. J., Casey, L. S., & Benson, J. M. (2017). Public opinion and trump's jobs and trade policies. *Challenge*, 60(3), 228–244.

rights (IPR), and energy sectors. The reasons this administration gave to pursue an economic policy with a protectionist bias, using economic barriers to preserve the interests of American companies and to consequently boost job creation, found support in domestic politics and received recognition from the electorate during the election. This rhetoric galvanized the angry feelings of the American public but assured that the internal demands of economic groups affected by external competition were being met and that concrete actions were being taken to resolve this issue, despite evidence that such actions already had unfavorable consequences and impacts. These objectives, motivated by economic nationalism with respect to external economic relations and the unwinding of Obama's policies on domestic matters, particularly focused on measures involving deregulation. These policies have been unconventional combinations of free-market and protectionist measures and intentions to reduce the federal deficit while, at the same time, boosting expenditures on infrastructure and the military.[14]

According to Guillen,[15] there is an ongoing process of stagnation, deglobalization, and deflation that condition the foreign policy of the United States and its trade policy. The social discontent against neoliberalism took root in large sections of the population. The neoliberal consensus between social democrats and traditional right-wing parties began to fracture. The triumph of Donald Trump in the United States, through a fascist, xenophobic, protectionist, and deglobalizing discourse, is a reflection of these processes of fragmenting the world economy. We will try to define some elements of the characteristics of the current phase of deindustrialization that the economies of the United States and most developed countries have been facing. We intend to seek scientific reasons beyond the propagated "China Effect."

[14] Pham, H. N. A., Ramiah, V., Moosa, N., Huynh, T., & Pham, N. (2018). The financial effects of Trumpism. *Economic Modelling*, 74, 264–274.

[15] Guillén, A. (2019). USA's trade policy in the context of global crisis and the decline of North American hegemony. *Brazilian Journal of Political Economy*, 39(3), 387–407.

The report of United Nations Conference on Trade and Development (UNCTAD)[16] "Capital accumulation, economic growth and structural change" (2003) elaborated a concept of different types of deindustrialization after the 1990s during which most developed countries (the United States, Canada, European Union, and Japan) increased their economic power over developing countries. After a historic process of industrialization and urbanization maturity, with the informatization of the economy and automation of industrialization, the services sector expanded and diversified, with a higher growth rate than industry, causing the transformation of industry in developed countries to continuously shrink in regard to its percentage of the Gross National Product[17] (Cano, 2014). In developed countries such as the United States, industry started to grow with different characteristics. Despite large public investments, there were private investments with a greater share of financial capital and investment funds, science and technology development, industrial automation, increased productivity, and international competitiveness. According to UNCTAD, developed countries started to be characterized by "normal or positive deindustrialization," but underdeveloped countries were characterized by "early or negative deindustrialization." In underdeveloped countries, on the other hand, even if industries were growing, they were growing at reduced rates, with lower investment rates, stagnation or a drop in productivity, loss of external and internal competitiveness or drop in the share of their manufactured exports, and, in many cases, a dependence on commodity prices to reduce the transaction deficit.

The empirical studies of Leif van Neuss[18] (2018) of 15 advanced OECD countries suggest that the contribution of globalization to deindustrialization in advanced countries—especially by the growing North-South integration—may be revised upward when using better-suited indicators of trade. Furthermore, the role and relative importance of the "internal" and "external" factors—those linked to globalization and

[16] UNCTAD (2003). Capital accumulation, economic growth and structural change. Trade and Development Report, Geneva.

[17] Cano, W. (2014). (Des)Industrialização e (Sub)Desenvolvimento. IE/Unicamp, Campinas, n. 244.

[18] Van Neuss, L. (2018). Globalization and deindustrialization in advanced countries. *Structural Change and Economic Dynamics*, 45, 49–63.

trade—are still very far from being consensual. This study demonstrates that the manufacturing share of employment decreased from 28.2% to 15.6% in the EU15 between 1970 and 2007, while it dropped from 22.4% to 9.9% in the United States. Over the same period, the manufacturing share of nominal value-added declined from 26.6% to 18.1% in the EU15, while it dropped from 23.5% to 13.1% in the United States. Four primary sources of deindustrialization were identified: (1) nonhomothetic tastes, (2) technology, (3) outsourcing, and (4) international trade. Besides, Ness (2018) concluded that the causes and consequences of deindustrialization are still far from being fully understood. Such concepts are also shared by Xiuying Du and Zixiong Xie[19] (2019), and Rowthorn and Wells[20] (1987). They developed the concept of deindustrialization by classifying the causes and consequences of deindustrialization into premature deindustrialization, positive and negative deindustrialization, and (de)industrialization efficiency.

The developed countries that underwent normal deindustrialization showed declining participation of the manufacturing industry compared with the total amount between 1990 and 2012, with this sector in the United States falling from 18.2% to 12.3%, in Canada from 17.1% to 10.8%, in France from 17.6% to 10%, and in Japan from 25 to 18.7%, with Germany being the exception because of its usual high rate, which showed a slight drop in deindustrialization of 27.1–23.8%. Note that the loss of production in developed countries also occurred due to the internationalization of companies and foreign direct investments. In reality, there was a change due to a geographical shift in production mostly in favor of China, India, and East Asia. The investor countries have continued to appropriate a substantial part of the added value of this production through the receipt of royalties, profits, and other rights (intellectual property, brands, and others).

Although the American manufacturing industry had an average annual rate of 3.8% (1990–2000) and 1.9% (2000–2007), it had a negative rate of 0.5% (2007–2012), showing the impacts of the financial crisis of

---

[19] Du, X., & Xie, Z. (2020). Occurrence of turning point on environmental Kuznets curve in the process of (de) industrialization. *Structural Change and Economic Dynamics*, 53, 359–369.

[20] Rowthorn, R., & Wells, J. (1987). *De-Industrialization Foreign Trade*. Cambridge University Press, Cambridge.

2008. Also, the Gross Domestic Product (GDP) participation of American industry was 19.7% in 2010 and 18.5% in 2017. The services sector and others in the same period increased from 79.3% to 80.7%. This change occurred even with an increase in the percentage of workers employed in the manufacturing industry from 18.5% in 2010 to 18.7% in 2019.

An Aggressive Foreign Policy

The measures taken by Trump in the trade war follow the unilateralist orientation of American foreign policy, as he expresses his preference for the one-sided approach, weakening the international system to the detriment of multilateral mechanisms. The unilateralism of American foreign policy, denounced by several countries and members of international multilateral organizations, is a threat to international security and represents another example of the countless unilateralist practices of the United States, such as the American invasion of Iraq (2003) by the Bush administration without UN consent and the assassination of the Iranian General Qasem Soleimani (2020) by the Trump administration without authorization from the U.S. Congress, that make Washington's decisions even more explosive and unstable.

Regarding international trade, the greatest example of this unilateralist practice occurred in December 2019 with the U.S. boycott of the World Trade Organization (WTO) Dispute Settlement Body (DS). This was a new attack on the Bretton Woods Institutions, which were created by the United States and its European partners and controlled by them for decades. Trump demanded a "totally new structure" for the Dispute Settlement Body (DS) because he thinks it is unfair to American interests. Contradictorily, Trump praised the WTO decision in the Boeing and Airbus case (October 2019), authorizing the United States to impose rates of up to US$7.5 billion on European goods for 1 year. That is, the WTO is necessary only when it favors American interests in multilateral entities.

During the presidencies of Bill Clinton (1993–2001) and George W. Bush (2001–2009), with the predictable differences between the

Democratic and Republican administrations, the American trade policy of these administrations followed the trend of expanding trade policy and opening free-trade treaties. In the Barack Obama administration (2009–2017), trade policies to contain China, such as the Transatlantic Trade and Investment Partnership (TTIP)/Trans-Pacific Partnership (TPP) treaties, had already been drawn up and complemented WTO negotiations[21] (Nascimento, 2017). After the financial crisis of 2008 and with the increasing rise of China, a fertile environment was created for the return of speeches on fair trade by the Obama administration. As mentioned, anti-China rhetorical speeches in the 2016 election led Trump to the presidency.

Still, during the administrations of Presidents Bush and Hu Jintao in 2006, the Strategic Economic Dialogue between China and the United States was created, and steps were taken to create institutions to promote dialogue and cooperation[22] (Mendes, 2017). In 2009, Presidents Obama and Hu Jintao renamed this forum the U.S.-China Strategic and Economic Dialogue. A set of topics were discussed, such as economy, trade, counterterrorism, science and technology, education, culture, health, energy, environment and climate change, nonproliferation of nuclear weapons, and human rights[23] (Morrison, 2014).

During the Obama and Hu administrations, with the installation of the U.S.-China Strategic and Economic Dialogue, several points of tension were identified in the countries' relationship, which would later be incorporated by the Trump administration. Questions about the trade deficit were already debated, as well as criticisms of the Chinese monetary policy, with the United States accusing China of maintaining currency stability as an indirect way of subsidizing exports, which hindered American competitiveness, along with Chinese state intervention in the economy, undue product-dumping actions, and other barriers to market access.

---

[21] Nascimento, D. F. (2017). TISA/TTIP/TPP and the Exclusion of the BRICS: The possible impacts in Brazil. *Revista Contexto Internacional*, 17, 13–22. Rosário, Argentina.

[22] Mendes, Nuno (2017). As relações dos EUA com a China: Uma perspectiva geoeconômica. In: A economia política do governo Obama. Editora UFPB.

[23] Morrison, W. M. (2014). China-US trade issues (CRS Report for Congress RL33536). *Washington, DC: Congressional Research Service.*

Tensions continued to rise with China not adhering to the WTO plurilateral agreement on public markets and the renegotiation of the Bilateral Investment Treaty (BIT) on the protection of intellectual property. Questions rose about China's cyberattacks for the purposes of economic, governmental, and military espionage. In a report by the Commission on the Theft of American Intellectual Property (2013), an impact of US$300 billion on the American economy due to intellectual property theft was estimated, of which 50–80% was attributed to China[24] (Lawrence, 2013). In fact, Trump's trade policy has a historical precedent: the Ronald Reagan administration (1981–1989), during which Reagan targeted Japan with intensifying fair trade discourse, aggressive unilateralism, and the creation of domestic retaliatory devices.

Regarding the U.S. economic and trade deficit, Mendonça, Thomaz, Lima, and Vigevani[25] (2019) explain that although competitiveness problems had little relation to policies adopted in other countries and could be more attributed to the value of the dollar, blaming other countries' disloyalty and demanding a more aggressive and nationalist attitude from the government were attitudes that generated electoral appeal. The economic difficulties stimulated the activities of interest groups, mainly lobbyists, to pressure congressmen for political changes.

To find some answers as to why Trump started trade battles with China, the European Union, and even with the NAFTA (North American Free Trade Agreement) signatories, we can seek evidence by examining the economic advisers of this administration. These economic advisers have been together since the campaign, and they reached a consensus that, in the past, the United States gave in to trade preferences for greater openness in the American market, so they became victims of the international system that they helped to create. These hardcore economic advisers, including Peter Navarro (Assistant to the President and Director of the Office of Trade and Manufacturing Policy), Wilbur Ross (Secretary of Commerce), Robert Lighthizer (U.S. Trade Representative), and Mike

[24] Lawrence, S. V. (2013, August). US-China Relations: An overview of policy. In *Congressional Research Service: CRS Report for Congress-Prepared for Members and Committees of Congress* (Vol. 1).

[25] Mendonça, F., Thomaz, L. F., Lima, T., & Vigevan, T. (2019). "America first but not alone": uma (nem tão) nova política comercial dos Estados Unidos com Donald Trump, Tempo do mundo/Instituto de Pesquisa Econômica Aplicada. Brasília, 107–142.

Pompeo (Secretary of State), share a common rhetoric about the loss of U.S. international influence, caused mainly by China, which must be combated with the instruments of geopolitical and commercial disputation.

The reasons Trump and his team give are often expressed in terms of fear. The reasons for the United States to fear China are manifold. Roughly speaking, the reasons include the hidden subsidies that China provides to state-owned enterprises through cheap and easily obtained credit from state-owned banks, the large trade deficit that China has with the United States, the forced technology transfers by American firms to China, the lack of enforcement of intellectual property rights protection by China, the military buildup of China, the economic expansion of China through the Belt and Road Initiative (BRI), and the fear of the dependency of American firms on Chinese suppliers.[26] To be more specific, the central ideas that were drafted into the document "Scoring the Trump economic plan: trade, regulatory, & energy policy impacts"[27] by the economic advisers Navarro and Ross (2016) emphasize that the trade agreements of the last few decades, especially those that allowed China's entry into the WTO in 2001, ended up taking productive investment out of the United States and contributed to the dispersion of offshore production. For this reason, among other reasons, the mismanagement of these agreements ended up expanding the purchase of goods produced and traded unfairly. The document presents numerous quotes about the role that China plays in the economic imbalances that the United States suffers and the victimization of the country in the face of practices that inhibit the fair competition that American products, whether at home or abroad, deserve. The document also notes that U.S. direct investments that flow to China were "fairly stable at about $1.6 billion per year in the period 1999–2003" but "jumped in the period 2004–2008 to an annual average of $6.4 billion." Additionally, the document attributes most of the decline in U.S. manufacturing jobs from 2001 to 2007 to China.

[26] Lai, E. L. C. (2019). The US–China trade war, the American public opinions and its effects on China. *Economic and Political Studies*, 7(2), 169–184.

[27] Navarro and Ross (2016). *Scoring the Trump economic plan: trade, regulatory, & energy policy impacts*. Peterson Institute for International Economics (PIIE), Washington, D.C., Disponível em: https://bit.ly/2daD7H3.

They describe the "China trade shock" that has raised the unemployment rate, depressed wages and the labor participation rate, and reduced the lifetime income of workers in American manufacturing, which was most "exposed" to the shock.

In this document, the economic advisers criticize the fact that auto companies such as GM and Ford have built new factories in China or Mexico and that additional jobs have been lost throughout the economy. Many more jobs have been created downstream in industries ranging from aluminum, plastics, rubber, and steel to glass, rubber, textiles, and computer chips. As we had previously mentioned regarding the boycott by the American delegation of the renewal of names in the WTO Dispute Settlement Body, the text of the U.S. boycott shows the discontent of the Trump economic team with multilateral instruments, to the point of ending the unequal value-added tax (VAT) treatment under WTO rules. For Navarro and Ross, it is an obvious problem of relatively high corporate tax rates pushing American capital offshore, which relates to unequal treatment in the U.S. income tax system.

In the document, the authors state a belief that the dispute resolution mechanisms that exist within the WTO make it a lengthy and uncertain process to obtain relief against even the most egregious behavior, including the dumping of steel into global markets by countries ranging from China, India, and Italy to South Korea and Taiwan and the use of non-tariff barriers to offset the lower tariffs required under WTO rules. It is currently dumping over 100 million tons of steel alone into global markets. China is hardly the only cheater in the world. It is no accident that Navarro and Ross set the example of the global steel market as a disadvantaged sector in the United States. Navarro, who authored the book *Death by China*[28] and has published articles and made videos about China, and Ross, an investor in the steel and coal sector, seek to protect American investors from Chinese steel competition.

The Trump administration announced a 25% tariff on steel and a 10% tariff on aluminum imports. The dependence on imported metals threatens America's ability to make weapons. America is the world's largest steel

[28] NAVARRO, P.; AUTRY, G. (2011). Death by China: confronting the dragon—A global call to action. New York: Pearson Prentice Hall.

importer. Steel importers employ 6.5 million workers compared with 147,000 steel export workers in the United States.[29] As shown in the tables below, China's production between 2007 and 2016 of crude steel and steel semi-finished products is well above that of the United States. The production capacity of crude steel in the United States (78,400 thousand metric tons in 2016) is 10% that of China (808,000 thousand metric tons in 2016) (Fig. 2.1).

Besides, the dimensions in relation to the production of iron ores and concentrates show a quantitative decrease for the two countries, but production in China is still higher (123,000 thousand metric tons in 2015) than U.S. production (43,100 thousand metric tons in 2015), which represented 35% of the Chinese output (Fig. 2.2).

The investment capacity in the energy matrix is an important indicator for assessing the increase in productive structures in a country. The energy

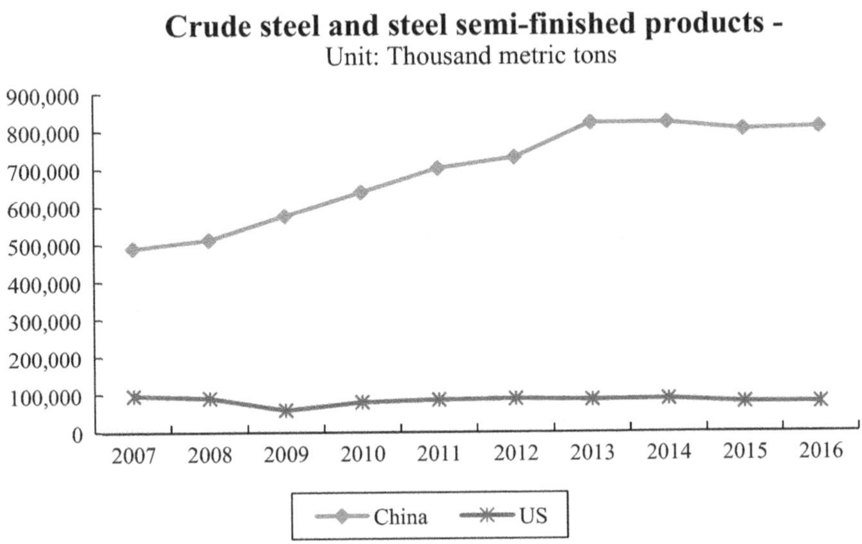

Fig. 2.1 Crude steel and steel semi-finished products in China and the United States (Unit: thousand metric tons). (*Data Source: UNTAD—Industrial Commodity Statistics Yearbook, Production Statistics [2007–2016]*)

[29] Kimberly, A. (2019, December). Trade Wars and their Effect on the Economy and You: Why Trade Wars Are Bad and Nobody Wins. *The Balance*.

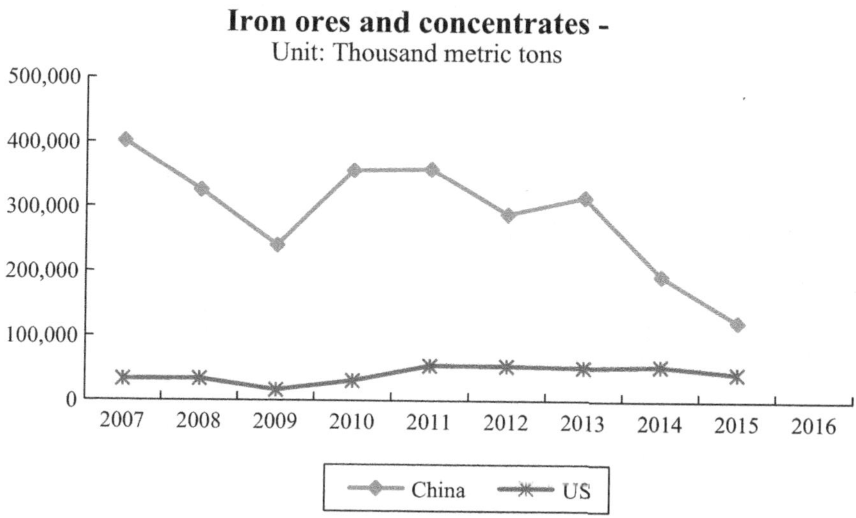

Fig. 2.2 Iron ores and concentrates in China and the United States (Unit: thousand metric tons). (*Data Source: UNTAD—Industrial Commodity Statistics Yearbook, Production Statistics [2007–2016]*)

issue was one of the main strategic concerns of the Chinese model of development. Even with oil and gas reserves, investments in hydroelectric constructions were made, and the use of coal for energy purposes is still part of the matrix, causing, among other impacts, levels of pollution that are equal to the pollution levels of developed countries. Both Chinese and American production of hard coal has declined over the years. China is slowly changing its energy model toward other sources (Fig. 2.3).

As an example of the gradual change in Chinese investments in the energy matrix, in addition to coal, we can see in the graph below that in 2011, there was a turnaround with the greater production of electrical energy in China, which produced 30% more than the United States by 2016 (Fig. 2.4).

Another change in China in the framework of the energy matrix was the drastic decrease in the highly polluting production of gasworks gas between 2009 and 2010, though there was an increase from 2010 to 2016. As we can see in the graph, U.S. production represents 10% of China's gasworks (Fig. 2.5).

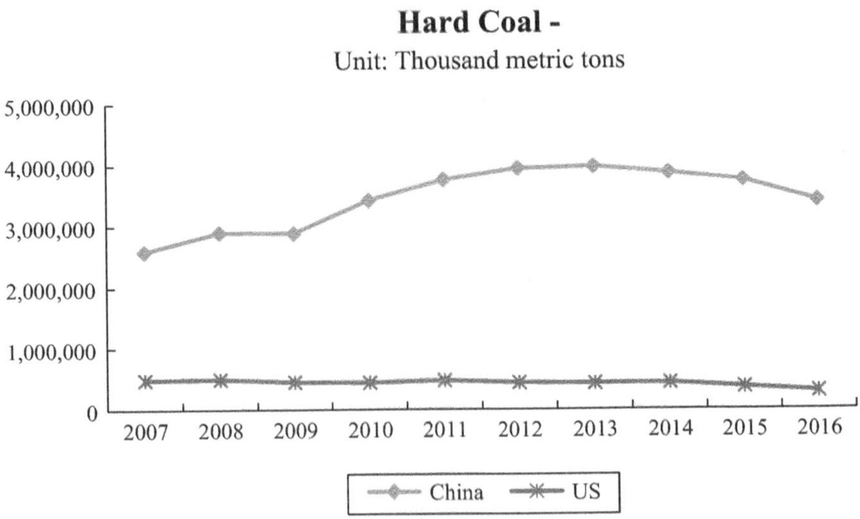

Fig. 2.3 Hard coal in China and the United States (Unit: thousand metric tons). (*Data Source: UNTAD—Industrial Commodity Statistics Yearbook, Production Statistics [2007–2016]*)

However, there are two areas in which the United States has greater production and generation capacity than China: natural gas and crude petroleum. Even with China showing a steady increase from 2600 PJ in 2007 to 5500 PJ in 2016 of natural gas, these figures represent 19% of U.S. production (Fig. 2.6).

U.S. oil production has seen a huge increase since the start of shale extraction. Between 2011 and 2016, the United States increased production from 278,000 thousand metric tons to 438,000 thousand metric tons. The United States imported US$157 billion in 2018 and US$127 billion in 2019 of oil from other countries and exported US$47 billion in 2018 and US$65.3 billion in 2019 worldwide. China is the largest oil importer in the world. The United States exported US$5.3 billion to China in 2018 and US$2.9 billion in 2019 (Fig. 2.7).

According to the authors Yan Xia, Yishu Kong, Qiang Ji, and Dayong Zhang (2019), it is already possible to perceive the different levels of impacts on the energy sector directly or indirectly from the trade war between the two countries. For the characteristics of the energy-related

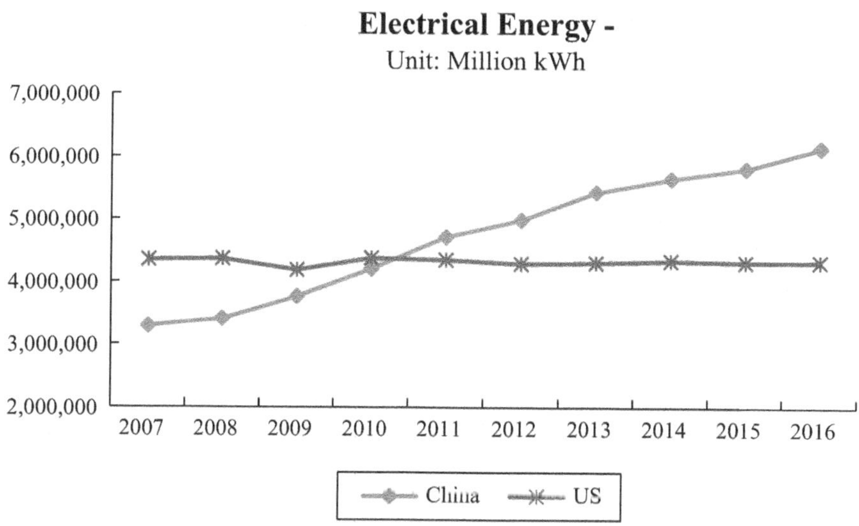

Fig. 2.4 Electrical energy in China and the United States (Unit: million kWh). (*Data Source: UNTAD—Industrial Commodity Statistics Yearbook, Production Statistics [2007–2016]*)

products subject to additional tariffs, the share of direct energy products (such as coal, gas, and petroleum) is relatively low, while the share of indirect energy-related products (in particular, electric equipment) is much higher. To date, US$0.5 billion worth of direct energy products have been targeted; these are restricted to diesel fuel and kerosene. These products are subject to additional tariffs but account for only 2% of China's direct energy exports and 1.75% of the U.S. direct energy imports. Thus, the impact of the additional tariffs on direct energy products is limited. In contrast, the value of indirect energy-related products that will be subject to additional tariffs, such as electric transformers, vinyl chloride and polymers, and steel products, is significantly higher. If these indirect energy-related products are classified by the production sector, the electric equipment sector is primarily involved.[30]

According to Navarro and Ross, with their tariff policies in place, the U.S. dollar would weaken and the Chinese yuan would strengthen

[30] Xia, Y., Kong, Y., Ji, Q., & Zhang, D. (2019). Impacts of China-US trade conflicts on the energy sector. *China Economic Review*, 58, 101360.

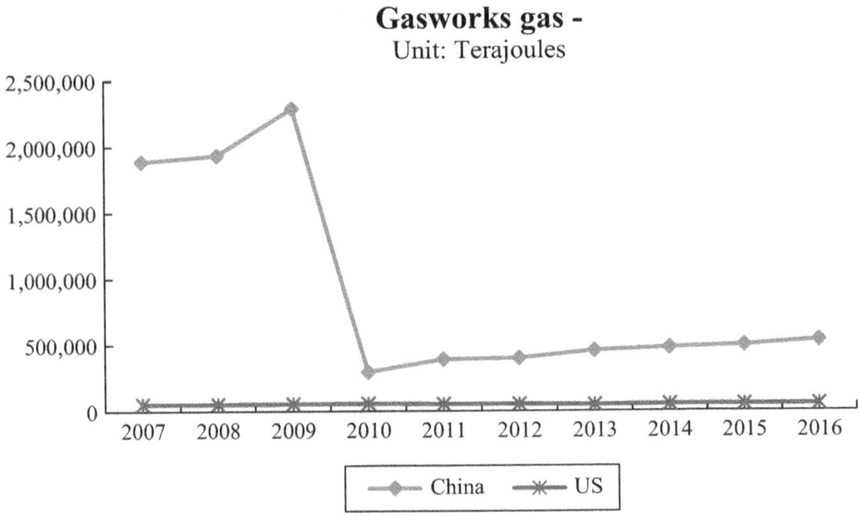

Fig. 2.5 Gasworks gas in China and the United States (Unit: terajoules). (*Data Source: UNTAD—Industrial Commodity Statistics Yearbook, Production Statistics [2007–2016]*)

because the United States runs a large trade deficit with China and the rest of the world. With adjustments, American exports to China would then rise, Chinese imports to America would fall, and trade should balance. The problem, however, is that China has stymied these major adjustments. China's purchasing of U.S. Treasury securities is one way the Chinese government holds down its currency relative to the U.S. dollar. By maintaining its manipulated currency peg, China perpetuates the trade imbalance.

This text also addresses *Inflation and Trade War Critiques of the Trump Plan*, which was released in 2016. Since the release of that plan, many predicted that there would be a trade war (which, in fact, is occurring), that the American economy would enter into a recession (which it has due to the COVID-19 epidemic), and that China would not reduce its import of soybeans (not only has China reduced the import of soybeans, but it has also taxed them). The Trump plan ends with a call for other economic wars because there are many markets in the world and China

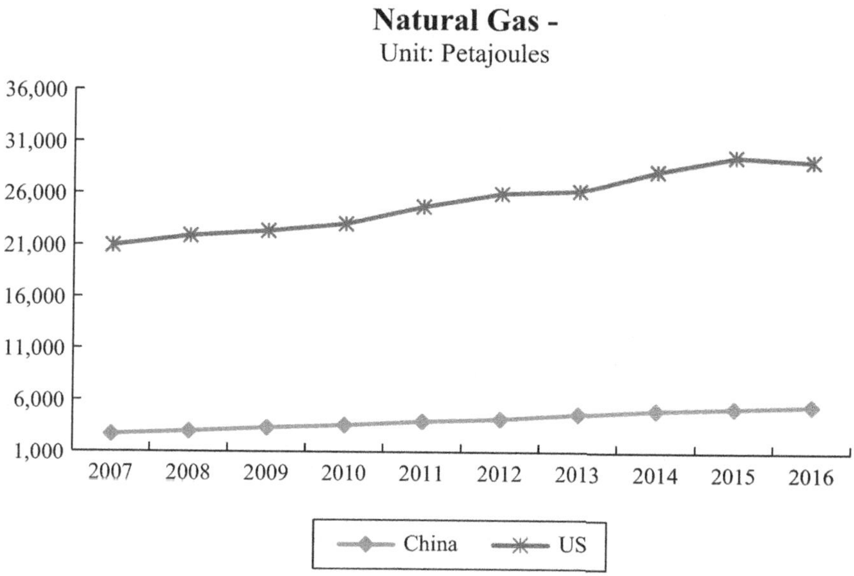

Fig. 2.6 Natural gas in China and the United States (Unit: petajoules). (*Data Source: UNTAD—Industrial Commodity Statistics Yearbook, Production Statistics [2007–2016]*)

is only one of them. We simply cannot trade based on any country's one-sided terms as they are too destructive to the U.S. growth process.[31]

When evaluating the main documents of the U.S. Trade Representative (USTR) Report (Trade Agenda 2019/2020 and Annual Report 2018/2019) led by Ambassador Robert E. Lighthizer on the trade war with China, we find the elements that guide American trade policy as well as the administration's self-evaluation of the measures undertaken, without the evident demonstration of real effects. We can characterize these reports more as self-promotion documents from the Trump administration; despite presenting technical data, they have a substantial political undertone that reinforces the president's speeches. In these reports covering the period from the beginning of the trade war in 2018 until the

[31] Navarro and Ross (2016). *Scoring the Trump economic plan: trade, regulatory, & energy policy impacts*. September 29. Peterson Institute for International Economics (PIIE), Washington, D.C., 29 Sept. 2016. Disponível em: https://bit.ly/2daD7H3.

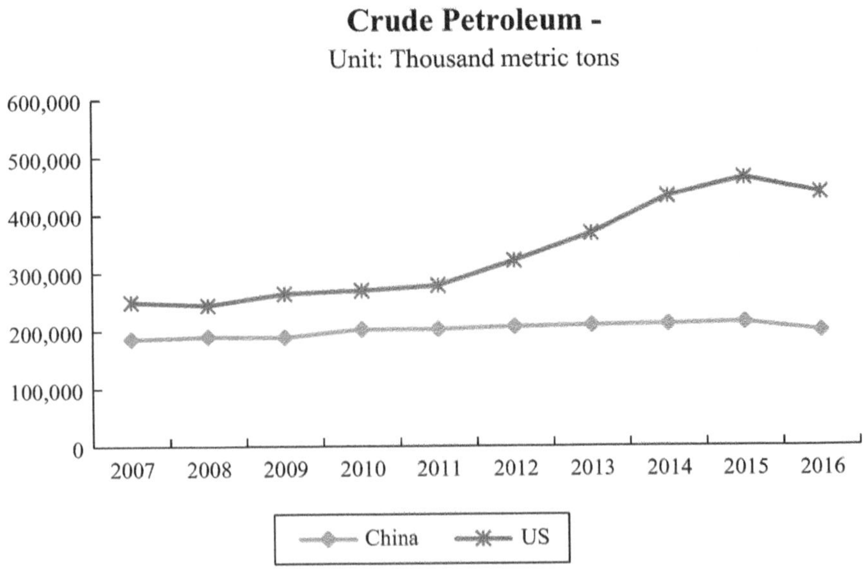

Fig. 2.7 Crude petroleum in China and the United States (Unit: thousand metric tons). (*Data Source: UNTAD—Industrial Commodity Statistics Yearbook, Production Statistics [2007–2016]*)

signing of the first phase of the agreement in 2020, we can see a process that signals the supposed victory of American willpower reflected in the signed agreements and the extent of Trump's campaign promises.

According to the USTR, the path taken by Trump presents concrete and promising results for American workers and entrepreneurs. First, in generating increased work income, the report states that U.S. job creation grew from 2.2 million in 2017 to 2.7 million in 2018. From 2013 to 2016, an average of 8000 manufacturing jobs were created per month. In the first two years of the Trump administration, that average has grown to approximately 20,000 manufacturing jobs per month. In 2018, the United States created 264,000 new manufacturing jobs, the largest such increase in 21 years. While 15,000 manufacturing jobs were lost in the 12 months prior to President Trump's election, more than 500,000 manufacturing jobs have been added to the American economy since then.

While Trump makes speeches stating that there is an unprecedented blue-collar boom, increased wealth for the bottom half of American households, and faster wage growth for historically disadvantaged Americans, it seems that the reality does not quite reflect that rhetoric. According to Tom Hall,[32] the reality is very different than the fantasy Trump has presented over the country's airwaves. Corporate profits, dividends, and the income of wealthy executives are higher than ever before—the direct result of unprecedented levels of socioeconomic disparity. Hall stated that in 2019, at least 24,000 auto workers lost their jobs. While Trump never tires of making nationalist tirades against Mexican and Chinese workers stealing "American" jobs, these cuts were part of a global jobs massacre in the auto industry, which eliminated over 500,000 jobs worldwide last year. Auto companies are pursuing an international strategy to force workers in every country to bear the cost of the emerging downturn in the industry and to prepare for the transition to electric and autonomous vehicles, which will require a vastly reduced workforce. While Trump's propaganda states that there is an increase in employment, a large part of this increase is due to the increase in part-time jobs; full-time employment has fallen by 6.8% since the turn of the century, while part-time employment has risen by 3.4%, that is, precarious jobs have supplanted good jobs.

There is an emphasis in the 2018 USTR Report on retaliatory measures for trade relations with China, the renegotiating and renaming of NAFTA by the American side as the USMCA (United States-Mexico-Canada Agreement) and trade with South Korea. The document continually expresses itself as if the United States was the great victim of the international trading system that they themselves helped to build. This is why the document makes a call to carry out trade wars, even if of a unilateral scope, to save the jobs of American workers. Products such as steel, aluminum, washing machines, and solar and agricultural panels receive a special emphasis in the document. The document even addresses the issue of national security, the import effects of automobile imports and uranium imports, and the need to take unilateral action or risk permanent long-term damage to steel and aluminum production in the United States.

[32] Hall, Tom. (2020, February 15). Trump's "Blue Collar Boom": Myth vs Reality. https://www.wsws.org/en/articles/2020/02/15/boom-f15.html.

There is a systematic attack in the document on the WTO. The United States presents itself as the real loser in trade disputes and charges that the organization has become obsolete and too open to the demands of developing countries. If, from the American perspective, the WTO has proven to be an obstacle to American interests, the reverse has happened with China. For the American representation, the WTO is not well equipped to handle the fundamental challenge posed by a nonmarket economy such as China's. China has no fear of WTO dispute settlements, even as it continues to embrace a state-led, mercantilist approach to the economy and trade that is fundamentally incompatible with the open, market-based approach expressly envisioned and followed by other WTO members. As the United States has repeatedly made clear at the WTO, China pursues an array of nonmarket industrial policies and other unfair competitive practices aimed at promoting and supporting its domestic industries (p. 26). The United States repeatedly claims that the trading system is deeply flawed and is generating harmful outcomes for American workers in many instances.

For the United States, China deceives the mechanisms of the WTO. According to the *2018 USTR Report to Congress on China's WTO Compliance*, China's use of export and import substitution subsidies has been ubiquitous throughout the past two decades in sectors as diverse as automobiles, textiles, advanced materials, medical products, and agriculture, despite explicit prohibitions in the WTO Agreement and repeatedly deployed illegal export restraints, such as export quotas, export licensing, minimum export prices, export duties, and other restrictions on scores of raw material inputs, as determined in multiple WTO cases brought by the United States and other WTO members. China has used these illegal export restraints to provide substantial cost advantages to a wide range of downstream producers in China at the expense of foreign producers while creating pressure on foreign producers to move their operations, technologies, and jobs to China.

A summary of China's inconsistencies regarding trade with the United States has been documented by the WTO. Such activities pursued by China include the following: (1) local content requirements in the automobile sector, (2) discriminatory taxes in the integrated circuit sector, (3) hundreds of prohibited subsidies in a wide range of manufacturing sectors, (4) inadequate intellectual property rights (IPR) enforcement in the copyright area, (5) significant market access barriers in copyright-intensive industries, (6) severe restrictions on foreign suppliers of financial information services, (7) export restraints on numerous raw materials, (8) denial of market access for foreign suppliers of electronic payment services, (9) repeated abusive use of trade remedies, (10) excessive domestic support for key agricultural commodities, (11) opaque and protectionist administration of tariff rate quotas for key agricultural commodities, and (12) discriminatory regulations on technology licensing.

However, the biggest criticism in terms of the economic policy that the United States applies to China is an old argument of the nonmarket economy, in addition to the influence of the Communist Party in the market and in the financial sector. Again, the blame for the international system lies with the Communist Party. In support of the American charges, Article 7 of the Constitution of the People's Republic of China provides that "[t] he state-owned economy, that is, the socialist economy with ownership by the whole people, is the leading force in the national economy. The state ensures the consolidation and development of the state-owned economy."

In trying to find a culprit for their loss of hegemony, Americans point to China's strategic plans for economic development in the Belt and Road Initiative (BRI), which the United States labels as a nonmarket economic model extended to other countries. As is now well known, China has invoked this initiative and offers to build large infrastructure projects in countries throughout Asia and other parts of the world, especially in strategically located or developing countries. China claims that the Belt and Road Initiative is open to all, but virtually all of the projects are financed by Chinese banks, run by Chinese state-owned enterprises, and built by Chinese workers. The Belt and Road Initiative (BRI) is especially important to the Chinese Communist Party, which has incorporated the Belt and Road Initiative into its Constitution and has called for using this initiative to develop relations with surrounding countries through discussion, collaboration, and unity. However, Belt and Road Initiative projects are often opaque, one-sided, and divisive. These projects generally ignore market principles and fail to adhere to internationally accepted best practices for financing, infrastructure development, and government procurement. Too often, these projects also create unsustainable debt burdens for the recipient countries.

The U.S.-China FDI: Why Interrupt a Positive History?

From a historical perspective, despite ideological differences in the context of the Cold War, the restoration of Sino-American relations, with then the Former Richard Nixon in the 1970s, provided periods of cooperation that strengthened the mainly economic ties between countries. Taking advantage of the conflicts in the Socialist Bloc between the USSR and China, the United States realized the importance of not only geopolitical, of the Chinese economic opening, from the perspective of a new consumer market integrated into the global economy. China's economic opening and diplomatic rapprochement with the United States brought the "American way" in introducing techniques and other elements into the world of work. Far beyond Fordism, new forms of organization of scale production and management have modernized the environment of companies, developing standards for rationalization and handling of new technologies. The Special Industrialization Zones themselves are an example of the American influence on China's development. The participation of companies, investments, and U.S. capital boosted the formation of companies that brought their experience in different areas of manufacturing and technology.

The first phases of the opening and industrialization of "Made in China" products were partly due to incentives given by American companies and investment funds that found a favorable environment to settle. We can show that the phase of harmony and cooperation between countries was guided by the win-win logic during the decades. Even during the administrations of George W. Bush (2001–2009) and Barack Obama (2009–2017), economic cooperation was placed as a guarantee of security for American investments in the country, sharing a series of value chains and technologies. There was a large volume of growing American foreign direct investments (FDIs) that were applied, in the installation of industries, in the strengthening of foreign trade and companies from different branches of the United States in China.

Despite the data showing some divergences, in the sources on the investments of both countries, it was noteworthy during 1990–2015. There were large U.S. FDI investments in China. In the case of FDI China, investments gradually increased after 2010. In practically all sectors of the economy, American investments in China were proportionately higher. From the Rhodium Group (RHG)[33] data used by the National Committee on U.S.-China relations,[34] different FDI values are observed compared to data from the U.S. Bureau of Economic Analysis (BEA) and the Ministry of Commerce (MOFCOM/China). In the report[35] the Rhodium Group argues that

> offer an alternative perspective on the scope and patterns of US FDI in China, by introducing a new transactions-based dataset created by identifying, qualifying, and counting every single FDI transaction over $ 1 million since 1990, count nearly 6700 American investments in China with a combined value of $ 228 billion, and dataset included more than 1300 US companies that have built significant operations in China, 430 of them investing more than $ 50 million and 56 with billion-dollar bets.

There was between 1990 and 2015 the cumulative U.S. FDI transactions in China from $228 billion, for the Bureau of Economic Analysis it was $75 billion, and for MOFCOM is $70 billion. In the case of the Chinese FDI Stock in the United States for the Rhodium group, it was $63.8 billion, for MOFCOM $40.8 billion, and for the Bureau of Economic Analysis is $20.8 billion between 1990 and 2015. Of this accumulation of $228 billion, between 1990 and 2015 the cumulative value of U.S. FDI transactions in China by industry: 14% in information communications technology (ICT); 13% in chemicals, metals, and basic materials; 9% in automotive and transportation stand out equipment;

---

[33] Rhodium Group (RHG) is an economic research firm that combines policy experience, quantitative economic tools and on-the-ground research to analyze disruptive global trends.

[34] The National Committee on U.S.-China Relations is an American nonprofit, nonpartisan educational organization that encourages understanding and cooperation between the United States and Greater China.

[35] Hanemann, T., Rosen, D. H., & Gao, C. (2016). Two-way street: 25 years of US-China direct investment. *National Committee on United States-China Relations, www.us-china-fdi.com.*

10% in energy; 7% in real estate and hospitality; 7% in agriculture and food; 6% in healthcare, pharmaceuticals, and biotechnology; 9% in financial and business services; 5% in consumer products and services; 4% in electronics and electrical equipment; 3% in transport and infrastructure; 2% in entertainment, media, and education; and 1% in aviation. In absolute values, $31.5 billion in ICT; $20.8 billion in financial and business services; $19 billion in machinery; $14.3 billion in healthcare, pharmaceuticals, and biotechnology; $16.4 billion in real estate and hospitality; and US$7.7 billion in transport and infrastructure. Major U.S. FDI investments in China were in Shanghai ($52.6 billion), Beijing ($35.8 billion), Jiangsu ($33.1 billion), and Guangdong ($21.2 billion).

There is a clear superiority of American investments in China in the period 1990–2015, questioning the reasons that Donald Trump is based on the trade war. But 2014 was a turning point, when there was more Chinese investment in the United States than the reverse. The characteristics of American investments were in greenfield investments, in the case of China, in acquisitions. In a world where foreign direct investment (FDI) is increasingly scarce, Trump has another dilemma to face in the trade war with China.

China is one of the major investors in the United States, which means that China is not limited to international trade, which in itself would already be a large challenge for Trump, but China is also a major purchaser of U.S. Treasury debt securities, as well as a purchaser of debt for Organization of the Petroleum Exporting Countries (OPEC). This means that Chinese capital is inserted in the varied productive forces of the United States: industry, finance, agriculture, logistics, technology, energy, tourism, and real estate. Therefore, the more instability there is between these two countries, the more that investments tend to descend into political, legal, and diplomatic insecurity.[36]

Chinese investments have expanded China's presence in the United States for years. From 2005 to 2019, more than US$180 billion was invested by China. In 2016 alone, this figure reached its highest value, with US$53 billion in investments. With the rise of Trump's presidency, these values dropped considerably by US$25 billion in 2017, with 30

[36] Sheng, L., & Gao, J. (2018). Foreign investors versus host communities: An urban political economy model for tourist cities. *Argumenta Oeconomica*, 41(2), 257–275.

contracts (or deals); US$8.1 billion in 2018, with 20 contracts (or deals); and US$3.2 billion in 2019, with 8 contracts (or deals)—the lowest value since 2011, when there was US$2.2 billion in 8 contracts (or deals). The main Chinese investment sectors in the United States between 2005 and 2019 were divided into real estate (US$29.8 billion), finance (US$23.2 billion), transportation (US$22.3 billion), technology (US$21.8 billion), and energy (US$16.8 billion).

According to data from the conservative American Enterprise Institute China Global Investment Tracker,[37] it is clear that Chinese investments in the technology sector are decreasing. Since the rhetorical and legal attacks on Chinese companies such as Huawei and ZTE, this branch has become more cautious about expanding its business in a hostile environment. The companies that made direct investments in the technology area that stand are Lenovo, with investments of US$2.1 billion in IBM (2014) and US$2.9 billion in Motorola Mobility (2014); Tsighua Holdings, which invested US$1.9 billion in Omnivision Technologies (2015); HNA group, with US$6 billion invested in Ingram Micro (2016); and Zhuhai Science & Technology, with US$3.4 billion invested in Lexmark (2016). However, since 2017, no major investments have been identified in this sector.

The question remains: is the goal of Trump and his team in the trade war to also decrease Chinese investments in the United States? The United States has expressed concerns about the rise of China in their rush for technological innovation and, consequently, in their acquisition of intellectual property. According to the USTR Report,[38] technology and intellectual property play a vital role in the U.S. economy, supporting 45.5 million American jobs and accounting for over 38% of U.S. GDP and 52% of U.S. exports. We know that when contracts are made between countries, whether for scientific and technological, military, or commercial cooperation, the transfer of technology is based on terms that the states sometimes carry out or that companies do themselves.

[37] China Global Investment Tracker—The American Enterprise Institute and the Heritage Foundation. The American Enterprise Institute and the Reagan Institute are part of conservative groups that take the political line of influencing the Trump administration against China's rise.

[38] USTR. 2019 Trade Policy Agenda and 2018 Annual Report of the President of the United States on the Trade Agreements Program.

Repeatedly, in the documents of American authorities, they blame China for pressuring the forced transfer of technology from American companies. These tactics included joint venture requirements and other foreign investment restrictions, which effectively pressured U.S. investors in China to partner with Chinese companies and provide access to the intellectual property of their U.S. counterparts. The American authorities complained that when U.S. intellectual property owners were permitted to license their technology in China, they had to do so under discriminatory regulations that barred U.S. owners from receiving market-rate returns and that Chinese companies implemented outbound foreign investment programs to obtain U.S. intellectual property through the acquisition of targeted U.S. companies, in addition to having targeted the confidential business information and other sensitive data of American companies.[39]

In the USTR Report 2018, the document tries to show that the economic war with China is not unilaterally with the United States but is shared with American allies, such as the EU and Japan. In the meeting held in September 2018, it was exposed that the EU ministers called these practices "deplorable" and affirmed that they would use "effective means" to halt forced technology transfer and would further discuss enforcement and rule-making as tools to address this problem.

The Impact of the Trade War on U.S. Agriculture

The challenge of understanding explanations for the dilemmas of the American economy is that it is necessary to confront how the interests of internal groups influence the country's foreign policy. The support base of Trump, and consequently the Republican Party, is the white population, located in rural and less-urban areas, in deindustrialized and resource-extracting regions.

In the 2016 elections, Donald Trump had broad support from the American agricultural-livestock sector, agribusiness and ranchers as well

[39] Idem.

as interest groups (agribusiness companies, large- and medium-sized farmers), and the populations of the states of the Midwest and South, Texas, Oklahoma, Louisiana, and Mississippi, where agriculture, fishing, fish farms, and livestock are the main economic activities. Even though this sector represents 1% of Gross Domestic Product and 1.6% of employed labor, the agricultural production indices[40] have increased from 106 in 2010 to 117 in 2019. Among the sectors that contributed the most to the Trump campaign[41] in 2016 were agribusiness, at US$5 million, which was more than sectors such as construction (US$4 million), energy and natural resources (US$2 million), and defense (US$1 million). The agribusiness sector also contributed US$6.5 million to the campaign of Republican Florida Senator Marco Rubio. Primary sector interest groups and lobbyists are traditionally among the strongest such organizations that seek to influence the U.S. Congress. In this case, according to Open Secrets data, the annual lobbying on agribusiness was between $127.84 M in 2016 and $101.29 M in 2019. Among the lobbyists of the companies that are present in the Trump administration in the agriculture department are CropLife America, the National Corn Growers Association, the American Farm Bureau, and the American Horse Council, among others. Trump, in return for support from this sector, signed the Farm Bill, which was passed in the House and Senate between June and December 2018. The project envisaged US$867 billion. The Farm Bill included funding for commodity support, conservation, trade and international food aid, nutrition assistance, farm credit, rural development, research and extension activities, forestry, horticulture, and crop insurance. The Secretary of Agriculture, Sonny Perdue, justified the announced $12 billion as an aid package for farmers affected by tariffs imposed by other nations, especially China's retaliation against illegal trade practices. This package included the Market Facilitation Program, Food Purchase and Distribution Program, and Trade Promotion Program.

The United States is the largest food exporter in the world; in 2018, US$135.9 billion were exported, 1.5 billion more than in 2017. Products

[40] UN Stat.

[41] Opensecrets.org.

such as soybeans, corn, nuts, beef, and cotton are the main items. China is the fifth-largest destination for agricultural exports from the United States. However, between 2008 and 2018, there was a decrease of 24% (US$12.1 billion down to US$9.2 billion). In addition, the outlook for 2019 was US$6.5 billion. The pattern of export trade to China is varied, with the main export sector in the industrial area of airplanes, helicopters, and parts for civil aviation at US$13.4 billion in 2017, followed by cars and integrated circuits. However, there were also considerable exports of vegetable products, especially soybeans, totaling US$15.3 billion.

The example of the impacts of the economic war can be seen from what happened to soybeans. The price of soybeans, which was above US$420 per ton in March 2018, dropped to almost US$350 per ton in July 2018 after China's retaliation, and the levels reach below US$310 per ton. After the 90-day truce with China, the price rose to US$330 per ton. During this period, there was an increase in supply and a decrease in planted area. In 2017, the value of soybeans imported by China was US$12.4 billion; in 2018, it was US$3.14 billion, with a recovery in 2019 of US$7.9 billion. However, if we take soy oil data, the fall was much more accentuated. In 2017, the United States exported US$102 million to China and Hong Kong; this amount dropped to US$1800 in 2018 and US$1000 in 2019. Although the Food Price Indices did not drop for exports, they also suffered a decline from US$1.6 billion in 2018 to US$1.3 billion in 2019.

The Congressional Research Service's "China's Retaliatory Tariffs on U.S. Agriculture: In Brief" report (Sep, 2019) presents some immediate results from the impacts of the trade war. In its introduction, the report presents these impacts. The result of this trade war was a decline in trade between the United States and China. In 2018, U.S. agricultural exports to China declined by 53% in value to $9 billion from $19 billion in the calendar year 2017. In 2019, China's market had shrunk, becoming the fourth-largest destination for U.S. agricultural exports behind Canada, Mexico, and Japan. Among the measures discussed, China levied an additional 5% or 10% tariffs on U.S. imports, including tariffs on 695 different U.S. agricultural products but granted tariff exemptions on some U.S. imports, including alfalfa, feed whey, and other feed. The forecasted decline in China's imports accounted for most of the reduction in

FY2019 total U.S. agricultural exports. In FY2019, U.S. agricultural imports were projected at $129.3 billion, an increase of 1.4%. This would have resulted in an agricultural trade surplus of $5.2 billion, which would be the lowest since 2006.

Since 2017, Brazil overtook the United States as China's largest agricultural supplier. Due to the imposition of the retaliatory tariffs on U.S. imports in 2018, U.S. agricultural shipments to China declined to $15 billion as overall Chinese imports increased to $127 billion. When China's total agricultural imports were at $127 billion, the U.S. market share was 12%. A USDA study reports that over 1300 Chinese enterprises had overseas investments in agriculture, forestry, and fisheries valued at $26 billion in 2016. The report also notes that other countries have taken the place of the United States as exporters of agricultural products to China. For example, Brazil increased its shipments of soybeans, cotton, tobacco, pork, and certain oilseeds. Australia increased its shipments of cotton, sorghum, pulses, fruit and nuts, dairy, and hides and skins. Canada increased its shipments of feed and fodder products, hides and skins, and wheat. New Zealand increased its shipments of dairy and hides and skins. Other countries exporting to China include Thailand, Indonesia, Russia, Ukraine, and countries from Central, South and Southeast Asia as well as from Africa.

The Belt and Road Initiative prioritizes investing in port, rail, and air infrastructure with competing countries, such as Russia, Vietnam, and Myanmar. Trade agreements between China and other exporting countries have put U.S. products at a price disadvantage. This means that American agricultural products are not essential and can be replaced by products from other markets. The question remains as to why Trump, even with China's first measures in retaliation against agriculture in particular, still continued to break previous agreements. Agriculture has remained the most affected sector. Was Trump using the agricultural sector in the trade war only as a side effect?

Perhaps Trump's goal was to take measures against China's industrial and high-tech products, and China's retaliation in the agricultural sector would be only a minor undesirable consequence. This view reaffirms that the main objective of the trade war would be to protect the American industrial sector, which has been losing ground internally and externally.

The American agricultural sector, however, is competitive and uses high technology in production, even though the added value is much lower than in other sectors. The political consequences for Trump in the 2020 election might be seen in states where the agricultural sector was most affected. Farmers were already frustrated by the decline in soybean, sorghum, ethanol, and corn-based livestock feed exports as a result of the U.S. trade war with China. In northwest Iowa's fourth congressional district, goods exports to China fell by $558 M in 2018 because of higher tariffs, the largest decline of any district in the country, according to the U.S.-China Business Council.[42]

Although China is one of the largest importers of U.S. agricultural products, Americans still use dispute settlement mechanisms to support their interests, as was the case with the WTO panel on China—Domestic Support for Agricultural Producers (DS-511) and China's administration of its tariff rate quotas, including those for wheat, short- and medium-grain rice, long grain rice, and corn (DS-517).

The "Aggressive Enforcement Strategy": The Phase One Trade Agreement with China

If in the 2018 USTR Report we find a call for a trade war by the Trump administration, with its varied justifications, in the 2019 USTR Report we find almost an exaggeration of the supposed victories that American trade policy has achieved on all fronts. In the language of the document, we observe the way Trump expresses himself to his opponents and enemies. The word synthesis could be "aggressive enforcement strategy," which was mentioned several times: a real propaganda piece.

With the American elections to be held in November 2020, there are still doubts about the continuing effects of the COVID-19 epidemic and its impact on the elections, but the document provides the basis for Trump's election campaign. Campaign flags such as generating jobs in the manufacturing industry, defending the return of investments and companies to the country, increasing workers' income, the blue-collar

[42] Financial Times. Why US farmers are falling out of love with Trump. Nov/2019.

boom, and finally, the imposition of American interests in bilateral negotiations, mainly with China, were highlighted as promises kept, and now they are seen as trophies to be celebrated.

The document summarizes the main achievements from the promises Trump made in the 2016 campaign, with Trump undoing the mistakes of the past in the decades following the implementation of North American Free Trade Agreement (NAFTA) and China's accession to the WTO, when America lost one in four manufacturing jobs, more than 60,000 American factories were shut down, and millions of high-paying U.S. jobs were shipped overseas. President Trump committed to ending the disastrous trade deals of the past, and he delivered.

The results of the Phase One trade agreement with China; the replacement of NAFTA with the USMCA, the U.S. trade relationship with Mexico and Canada; the agreements with Japan, which initiated action against France for its unfair and discriminatory "digital services tax"; the EU Member States' subsidies to Airbus; and the proposal to change and rethink the World Trade Organization are great victories for U.S. trade policy. On December 2019, the conclusion of the U.S.–China Economic and Trade Agreement (Phase One Agreement) was announced. President Trump and Vice Premier Liu He signed the Phase One Agreement on January 2020.

In summary, the main elements of the Phase One Agreement are as follows: (1) the agreement includes enforceable obligations on trade secrets, patents, trademarks, geographical indications, pharmaceutical-related intellectual property, and enforcement against pirated and counterfeit goods; (2) the agreement prohibits China from forcing or pressuring U.S. companies to turn over their technology as a condition for market access, to gain administrative or licensing approvals, or to receive advantages from the Chinese government. Any transfer of technology must be voluntary and take place on market terms. In addition, China has committed to not direct or support outbound investments aimed at acquiring foreign technology to meet its market-distorting industrial plans. (3) The agriculture chapter of the agreement addresses a number of structural barriers to U.S. exports. China must implement a fair, predictable, science-based, and risk-based regulatory process that will facilitate exports of U.S. meat, poultry, seafood, rice, dairy, infant formula, horticultural products, animal feed, pet food, and so on. Importantly, this agreement includes requirements to approve certain U.S. biotech products more promptly. (4) The agreement removes a wide range of discriminatory regulatory requirements and limitations that have stifled U.S. companies seeking to operate in China's financial services market. This change will allow U.S. banks, insurance companies, credit rating services, electronic payment services, and other financial services to compete on a more level playing field.

In addition, the agreement requires China to increase purchases of U.S. exports by no less than $200 billion over the next two years in four major areas: manufactured goods, agriculture, energy, and services. The United States agreed to reduce the increased tariff rate on $120 billion in Chinese goods from 15% to 7.5%, but it maintained the additional tariffs on $250 billion in Chinese goods at 25%. Despite commitments establishing a bilateral evaluation and dispute resolution office to assess implementation and attempt to resolve disputes, if a dispute is not resolved, the complaining party has the right to take action, including by suspending an obligation under the agreement or adopting a trade measure in a proportionate way. We can interpret that there will be an attempt to bilaterally coordinate the adopted measures, with less participation of the WTO in the resolution of disputes between the two countries. Moreover, the United States, in partnership with Japan and the EU, calls for the reform of the WTO with a specific focus on measures against China. This arrangement creates regular bilateral consultations at the main level, the deputy level, and the working level. This arrangement also establishes strong procedures for addressing disputes related to the agreement and allows each side to take proportionate responsive actions that it deems appropriate when a dispute is not otherwise resolved.

The USTR Report to Congress on China's WTO Compliance 2019, which was presented in March 2020 in a difficult global situation due to the COVID-19 epidemic, was already prepared with the elements of the Phase One economic and trade agreement in January 2020. Despite presenting repetitive elements of the USTR Report to Congress on China's WTO Compliance 2018, this document tries to deepen the characteristics, practices, and policies of China's nonmarket economy, which it exposes based on arguments such as (1) state-sponsored, cyber-enabled theft of intellectual property, trade secrets, and know-how is conducted for the commercial benefit of Chinese companies; (2) forced technology transfer is conducted through various means; (3) state-owned enterprises play a large role in the economy and provide Chinese companies with numerous competitive preferences, to the detriment of foreign companies, both in China's market and abroad; (4) competition law enforcement achieve industrial policy objectives; (5) cybersecurity acts as a pretext to discriminate against foreign information communications technology (ICT) products and services and to promote the substitution of domestic ICT products and services in sectors throughout the Chinese economy; (6) China manages the export of many primary, intermediate, and downstream industrial products by strategically raising or lowering the value-added tax (VAT) rebate available upon export; and (7) China is rolling out a new social credit system, which will apparently be used to monitor, rate, and condition the conduct of all companies in China, including foreign companies.

In addition to arguing that the American government's view of the Chinese economy is also shared by other foreign companies doing business in China, the administration understands that the state's role in China's economy has increased in recent years. The problem is China's inadequate transparency and its disregard of many of its WTO transparency obligations, which place its trading partners at a disadvantage and often serves as a cloak for China to conceal unfair trade policies and practices from scrutiny.

The Globalization Paradox

Common sense advises never giving up on foreign engagement and domestic reforms. This wisdom has been confirmed by positive and negative experiences in international relations. Engaging with other countries brings many benefits that are useful to a country in solving a dilemma. First, engagement with others can be conducive to international stability and harmony, leading to collaboration, cooperation, confidence, and faith and helping to promote a win-win situation. Engaging with other countries makes possible the use of overseas resources to diminish domestic dilemmas. Second, engagement opens the door for a country to solve disputes between itself and other countries, which may provide more solutions for future problem tackling. However, political engagement still needs to find a balance between allowing the domestic political process to develop through the initiative of national leaders and enhancing the opening up of this political process to external power holders.[43] Furthermore, engagement also makes it possible for a superpower to be rewarded by other world powers. Alternatively, giving up on engagement can incur strong reactions from others, which may endanger the interests of a country. The three benefits listed here can not only help to consolidate a country's interests but also act as a guarantee to maintain a healthy international environment for its domestic reforms.

Since World War II, the United States, as the leader of the multilateral trading system, has promoted the implementation of many economic and trade rules that have been conducive to itself and therefore has become the biggest beneficiary of these rules. It is undeniable that globalization has strengthened the links between countries, as trade has changed in a new way that connects various national economies together at a deeper level than in the past,[44] enabling capital and talent to flow at the global scale and creating a large amount of wealth. However, deeper globalization, which follows market-oriented fundamentalism[45] and has

[43] Papagianni, K. (2010). Mediation, Political Engagement, and Peacebuilding. Global Governance: *A Review of Multilateralism and International Organizations*, 16(2), 243–263.

[44] Held, D., McGrew, A., Goldblatt, D., & Perraton, J. (1999). Globalization. *Global Governance*, 5(4), 483–496.

[45] Market fundamentalism refers, in part, to the transformation of the global economy and economic policy in the wake of the 1970s' crises. The principles of market fundamentalism—free markets, free trade, free investment, and pervasive commodification—were laid out decades earlier by economists such as Friedrich von Hayek and Milton Friedman. Only in the last three decades has market fundamentalism become the rallying cry that accompanied and legitimated deregulation within and between nations. Commodification was expanded to include not only goods, services, and financial instruments but also everything from intellectual property and carbon offsets to basic necessities such as water. The language of markets permeates all realms. We speak of human capital (and not skills, preferences, or capabilities), social capital (and not class or community), and cultural capital (and not values or shared knowledge and ways of life). Instead of being urged to participate, people are told to become stakeholders. Instead of committing themselves to a vision or project or choice, they "own" it. The discourse begins and ends with individual in a world of endless markets and unlimited, ostensibly free choice, coordinated only by the invisible hand.

Nolan, M. (2011). Gender and Utopian Visions in a Post-Utopian Era: Americanism, Human Rights, Market Fundamentalism. *Central European History*, 44(1), 13–36.

been promoted by the United States, has also brought a series of challenges. A country that agrees with deeper globalization will inevitably pursue the optimality of capital efficiency, which will lead to the outflow of capital from these countries to other countries or regions that can eventually obtain greater profit returns. When a country adopts market fundamentalism, which is considered to be the best choice based on market regulation and avoids government intervention, a large number of cross-border investments in financial capital will become a reality. This is the realistic background in which U.S. financial capital seeks global opportunities and U.S. companies try to expand outsourcers globally as the United States historically has tried to promote deeper globalization.[46] These financial and industrial companies can indeed achieve more financial value in the short term. However, in the long run, such an economic model undermines the employment opportunities of the middle and lower classes of the United States and the long-term competitiveness of the domestic manufacturing industry.[47]

The immediate cause of the trade war between China and the United States today is that Trump needs to implement his commitment of making America great again. For the middle and lower classes of the United States, this means finding a solution to restore the pre-1990s' glory. Faced with the pressure of middle- and lower-class voters, Trump must attack all other countries that pose a potential threat to the recovery of U.S. manufacturing employment while also strategically curbing long-term competitors such as China.

As a result, this is the internationalization of the U.S. domestic dilemma. Trump argued that the globalized free-trade policy destroyed the manufacturing industries in the United States, which made the life of American workers much more difficult. For Trump, the "logic" of globalism was a kind of "foolishness" and "arrogance," leading to foreign policy disasters and making money for "large corporations" that triggered the

---

[46] Sheng, Li (2016) Explaining US-China Economic Imbalances: A Social Perspective. *Cambridge Review of International Affairs*, 29(3), 1097–1111.

[47] Sheng, L. (2011). Theorising free capital mobility: the perspective of developing countries. *Review of International Studies*, 2519–2534.

outflow of capital.[48]As a consequence, to achieve the commitment of making America great again, Trump had taken several anti-globalization actions. On the one hand, the United States directly withdrew from global multilateral mechanisms, such as UNESCO and the Paris Climate Agreement; on the other hand, the United States has criticized some international organizations. For example, Trump has assumed a victim posture, accusing the WTO of rules not favoring the United States and insisting that the WTO unfairly sides with China. In addition, he complained that NAFTA, the TPP, and the WTO have caused losses of thousands of manufacturing jobs in the United States and that those agreements were responsible for the $1 trillion trade deficit the United States had with the rest of the world.[49]

Regarding the issue of the U.S. trade deficit, much research has been performed by scholars domestically and abroad. It is believed that there are four main reasons for this deficit: the status of the U.S. international reserve currency,[50] the low savings model of U.S. overconsumption,[51] the

[48] Edwards, J. A. (2018). Make America great again: Donald Trump and redefining the US role in the world. *Communication Quarterly*, 66(2), 176–195.

[49] Edwards, J. A. (2018). Make America great again: Donald Trump and redefining the US role in the world. *Communication Quarterly*, 66(2), 176–195.

[50] The dollar's status as the global reserve currency has resulted in high foreign demand for dollars, which means an appreciation in its exchange rate. Therefore, U.S. exports are more expensive and U.S. imports are cheaper, irrespective of trade practices. This dynamic reinforces America's trade deficit. A rebalancing of the international trading system would necessitate a decrease in the global demand for dollars. Reforming the international monetary system would help rebalance trade.

Carbaugh, B. (2019). Trump's America First Program: A Flawed Approach. *Challenge*, 62(2), 144–162.

[51] Trump's fixation on the balance of trade in trade negotiations misses a fundamental economic principle. The balance of trade is ultimately determined by macroeconomic forces, not by trade barriers or trade agreements. America's total trade deficit reflects the shortage of savings by U.S. households, businesses, and governments—that is, the surplus of their combined spending over their income. Tariffs can result in trade moving into balance only if they somehow promote a rise in national saving or a reduction in investment. If the United States imposes tariffs on China's merchandise, and if nothing else changes, Americans will purchase less Chinese merchandise. However, unless Americans modify their total spending and saving, they will purchase more merchandise from some other country. In the long run, the impact of trade policies on the balance of trade tends to be outweighed by the more fundamental determinants of investment and saving, such as expectations about future profits and the costs of borrowing, expected future interest rates, and income levels.

Carbaugh, B. (2019). Trump's America First Program: A Flawed Approach. *Challenge*, 62(2), 144–162.

division of labor in the global value chain,[52] and the U.S. high-tech export restrictions[53] on China. Therefore, the trade imbalance between China and the United States is not China's responsibility but the result of defects in the U.S. domestic system. The deficit was just an excuse for Trump to initiate the trade war with China.

As the U.S. dollar's status as the global reserve currency, other countries, especially China, sorely demand U.S. dollars in the chaos of fluctuating exchange rates. According to the Official Reserve Assets report published on May 7, 2020, by the State Administration of Foreign Exchange of China, at the end of April 2020, the scale of foreign exchange reserves is anticipated to be 3.0915 trillion U.S. dollars.[54] The consistently positive and substantial trade balance can be attributed to China's accumulation of foreign currency. Since China accepts foreign currency, especially U.S. dollars, for exported goods and services, it maintains that currency in the national reserve.

Foreign countries usually stockpile U.S. dollars to defend against crises that arise when the decisions and policies of central bankers in large economies such as the United States influence their currencies to float up and

[52] From the 1990s, research in the field of international economics had begun to pay attention to the phenomenon that increasingly various countries participate in different sections of supply or the production of specific products. For example, Krugman (1996) called it slicing the value chain; Arndt (1997) thought that this international division included global sourcing, offshore sourcing, subcontracting and intraproduct specialization; and Feenstra (1998) used the phrase "disintegration of production and integration of trade in the global economy." Some recent research (Plasschaert 2011) has already paid attention to the role of multinational companies in the U.S.-China trade deficit as "exports attributed to China usually contain a large percentage of imported components with modest value-added attributed to China itself." Koopman, Wang, and Wei (2012) have already pointed out that almost all of the U.S.-China trade deficits for advanced technology products (ATPs) are finished by wholly foreign-owned enterprises or joint ventures. The U.S.-China trade imbalance is actually an imbalance through the "global production network," which is the result of the international division of labor.

Gao, Y., Cheng, W., & Yuan, Q. (2018). Understanding the global imbalance from the perspective of processing trade value added of China. *Journal of Chinese Economic and Business Studies*, 16(4), 337–356.

[53] Some people criticized that the increased tariffs on U.S. high-tech exports proposed by Trump would raise prices and reduce investment in the types of machinery, equipment, and other technology that drive innovation and productivity throughout the U.S. economy.

Carbaugh, B. (2019). Trump's America First Program: A Flawed Approach. *Challenge*, 62(2), 144–162.

[54] Official Reserve Assets (2020), State Administration of Foreign Exchange of China, URL: http://m.safe.gov.cn/safe/2020/0207/15341.html.

down as well as destroy the stability of their economies, particularly when experiencing the significant monetary easing and depreciation of U.S. dollars. Including China, most countries hold foreign exchange reserves, not only facilitating international trade but also undertaking their currencies' steadiness and boosting other foreign transactions. The world's total foreign exchange reserves were approximately $527 billion (in 2020 dollars) in 1973, drastically rising to $11829.54 billion in the last quarter of 2019,[55] a 22.5-fold increase. In all the shares of allocated reserves, the U.S. dollar has the largest proportion, at 60.89%,[56] such that approximately two-thirds of the world's total reserves are claimed in U.S. dollars.

Such a high global demand will lead to the appreciation of the U.S. dollar in its exchange rate, strengthening its dominant international position. Thus, U.S. exports cost more and imports cost less, despite trade practices. This tendency dilates America's trade deficits and budget in tandem. Therefore, American enterprises have found it challenging to provide more jobs in the manufacturing industry inside the country. Meanwhile, propelled by the benefits of trading currencies and hedging the related risks, the portion of the contribution of the finance industry to GDP has increased from 2% to 9%.

In contrast to the opinion of some trade hawks, the cause of America's hefty and constant trade deficit is not predominantly harmful trade deals. The status of the global reserve currency for U.S. dollars is just as irresponsible as any free-trade agreement or unfair behaviors. Overloaded demand for dollars has made the competitive environment for U.S. exporters and workers even more slanted. Those electorates who opposed tariffs, specifically blue-collar voters, should concentrate more on the reform of the international monetary system.

In the "Monetary Reform Would Rebalance Trade," Rushton suggested three effective procedures to establish a level playing field for the U.S. dollar, which requires shrinking global demand by plateauing the

[55] World—Official Foreign Exchange Reserves by Currency, Currency Composition of Official Foreign Exchange Reserves (COFER), International Monetary Fund (IMF) data, URL: https://data.imf.org/?sk=E6A5F467-C14B-4AA8-9F6D-5A09EC4E62A4.

[56] World—Allocated Reserves by Currency, Currency Composition of Official Foreign Exchange Reserves (COFER), International Monetary Fund (IMF) data, URL: https://data.imf.org/?sk=E6A5F467-C14B-4AA8-9F6D-5A09EC4E62A4.

U.S. dollar and other major currencies and launching a brand-new international reserve currency[57] (Rushton, 2018). First, for the guidance of monetary policy, Federal Reserve appointors should aim to target the real-time prices of commodity indices, foreign currencies and bonds, which can be an approach to avoid the Fed's most recent mistakes. The loose monetary policies of the 1970s and 2000s led to a substantial increase in world dollar assets, a price bubble, and an economic collapse. Second, the United States should court other major currencies to stabilize the dollar. America can initially cooperate with the second most commonly held reserve currency, the euro, to construct a dollar-euro stableness protocol. Subsequently, the United States can invite other democratic countries' currencies into the pact, reducing and stabilizing the demand for dollars. An International Monetary Fund (IMF) communiqué presented a positive view in this regard that they acknowledged that undue volatility or disorderly variation in exchange rates could adversely influence financial and economic stability by avoiding competitive devaluation or not objecting to the exchange rate for rival purposes. Last and most contentious, the United States and other influential economies should innovate a new international currency to value commodities globally and establish trade accounts. Countries would retain their national currencies for domestic use, converting them into international currencies at constant rates. Robert Mundell, the Nobel Prize laureate, proposed a similar international currency, which would be backed 50% by gold and 50% by the five most powerful currencies. Rep. Jack Kemp once put forward resolving the "reserve currency curse" with a return to the sufficient international gold standard. In addition, such plans as developing the use of the IMF's reserve asset could also be taken into consideration.

However, Trump's obsession with the negotiation of the trade balance ignored the elemental economic principle. The large trade deficit is fundamentally aroused by forces of macroeconomics instead of trade agreements or trade barriers. Trade agreements and trade barriers tend to change the composition of the trade deficit with different trading partners and compound goods and services, while they do not affect the total

[57] Sean Rushton (2018), Monetary Reform Would Rebalance Trade, Wall Street Journal, 29 Mar 2018: A.17.

size of the trade deficit. The consequence of trade policy on the trade balance is believed to be masked by more basic saving and investment determinants in the long run.[58] These factors include wealth, present income, and future expected income, as well as private savings and government savings. U.S. private and public savings and investments are essential to increasing trade deficits, which were neglected by the government due to it failing to consider the conceivable influence of its own tax and expenditure policies on the future trade balance.[59]

The U.S. cumulative trade deficit indicates the deficiency in both private savings by households and enterprises, plus government savings, which means that their total expenditures exceed their income. Only if tariffs facilitate an increase in national savings or a decrease in investment by some methods can the government balance trade. Since foreign capital inflows bridge the gulf between supply of and demand for domestic capital, or between the total amount of the economic savings relevant to investments, they perform a vital role in the present structure of the U.S. economy.[60] The graph below shows the net savings by three main components of the savings-investment balance in the United States: the economy, households and businesses in private saving, government saving, and net national saving (Fig. 2.8).

Conventionally, the funds invested by businesses and utilized by the government are supplied by households. When the sum of these three zones combines the negative net savings, it leads to rising interest rates and the inflow of foreign capital. Therefore, it also pressures the exchange rate of the U.S. dollars upward, driving the relative value of the dollar up compared to that of other currencies. Similar to the situation of the high global demand of the U.S. dollar, it tends to increase the deficit of the current account.

Americans have a low saving rate compared with other countries around the world; it is especially much lower than that of Chinese

---

[58] Lawrence, R. Z. (2018). *Five Reasons Why the Focus on Trade Deficits is Misleading* (No. PB18-6).

[59] Sheng, L. (2015). Theorizing income inequality in the face of financial globalization. *The Social Science Journal*, 52(3), 415–424.

[60] Jackson, J. K. (2018). *The Economic Effects of Trade: Overview and Policy Challenges*, Congressional Research Service, 7–5700.

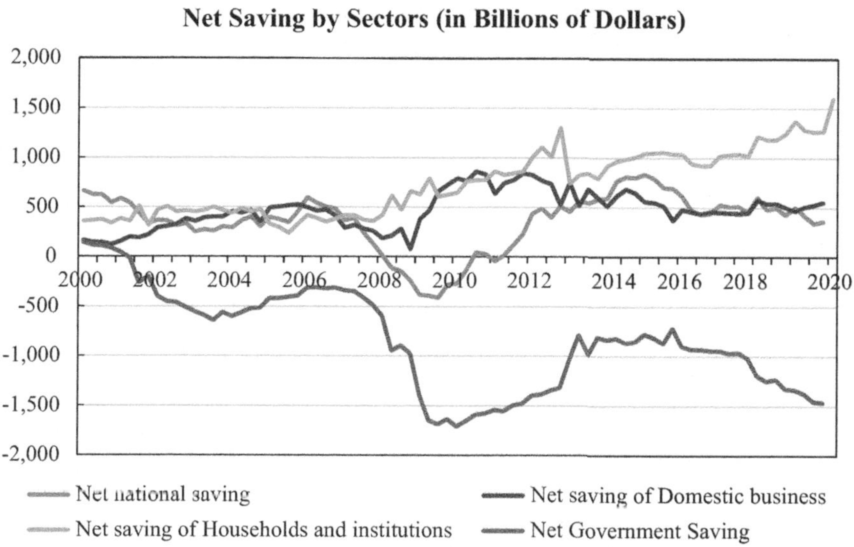

Fig. 2.8 Net saving by sectors in the United States (in billions of dollars). (*Data Source: U.S. Bureau of Economic Analysis, FRED economic data*)

households. The saving rate is not always high in developed countries, as they have better social welfare plus widespread use of credit cards. In contrast with China's saving tradition, Americans invest their money in bonds, stocks, and house assets, which have a high interest rate and a higher expected return than savings. Additionally, cultural differences matter. For example, American college students are more likely to request student loans to afford their college tuition fees and pay them later by themselves; by contrast, Chinese students prefer using savings from their family. Although Trump imposes tariffs on goods imported from China, as long as Americans do not modify their saving habits regarding their disposable income, spending merely changes from the consumption of Chinese commodities to goods of other countries (Fig. 2.9).

The low savings model of America's overconsumption has appeared for decades. The saving rate corresponds to net saving, which is equal to the variation between disposable income and the ultimate consumption expenditure. From the graph below, we can conclude that after the

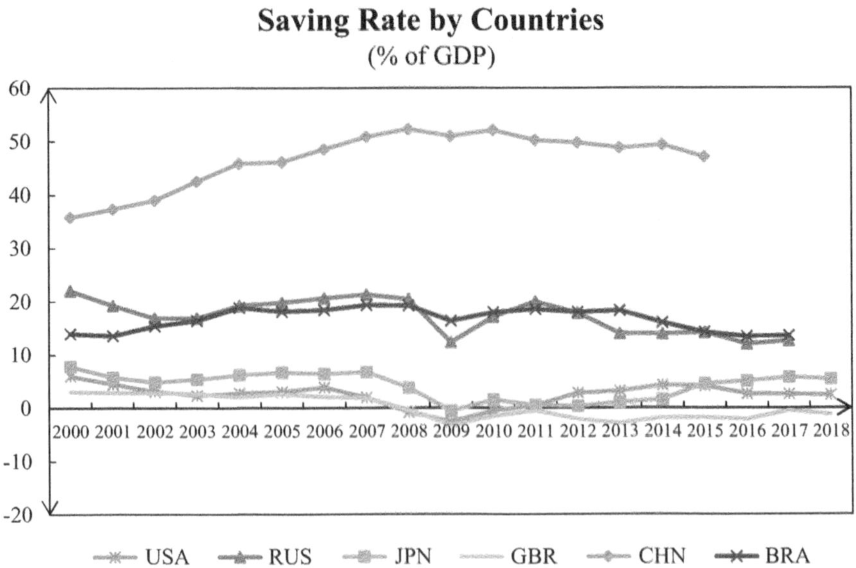

Fig. 2.9 Saving rate by countries (% of GDP). (*Data Source: Organisation for Economic Co-operation and Development [OCED] data*)

financial crisis in 2008, Americans started to increase their saving rates slowly, which reversed the decline of more than 25 years (Fig. 2.10).[61]

Before the deep recession caused by the financial crisis, household saving rates had decreased since the increasing value of stock markets and house assets made individuals wealthier, decreasing Americans need to save money for retirement. In addition, the availability of credit cards provided Americans with a greater chance to avoid saving as they purchased goods and services now and settled the payments later. However, after 2008, the situation of household assets abruptly exacerbated and house prices dropped 40%, suddenly erasing one-third of the equity of households with mortgages. The wealth of households was reduced by $10 trillion after the recession. With the demand for preparing for retirement and the consistently high unemployment rate, households had to

[61] Sheng, L. (2012). Dealing with financial risks of international capital flows: a theoretical framework. *Cambridge Review of International Affairs*, 25(3), 463–474.

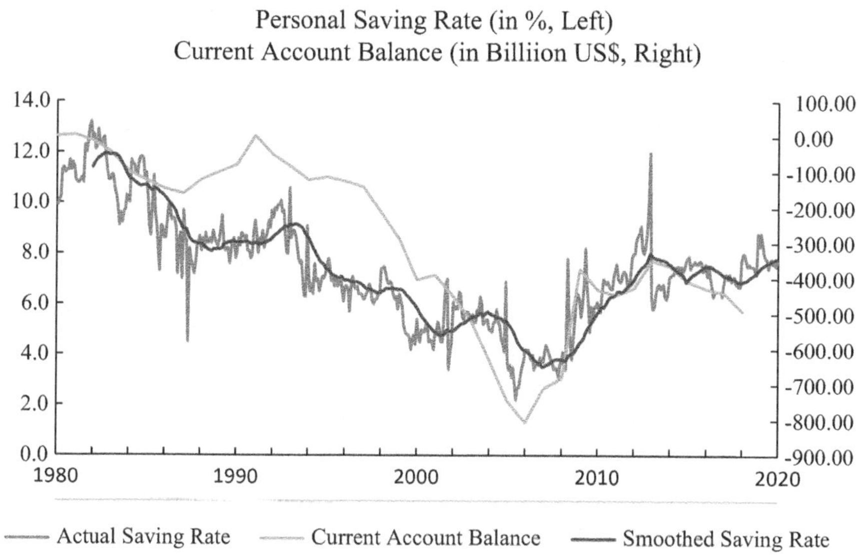

Fig. 2.10 Personal saving rate (in %, left) and current account balance in the United States (in billion U.S. dollars, right). (*Data Source: U.S. Bureau of Economic Analysis, FRED economic data, The World Bank Data*)

increase their savings rate so that they could hold more cash in case of job loss.

Since personal disposable income occupies approximately 75% of GDP, a personal saving rate of 8% converts into only 6% of GDP. Considering the depreciation of the existing equipment and plants, the average company's retained profits accounted for approximately 3% of GDP.[62] Hence, the private savings of households and enterprises can be summed to account for 9% of GDP. Unfortunately, the government has a deficit of approximately 5% of GDP, which would make the net national saving rate only 4% of GDP. Such a small percentage for the national saving rate is insufficient to fund new investment in the country's plant, equipment, and housing sectors. Therefore, despite the increase in household savings rates, unless the federal government changes policies to reduce the future budget deficit of the United States, it will

[62] Feldstein M. (2010). America's Saving Surprise. *Project Syndicate.*

continue to rely on capital inflows from other parts of the world. If this situation continues, global imbalances will continue to increase risks to the global economy. Both the status of the U.S. international reserve currency and the low savings model due to America's overconsumption can lead to continuous capital inflows. Such flows not only retain the strength of the U.S. dollar but also arouse the tendency of inhibiting exports and stimulating imports, thus causing the current account deficit.[63]

Global value chains (GVCs) and global production networks (GPNs) were established and developed in the late twentieth century and early twenty-first century during major changes in the international production system. With the swift pace of economic globalization, multinational corporations (MNCs) have emerged to allocate capital and arrange production activities at the global scale. The international division of labor has already achieved the level of interindustry, intraindustry, and product-specific specialization. With increasingly fierce competition and global market fluctuations, the competitive and cooperative relationships among countries, regions, industries, and companies are getting closer. As a result, MNCs became more prominent and influential in the trading system and manipulated economic globalization, enhancing the expansion of GVCs. In GVCs, production is spread across countries, and the procedures are much more complicated than a single-processed product. Trade and investment liberalization makes cross-border production possible with lower transportation costs, closer communication, and innovations in logistics. MNCs have integrated international business strengths in their kernel domains. MNCs have also become more potent through regulating and coordinating their foreign production networks, which composed of various companies. An evaluation indicates that GVCs "governed" by MNCs represent 80% of world trade every year.[64] Enterprises among different countries take part in GVCs by acting as upstream suppliers or downstream consumers of corporation goods or services. In addition, for developing countries aiming to engage new industries and learning to produce merchandise for export markets, how

[63] Gu, X., & Sheng, L. (2010). Sensible Policy Tool for Pareto Improvement: Capital Controls, *Journal of World Trade*, 44(3), 567–589.

[64] Industrial Analytics Platform (2019), What are global value chains and why do they matter?, URL: https://iap.unido.org/articles/what-are-global-value-chains-and-why-do-they-matter.

to provide inputs to enterprises is particularly important. However, these inputs are equivalently essential for industrial economies that supply complicated, professional, and high-value products.

After entering the WTO, China immediately waded into GVCs following the reinforcement of the open economy. Although China has the largest manufacturing industry in the world, manufacturers still lack competitiveness compared with their foreign counterparts in many aspects, such as advanced technology, resource utilization efficiency, the ability to innovate independently, and the application of information technology[65] (Cui & Liu, 2019).

There are also some negative outcomes generated by GVCs. Because of the division of labor, the risk of enlarging economic gaps between regions and countries exists. Other risks include the potential erosion of labor welfare, the collapse of social cohesion, and environmental degradation.[66] GVCs may have increased the external shocks of the local economy and driven some less developed countries into low-profit production over the long run.

As productivity and technology vary across regions, the share of intermediate goods counts differently than manufactured goods. For Oceania and Africa, exports are higher than imports, but for Asia and Europe, imports are higher. This situation can be attributed to the majority of exports for Oceania and Africa being raw materials and natural resources, such as agricultural products and minerals. Moreover, Europe is better off than Asia in regard to the intermediates' trade balance, which means it imports relatively low skill and technology required by intermediates and later processes these into more specialized goods.

Furthermore, Asia's trade deficit of intermediates demonstrates that this region processes more intermediates' assembly procedures than those from other regions. Thus, China is dedicated to representing higher valued and more specialized component assemblies. Recently, final and simple manufacturing has gradually moved to Southeast Asian countries. The outsourcing of MNCs may shift from China to other economies

[65] Cui Fengru and Liu Guitang (2019). *Global Value Chains and Production Networks: Case Studies of Siemens and Huawei*. Academic Press, ISBN: 978–0–12-814,847-1.

[66] Industrial Analytics Platform (2019), What are global value chains and why do they matter?, URL: https://iap.unido.org/articles/what-are-global-value-chains-and-why-do-they-matter.

with the advantage of cheap labor, but it will definitely not return to the United States.[67]

Research performed by the Asian Development Bank Institute finds that an iPhone exported from China to the United States sells for $179; the value added by China is only approximately $7. Even China did not add much value to a product unit when it was imported by the United States. This situation will lead to a $179 deduction in America's trade balance, which exacerbates the trade deficit (Fig. 2.11).

According to U.S. Census Bureau statistics, the U.S. trade deficit in goods with China in 2019 amounted to $346 billion, accounting for 40.5% of its total trade deficit. Over the past ten years, the proportion of Sino-U.S. trade deficit in total is 45.2% on average, which will definitely trigger the enmity of Trump and his administration.

As in the case of the iPhone mentioned above, the trade deficit can attribute a large portion to the division of labor in GVCs, the competitive market, and the discrepancy of industrial structures in the different

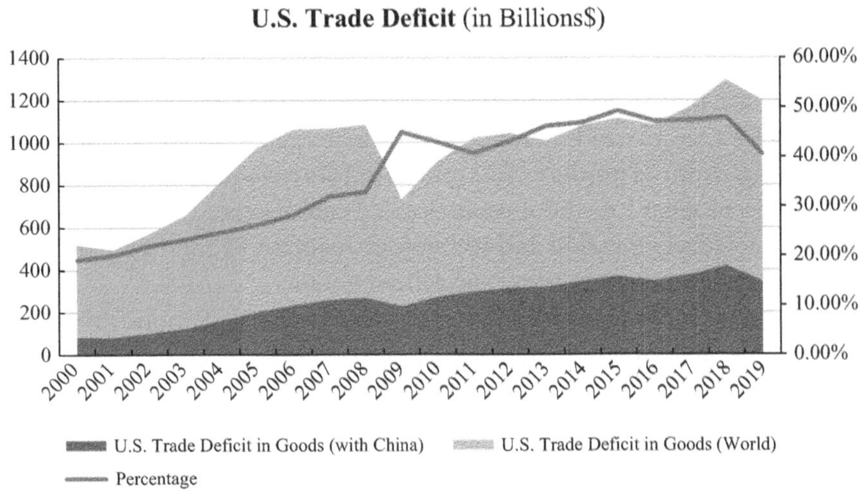

Fig. 2.11 U.S. trade deficit (in billions of U.S. dollar). (*Data Source: U.S. Census Bureau*)

[67] Sheng, Li (2014) Economic Structure, Cost Outsourcing, and Global Imbalances. *Journal of Australian Political Economy*, 74, 81–94.

countries. Although there is a large trade surplus for China, Chinese manufacturing industries are at the bottom or middle of GVCs, whereas the United States is at the top, guiding the world's innovation, production, and development of merchandise. Since the labor cost in the United States is much higher than in China, the United States does not have a comparative advantage in production. The well-developed and organized global production network due to unprecedented globalization, the repaid exploitation of fragmented multinational production, and low-cost but high-quality transportation all prompted rational companies to place their manufacturing plants in cheap labor-cost countries such as China. Such business decisions will directly widen the trade deficit. That is, the different trade balance between the United States and China is naturally generated from two nations' different economic structures.

However, scholars from Tsinghua University have analyzed the merchandise trade deficit between the United States and China by the comparative method of the international value-added distribution chain of products.[68] These scholars concluded that the traditional bilateral trade evaluation overestimates the deficit. The actual Sino-U.S. trade deficit is only half of the original statistics, particularly in the machinery and ICT industry. The Sino-U.S. trade imbalance is not the only reason for global imbalance; GVCs also cause the imbalance (Gao, Cheng & Yuan, 2018).

The function of those enterprises in Sino-U.S. trade is attributed to "exports attributed to imports." Generally, a large part of China's exports to the United States are imported; the added value owned by China is quite low and overestimated. In GVCs, almost all Sino-U.S. trade deficits of advanced technology products (ATPs) are accomplished by joint ventures or foreign invested companies. The sector's manufacturing exports, which require sophisticated, highly skilled labor, have a relatively low share of domestic content of 30% or less, such as electronic and telecommunication devices, computers, and scientific equipment.[69] Conversely,

---

[68] Gao, Y., Cheng, W., & Yuan, Q. (2018). Understanding the global imbalance from the perspective of processing trade value added of China. *Journal of Chinese Economic and Business Studies*, 16(4), 337–356.

[69] Koopman, R., Wang, Z., & Wei, S. J. (2012). Estimating domestic content in exports when processing trade is pervasive. *Journal of development economics*, 99(1), 178–189.

other sectors that require intensive, low-skilled labor, such as furniture and apparel, have a relatively high share. Furthermore, in the exports, both U.S.-owned enterprises and Sino-U.S. joint venture enterprises also tend to have a relatively low share of domestic content since they have lower domestic value added in processing exports (Koopman, Wang & Wei, 2012).

We have discussed how the status of the U.S. international reserve currency, the low savings model of the U.S. overconsumption, and the division of labor in the global value chain all influence and increase the U.S. trade deficit. The last influential reason is the U.S. high-tech export restrictions on China. The United States has imposed restrictions on high-technology exports toward China for a long time, even though China owns one of the world's largest markets with sufficient demand. The reasons for these restrictions are complicated and diversified, and military security is always considered the dominant cause. As the military power of China has strengthened and the military-to-military relationships between the two countries have reached precarious stability, the contradiction of the two economic models generates mistrust. The purpose of these restrictions is to control the advanced technology inflow to China by GVCs, stretch the imitation lag, and maximize the economic benefits.

Modeling the restrictions by the deadweight loss theory,[70] economists have found that controlling the export of technology leads to a decrease in social welfare. As free trade will maximize the total welfare of both exporters and importers, these restrictions serve as trade barriers, which damage not only the total profits of the United States and China but also the individual interests as well as change the distribution of resources between the two countries and lead to inefficient markets (Yang and Mai, 2016).

The econometric method of multilinear regression demonstrates that technology export is an essential variable to determine the growth of U.S. GDP and the technology industry. However, the United States is not the only source of technology inflow into China. Other countries,

[70] Chunmei, Y., & Wenyi, M. (2016). The US High Technology Export Control towards China. *Journal of Business*, 1(2), 13–16.

such as the European Union, Canada, Korea, and Japan, also participate in the Chinese technology market, earning huge profits. The limitation of America did not effectively hinder China's technological development.

China started concentrating on independent innovation for years after it recognized the difficulty and harm of importing technological merchandise from Western countries. With more technology expenditure of its GDP and considerable technical human resources, the development of Chinese scientific and technological enterprises accelerated. Hence, even though the restrictions do strike the Chinese technology industry and produce extra expenditure, the harm to the growth of U.S. GDP and the technology industry cannot be neglected. Stymieing advanced innovation in critical spheres and controlling exports can backfire on the United States. The Chinese government has launched the Made in China 2025 plan to facilitate domestic production in ten critical sectors, including information technology, biopharmaceuticals, and aerospace. Although America has suggested its allies should ban the fifth-generation (5G) mobile networks of Huawei, some Western countries still signed contracts and allowed the building of infrastructures using Huawei products.

Evaluating price data for 2018 from the Bureau of Labor statistics on imports from China indicates that the restrictions and tariffs were born by U.S. importers.[71] China's exports to the United States will decline significantly, while the impact on U.S. exports to China will be moderate. Since the post-tariff prices have increased after matching the magnitude, restricting trade will seriously harm low-income families (Sukar & Ahmed, 2016). If the unilateral restrictions are overly broad, international cooperation will become harder, which will ultimately impact American enterprises. The global nature of supply chains, commerce, and China's growing indigenous capabilities means that only the minimum real vital technologies should be controlled. The U.S. enterprises will be impacted by delays in implementing their own advanced technology without Sino-U.S. collaboration.

Since the restricted entity list included the technology enterprise Huawei, the U.S. firms that provide components for the P30 Mate

[71] Sukar, A., & Ahmed, S. (2019). Rise of trade protectionism: the case of US-Sino trade war. *Transnational Corporations Review*, 11(4), 279–289.

smartphone were harmed severely, including Skyworks Solutions and Qorvo, which provide the chips; Micron, which provides the memory; Synopsis and Mentor Graphics, which provide the design software; and Android, which provides the operating system[72] (Capri, 2020).

While the U.S. government is trying to block technology, MNCs of technology are finding ways to avoid the harsh restrictions to continue selling products to major customers. A recent report from the Hinrich Foundation indicates that the enterprises are doing this by exploiting legal loopholes and restructuring global supply chains.[73] These loopholes will drive the administration to enact stricter policies, which will lead to a higher cost and disrupt GVCs. Therefore, in the foreseeable future, the Sino-U.S. technology rivalry will continue to bring higher risks and uncertainties to technology companies.

The U.S. high-tech restrictions of protectionism on China as a passive policy will shrink the quota of exports and worsen the trade deficit. The sustainable solution would be that the U.S. government increases its investment in American talent and domestic companies while continuing to benefit from foreign talent, cooperation, and global innovation.

[72] Capri, A. (2020). Techno-nationalism: The US-China tech innovation race. *Hinrich Foundation*, August, URL: https://technode.com/2020/04/24/export-controls-and-the-rise-of-us-china-techno-nationalism/.

[73] Capri, A. (2020), Semiconductors at the Heart of the US-China Tech War. *Hinrich Foundation*, URL: https://hinrichfoundation.com/trade-research/global-trade-research/thought-leadership/semiconductors-at-the-heart-of-the-us-china-tech-war/

3

Geopolitics in the Trade War

When Did Love End?

The U.S.-China trade dispute is now continuously attracting global attention. Many countries are paying close attention to the development of Sino-U.S. economic and trade relations. Developing countries hope to take this opportunity to observe the attitude of the United States toward China's ascendance, whereas developed countries hope to capture relevant signals from a series of sanctions adopted by the White House. The Trump administration's tendency to prolong the trade war through other means suggests that, in principle, the disputes with China are not limited to economic issues. At present, geoeconomic conflict could be the beginning of a prolonged geopolitics battle, and only the future will reveal the consequences.

Former U.S. President Jimmy Carter (1977–1981) once explained his views on the rise of China in an interview.[1] Carter was one of those responsible for further opening up economic relations with China during his tenure. He mentioned that China has never had a war with any nation

[1] Brennan, D. (2019, May 15). Jimmy Carter took call about China from a concerned Donald Trump: 'China has not wasted a single penny on war'. Newsweek.

L. Sheng, D. Felix do Nascimento, *Love and Trade War*,
https://doi.org/10.1007/978-981-33-4897-4_3

since 1979, whereas the United States has been in a state of war. China has continuously built approximately 18,000 miles of high-speed railway, whereas the United States has spent US$3 trillion on military expenditures. Carter stated, "China has not wasted a single penny on war, and that's why they're ahead of us." In almost all respects, China's investments were spent on infrastructure projects, including intercontinental and transoceanic high-speed railways, fifth-generation (5G) and 6G technologies, robot intelligence, and resources for universities, hospitals, ports, and buildings, not just on military expenditures.

This does not mean that China's military expenditures have not gradually increased, nor does it mean that Chinese army has adopted more advanced modern technologies than the United States. What Carter declared was the perception that Chinese leaders had in combining a type of capitalist development with a purposeful international insertion in view of their domestic priorities and their strategic surroundings. The stages and challenges will be gradually implemented until the maturation of the "Made in China 2025" initiative. We understand that the trade war launched by the United States is one of the measures covering a wide range: the loss of U.S. hegemony in world political economy is triggered by a wide-ranging controversy in the geopolitical field. Therefore, this is the issue that most concerns Chinese leaders.

The author Yinxing Hong[2] states that the logic of China's 40-year economic reform is to clarify the stages of development according to four dimensions of reform: (1) the reform of the resource allocation mode, which is driven by the breakthrough of the theory of the socialist market economy. This theoretical breakthrough has clarified the direction of market-oriented reform. (2) The adjustment of ownership structure and the reform of public ownership, which is driven by the breakthrough of basic economic system theory in the primary stage of socialism. (3) The reform of the basic distribution system, which is driven by the breakthrough in factor payments theory. (4) Supply-side structural reform, which is driven by the breakthrough in economic operation theory. According to the author, China delegated more powers to lower-level

[2] Hong, Y. (2019). The logic of four decades of economic reform and major breakthroughs in political economy in China. *China Political Economy*, 2(1), 2–13.

governments and society, thereby improving regulation and optimizing services, improving macro control mechanism, and modernizing the national governance system and the governance capacity.

When we mention disputes in geopolitics between the United States and China, we understand that a new global phase of conflicts in different spheres has been initiated. Zhongliang Zheng[3] believes that the trade imbalance in the United States and the considerable differences in industrial structure and economic difficulties are the factors that led to the trade war between the United States and China. The huge trade deficit between the United States and China is the trade war's direct trigger, and thus "The purpose of the U.S. to stir up the trade disputes is to change the bad situation of its trade deficit." Yuhuan Zhang[4] believes that the change in U.S. economic and trade policies stems from the pursuit of fair trade.

Yifu Lin[5] questions the argument of the trade imbalance. He believes that the trade asymmetry between China and the United States has a long history, but it is not the root of the trade dispute. As the U.S. dollar is an international reserve currency, the United States can completely solve the problem of paying the deficit by increasing the circulation of U.S. dollars. Therefore, he stresses that when analyzing the motives underlying the Sino-U.S. trade war, the White House's policy intentions must be recognized. Apart from trade imbalance, the difference in industrial structure between China and the United States is also one of the important reasons for trade conflicts. Especially with the development of economic globalization, the commodity trade friction between China and the United States has become the current service trade friction. However, resistance to trade in services comes from the differences between the two countries in domestic laws, economy, and culture.

---

[3] Zheng, Zhongliang. (2018). Sino-US Trade Friction Seen from Sino-US Trade Structure. *China Business and Market,* 32(10), 80–92.

[4] Zhang, Yuhuan. (2018). Trump Administration's Foreign Trade Policy and Sino-US Trade Game, *Foreign Affairs Review*, 35(03), 12–36.

[5] Lin Yifu (2019). China's New Era and Sino-US Trade Disputes. *Wuhan University Journal of Social Science*, 72(02), 159–165.

Yanxiang Kuang[6] constructs a multistage dynamic game model and concludes that with the deepening of economic interdependence between China and the United States, the low-level trade friction between the two countries is also increasing. In other words, the deep economic interdependence between China and the United States is also a factor leading to trade friction. Considering that the U.S. real estate bubble has burst and the domestic economy has not recovered since the 2008 financial crisis, revitalizing the domestic industry and restoring the domestic economy is also one of the motivations for the United States to impose sanctions against China. The United States is trying to force the Chinese government to further open up its domestic market by pushing forward a trade war, which is believed to help the United States get out of its domestic economic predicament.

Tieliu Yu[7] believes that theoretically speaking, the primary cause of Sino-U.S. trade disputes is that the United States violates the basic rules of trade. He gives the reason that the most suitable pattern for Sino--U.S. trade should be that China exports labor-intensive products, whereas the United States exports technology and capital-intensive products. However, the United States runs counter to the ideal pattern, resulting in a trade deficit with China.

As Zhaohui Wang and Jinghan Zeng[8] describe, the recent trade tensions are rooted in the increasingly fierce strategic competition between the two countries. For the authors Wang and Zeng (2020), different phases in economic relations between the United States and China led to the current stage. First was a symbiotic relationship in the 1990s, when the United States consumed cheap Chinese exports and paid China in U.S. dollars. China held U.S. dollars and U.S. Treasury bonds and even provided loans to the United States. Second, after China joined the World Trade Organization (WTO) in 2001, China's low-cost

[6] Kuang Yanxiang (2010). Economic Interdependence and Sino-US Trade Friction: A Study Based on Multi-Stage Trade Model. *Journal of International Trade*, 2010(11), 36–43.

[7] Yu Tieliu (2004). Reasons for Sino-US Trade Friction and Countermeasures. *Management World*. 2004(09), 67–72.

[8] Wang, Z., & Zeng, J. (2020). From Economic Cooperation to Strategic Competition: Understanding the US-China Trade Disputes through the Transformed Relations. *Journal of Chinese Political Science*, 25(1), 49–69.

manufacturing and low-level exchange rate made Chinese goods particularly competitive in the world market, which generated large trade surpluses.

However, China's export-oriented industrialization suffered from external shock after the 2008 crisis. As a result, U.S.-China relations changed substantially in three phases. First, from 2009 to 2012, Chinese leadership was very aware of the disadvantages of overreliance on the U.S. market and the U.S. dollar, but gave priority first to growth and stability and second to domestic economic reforms. During the second phase, from 2013 to 2016, President Xi Jinping had great confidence and the ability to carry out substantive reforms in the domestic and international fields. In the third phase, from 2017 to 2019, the Trump administration defined China as a strategic competitor. In view of the structural changes in China's industrial and technology policies, this goal is driven by domestic consumption, new information technology, high-tech manufacturing, numerically controlled machine tools and robotics, aerospace equipment, and ocean engineering equipment and innovation, and China will become less dependent on foreign trade and less financially vulnerable to the United States.

Especially in the era of Trump-Xi, the reasons behind the ongoing changes mainly derive from China's series of domestic and global economic plans. In China's strategy in the financial field, China established an Asian Infrastructure Investment Bank (AIIB) in 2015 to focus on infrastructure development. A parallel initiative is the establishment of the "New Development Bank" (NDB) of BRICS for the financing of infrastructure and sustainable development projects in BRICS countries. A parallel BRICS initiative was to establish an International Monetary Fund (IMF)-style "Contingent Reserve Arrangement" (CRA) for emergency liquidity support to member countries. AIIB, NDB, and CRA are important new multilateral financial institutions that represent the Chinese initiative to seek greater financial autonomy.[9] With the internationalization of the Renminbi (RMB), China has reduced its reliance on the U.S. dollar to some extent, at least in terms of regional trade, invest-

[9] Bottelier Pieter (2018). *Economic Policy Making in China (1949–2016): The Role of Economists*, Taylor & Francis Group.

ment, and reserve currency arrangements. The launch of "the Belt and Road Initiative" and the establishment of the AIIB are aimed at promoting regional development and cooperation and creating a favorable environment for China's economic transformation and RMB internationalization.

According to economists Haiping Qiu and Min Zhao,[10] there have been serious contradictions in international trade, foreign exchange, and world reserves since the U.S. dollar was decoupled from gold in the 1970s, making it a new source of capital accumulation. This is clearly a strategy by the United States to compete with the Japanese yen and the German mark. What is more serious than the situation in the 1970s is the current contradiction between the excess of U.S. dollar capital and insufficient domestic investment. This means that the financial market has become the starting point for industrial capital decision-making in the United States. As a result, on the one hand, capital accumulation serves financial interests rather than social reproduction. As a result, the real economy is stagnant or even in recession. On the other hand, the huge wealth absorbed by financial capital has generated considerable investment demand, but financial capital does not have enough physical assets to invest and trade in a securitized way.

In view of the existing contradictions, Haiping Qiu and Min Zhao (2019) conclude that China is one of the greatest victims of the "US dollar problem." In this current unequal U.S. dollar-centered world currency system, China needs to participate in international cooperation through reform and opening up and actively integrate into the globalization process with developed capitalist countries at the center. After the RMB is included in the special drawing rights currency basket, it is necessary to continue promoting the internationalization of the RMB and enhance its status and role in the global trade and financial system.

[10] Qiu, H., & Zhao, M. (2019). The US dollar and new imperialism under the logic of capital accumulation. *China Political Economy*, 2(1), 98–107.

China: Strategic Competitor

Many factors have prompted the United States to list China as its main strategic competitor, mainly because of China's performance in the economic field over the past four decades. China accounted for 18% of global economic growth during the 1990s, and its contribution to global economic growth soared to 29% from 2000 to 2010. From 2008 to 2018, China accounted for 18% of the world's economic growth.[11]

Even though China's 6.1% growth (99.09 trillion yuan corresponding to US$14.14 trillion) in 2019 was more modest than in other years, a number of indicators show the continuity of the economic strategy that was implemented by Xi Jinping after 2013. In 2019, the tertiary industry accounts for 53.9% of GDP, whereas consumer spending contributed 57.8% to GDP growth. The foreign exchange reserve stood at $3.1 trillion, increasing by $35.2 billion annually. The average exchange rate for RMB against the U.S. dollar fell 4.1% to 6.8985. The total import and export of goods reached 31.5 trillion yuan, with an annual growth of 3.4%. Trade in services grew by 2.8% to 5.42 trillion yuan. In addition to banking, securities, and insurance, 40,888 foreign-funded enterprises were added, with foreign direct investment of 941.5 billion yuan, up 5.8%. Foreign nonfinancial investment amounted to 110.6 billion U.S. dollars, of which 15 billion U.S. dollars went to neighboring countries along the Belt and Road Initiative (BRI).[12]

Another thing that Trump and his aides cannot blame China for is the fact that the state's participation in the economy has been decreasing according to relevant indicators. According to Li (2020), in 2000, state-controlled industrial enterprises, referring to the industrial enterprises in which state-owned capital has a "controlling stake," usually defined as being the single largest equity owner but not necessarily owning more than 50% of the equity, still accounted for 50.2% of total sales revenue for all industrial enterprises "above designated sizes." By 2010, the share of state-controlled enterprises in industrial sales revenue fell sharply to

[11]Li, M. (2020). *Profit, Accumulation, and Crisis in Capitalism: Long-term Trends in the UK, US, Japan, and China, 1855–2018*. Routledge.

[12]Xinhua Português. (2020, March 3). Fatos e dados: Progressos econômicos e sociais da China em 2019. http://portuguese.xinhuanet.com/2020-03/02/c_138835771.htm.

27.9%. By 2017, the state-controlled share fell further to 23.4%. In 2017, state-owned enterprises accounted for 21.7% of the total fixed investment, whereas officially recognized domestic private enterprises accounted for 31.7%. Self-employed enterprises accounted for 1.8%; foreign-invested enterprises accounted for 1.8%; and Hong Kong-, Macao-, and Taiwan-invested enterprises accounted for 2.1%. The remainder reflects enterprises with mixed ownership. As a result, China's economy has undergone a fundamental change, and private capitalist enterprises at home and abroad have become the leading forces in China's industrial production, investment, and employment.

Li (2020) highlights the fact that from 2010 to 2016, China's share of profits fell from 35% to 26%. In 2017, profit increased by 1.1%. In 2018, the share of labor income was stable. The extra tax reduction for capitalists was offset by the increase in the share of fixed capital consumption, and the share of profits fell by 0.5%. The combination of rising capital-output ratio and falling profit share has led to an accelerated decline in China's profit rate. In 2018, China's economy-wide profit rate fell to 12.4%. In other words, Chinese leaders have given attention to encouraging private sector investments, but this occurs within the framework of combining productive capital and the interactive networks proposed by the BRI.

In the book *The US—China Trade War and China's Strategic Future*,[13] Alexander Lukin's view on the geopolitics of trade war is to some extent the same as that of Wang Zhaohui and Han Jing Zeng (2020). For Lukin (2019), Washington now argues that China's economic reforms have not only failed to make China more democratic and its foreign policy more pro-Western but have also emboldened Beijing to challenge the geopolitical advantages of the United States. The author mentions a speech by U.S. Vice President Mike Pence, who stated that "America had hoped that economic liberalization would bring China into a greater partnership with us and with the world. On the contrary, China chose economic aggression, which in turn contributed to its military strength." It also reports that China is too convinced that globalization is irreversible and that interdependence will force Washington to take action. Once the

[13] Lukin, A. (2019). The US–China Trade War and China's Strategic Future. *Survival*, 61(1), 23–50.

United Stated realized that China had benefited most from these processes and threatened to catch up with or even surpass the United States in economic strength, Washington rejected these processes and returned to its seemingly forgotten protectionist strategy.

Evgeny Pashentsev[14] shares the view that the United States runs a global campaign to discredit its opponents. Its focus is on its main economic and geopolitical competitor—China and its leading companies. According to data from the World Intellectual Property Organization, in 2019, China submitted 58,990 applications compared to 57,840 from the United States. Therefore, the main target is Huawei Technologies Co., Ltd., the world's largest telecommunications equipment manufacturer.

Political science scholars have pointed out that the pursuit of national interests, the domestic politics of the United States, economic interdependence, the international system, and other political factors cannot be ignored when studying the causes of the Sino-U.S. trade war. Interest groups also play an important role in the U.S. political system. The role of capital in the United States also indirectly influences the direction of U.S. foreign trade policy.

Kewei Guo[15] stresses that the trade war was launched not only to prepare Trump for the 2020 presidential election but also to coordinate with the expansionist fiscal policy of the United States. In 2018, when Trump was running for president in the midterm election, the policy of restricting China's exports to the United States should be regarded as his internal behavior designed to obtain more votes and political resources at this key node. In the era of globalization, the economies of all countries have been interdependent for a long time, but an increase in economic interdependence will often increase the frequency of trade conflicts between China and the United States. This is due to the United States' negative expectations of China's economic threat and traditional security. Guo also notes

[14] Evgeny Pashentsev (2020). Coronavirus Pandemics, Huawei 5G Technologies, Artificial Intelligence and Psychological Operations. http://www.eurocontinent.eu/2020/04/coronavirus-pandemics-huawei-5g-technologies-artificial-intelligence-and-psychological-operations-evgeny-pashentsev/.

[15] Guo Kewei. (2018). Sino-US Trade War: Motivation Analysis and Scenario Deduction. *Journal of International Economic Cooperation*. 2018(05), 14–24.

another important factor that triggered Sino-U.S. trade disputes, namely, the international system. At present, the existing international trade mechanism is not conducive to the realization of the best interests of the United States, which runs counter to Trump's consistent mantra of America First. Therefore, the United States' real intention in launching a trade war with China is to change the existing trade system and make international trade rules align with the interests of the United States. In addition, Trump's seemingly capricious but purposeful personality has also increased the uncertainty of the Sino-U.S. trade war. His unique shrewd businessperson character enables him to make good use of psychological tactics in the trade war, which also reflects the will of the United States.

Yaechan Lee[16] believes that Sino-U.S. economic cooperation is the result of the geopolitical interaction between the two countries. He also believes that the relaxation of Sino-U.S. geopolitical relations has promoted bilateral trade cooperation, whereas the U.S. attempts to prevent strategic rivals from appearing in Eurasia is the basis for the United States to promote the Trans-Pacific Partnership (TPP) to balance China's rise. After the 9/11 terrorist attacks, the consistent stances of the United States and China regarding international terrorism freed the two countries from tension over the Taiwan issue. The adjustment of Sino-U.S. geopolitical relations has expanded the scope of bilateral cooperation, thus deepening Sino-U.S. economic and trade cooperation. The purpose of the U.S. trade sanctions against China is to curb China's rise. Trump's current trade policy reflects the overall change in U.S. policy toward China. The Sino--U.S. trade war is actually an offshore check and balance by the United States against China, and some policy objectives are achieved by inhibiting China's economic development. The idea that China's related trade gains can be transformed into future military force reminds the United States that a strong China may pose a threat.

In addition, Lee also references the similarities and differences between the Sino-U.S. trade war and the U.S.-Japan trade war in the middle and late twentieth century. The direct cause of these two trade wars was the

[16] Lee, Y. (2018). Economic Interdependence and Peace: a Case Comparison Between the US-China and US-Japan Trade Disputes. *East Asia*, 35(3), 215–232.

serious foreign trade deficit of the United States. However, there are differences between these disputes. First, Japan's exports to the United States were mainly high value-added and high-tech products, while China's exports are mainly low-end and mid-end manufactured goods. Second, the market size is different, and the Chinese market is broader and has more potential than the Japanese market. According to the situation in Japan, Lee believes that the Sino-U.S. trade war will cause a trade deficit in the United States in a short period of one to three years, but will eventually be dominated by industrial advantages and economic structure. Historically, the U.S.-Japan trade war led to a decline in Japan's exports and temporarily suppressed economic growth. Meanwhile, it has also caused inflation in the United States. Although this created a small number of job opportunities, it was still far from offsetting the high unemployment rate. Lee believes that the Sino-U.S. trade war will have a much smaller impact on China than the U.S. Japan trade war had on Japan. The manufacturing of high-end semiconductors and electronic components is likely to be greatly affected. From a global perspective, the Sino--U.S. trade war is a confrontation between the world's two largest trading partners, which will not only affect the economic and social well-being of the two countries but also have a wider and systematic impact on other transition countries and the global trading system.

Sanjaya Baru,[17] an expert on India's national strategy, pointed out that Japan's efforts to transform geoeconomic power into geopolitical power from the mid-1950s to the early 1980s reflected the important role of geoeconomy in international politics after the Cold War. In his article, he pointed out that although Japan has not successfully transformed its economic strength into military and political influence, geoeconomy alone cannot replace geopolitics. Shortly after Japan's failed transformation attempt, during the Asian crisis of the late 1990s, China completed the transformation from geoeconomic power to geopolitical influence, which indicates that geoeconomy has replaced geopolitics as an important issue and method in the process of national gain. Geoeconomy plays an important role in shaping the political and security orders. After the end of the

[17] Baru, S. (2012). Geo-economics and strategy. *Survival* 2012, 54(3).

Cold War, state power began to accumulate wealth through market control rather than acquisition and territorial control.

Mikael Wigell[18] analyzes the geoeconomic strategies of large countries, and he defines geoeconomy as the geostrategic application of economic strength. He defines four ideal geoeconomic strategies, including neo-mercantilism, liberal institutionalism, imperialism, and hegemonism. Among the four strategies, the new mercantilist strategy and the new imperialist strategy originate from a competitive strategic framework that posits diplomatic relations as essentially a zero-sum game. The United States acts as an example. Economic strength is used as a lever to exert pressure on other countries or force them to give in. By contrast, the other two strategies emphasize mutual benefits. Geoeconomy is regarded as a strategy to govern the country.

John Morrissey[19] harkens back to the full operation of the U.S. Central Command in the 1990s in terms of military and economic security in the world's most critical areas, revealing the United States' deep-rooted geoeconomic desire to achieve global control. By adopting the concept of geoeconomy, he shows how the central command can make the commercial market a key factor in the overall strategy and use it as a means of geoeconomic deterrence.

Huotari and Heep[20] discuss China's experimental financial and monetary policies, believing that China's actions can be explained by its domestic concerns, especially the development path of the Chinese capitalism. China's move can be seen as aimed at managing the political and economic risks brought about by China's deepening ties with global financial flows rather than seeking a dominant position in international financial field in the future. China's geoeconomic strategy to promote export-oriented industrialization is based on macroeconomic policies. Seeking economic security and economic competitiveness and obtaining greater economic independence from large foreign suppliers with capital, brands, and technologies are all factors that China needs to consider.

[18] Wigell, M. (2016). Conceptualizing regional powers' geoeconomic strategies: neo-imperialism, neo-mercantilism, hegemony, and liberal institutionalism. *Asia Europe Journal*, 14(2), 135–151.

[19] Morrissey, J. (2017). Geoeconomics in the long war. *Antipode*, 49, 94–113.

[20] Huotari, M., & Heep, S. (2016). Learning geoeconomics: China's experimental financial and monetary initiatives. *Asia Europe Journal*, 14(2), 153–171.

Many of China's trade measures, including export credit, trade agreements, and tax rebate policies, are designed to allow global trade to flow to China's comparative advantage.

As shown by the above research results, many scholars have already recognized the characteristics of large countries using economic means to manipulate geopolitics. The United States and China are both using economic tools such as trade, finance, and energy to achieve their political and security goals. Geoeconomy provides a way for a country to implement power politics, which are different from territorial geopolitics. When dealing with international security issues such as the Iranian nuclear issue, Western countries prefer economic sanctions rather than military force. Most of the rising powers have also become the executors of economic policies. China has used financial, investment, and trade means to gain strategic influence, which to some extent has weakened the United States' strength and influence in the global economy and global politics. Today, a country's power and security are no longer linked only to the actual control of territory by military means but also to the command and control of economic ties. Economic ties play a decisive role in this globalized and highly interconnected world. The ability to exercise economic power is becoming a basic means of foreign policy for major powers.

The national strategy determines foreign policy objectives and makes them consistent. Theoretically, the tools to achieve geoeconomic goals include trade policies, investment policies, economic sanctions, cyberattacks, economic aid, financial and monetary policies, energy, and commodities. These goals are reflected in the implementation of geographical space. Power, capability, and means enable countries to deploy strategies and tactics for pursuing their own interests. In general, geoeconomic and geopolitical forces can predict the world's strategic patterns.

The geopolitical factors of confrontation in the U.S.-China confrontation are increasingly inevitable. In this way, the problem is beyond the scope of the trade war. What is the main means for the United States to contain China's rise? In view of reactions on the military field, since the priority of the economic front has been activated, other fronts can also be opened.

The Trade War as a False Justification: The U.S. Political-Military Structure Against China

Contemporary literature on the exercise of war in the twenty-first century, with different perspectives from Clausewitzian logic, has increasingly focused attention on the role of state and non-state actors in conducting Hybrid Wars over new geopolitical disputes. In the literature, the so-called Hybrid War, an unconventional war or asymmetrical war, includes the use and implementation of war by means other than military in their definition, aiming to weaken the enemy and force allied groups to change their strength. Russian general Valery Gerasimov is a proponent of Hybrid War theory in "The Value of Science Is in the Foresight: New Challenges Demand Rethinking the Forms and Methods of Carrying out Combat Operations"[21] and "Contemporary Warfare and Current Issues for the Defense of the Country,"[22] in which he calls the military and academic milieu Gerasimov's Doctrine. The Hybrid War method widely used by the United States and NATO allies has its own definitions because Gerasimov emphasizes that the confrontation method should be changed to incorporate the wide use of political, economic, diplomatic, information, and other nonmilitary measures, and should be implemented with the participation of potential public protests. Nonmilitary forms and means of struggle have undergone unprecedented development and have acquired a dangerous, sometimes violent nature. The practical use of nonmilitary methods and means can cause a collapse in energy, banking, economic, information, and other spheres of a state's daily activities. According to the Gerasimov Doctrine, we can find a targeted method of Hybrid War in nonmilitary measures, including economic sanctions, economic blockades, and pressure to transition from an economic route to a military route.

---

[21] Gerasimov, V. (2013, February 26). "The Value of Science Is in the Foresight: New Challenges Demand Rethinking the Forms and Methods of Carrying out Combat Operations", *Voyenno-Promyshlennyy Kurier* online, http://vpk-news.ru/articles/14632.

[22] Gerasimov, V. (2017). Contemporary warfare and current issues for the defense of the country. *Military Review*, 97(6), 22.

Frank Hoffman is an American officer and expert on this theory. In his book *Conflict in the 21st Century: The Rise of Hybrid Wars*[23] (2007), Hybrid Wars incorporate a range of different modes of warfare including conventional capabilities, irregular tactics and formations, terrorist acts including indiscriminate violence and coercion, and criminal disorder. At the strategic level, many wars have both regular and irregular components. However, in most conflicts, these components appear in different theaters or in significantly different formation. In Hybrid Wars, these forces become blurred into the same force in the same battle space. These definitions and methods of persuasion have become the necessary conditions for placing the trade war at the level of strategic disputes.

When we describe the process by which the United States began to identify China as a strategic competitor, we also note that the entire political, military, economic, governmental, administrative, and intelligence structures began to cooperate for the same purpose. The U.S. military and security mechanisms are still the most powerful in the world, with structures on all continents and regular battalions and military bases in several countries. According to the National Defense Strategy (NDS), "the central challenge to U.S. prosperity and security is the reemergence of long-term, strategic competition by revisionist powers," specifically China and Russia. It is becoming increasingly obvious that China and Russia want to shape a world consistent with their authoritarian model and gain veto power over the economic, diplomatic, and security decisions of other countries. To cope with the growing strength of hostile countries, the National Security Strategy (NSS) suggests returning to Cold War-style strategic competition: "An America that successfully competes is the best way to prevent conflict. Just as American weakness invites challenge, American strength and confidence deters war and promotes peace."[24]

For Brian D. Blankenship and Benjamin Denison,[25] a "return to Cold War style strategic competition is a mistaken view." Conflict during the

[23] Hoffman, F. G. (2007). *Conflict in the 21st century: The rise of hybrid wars* (p. 51). Arlington: Potomac Institute for Policy Studies.

[24] 2018 National Defense Strategy (NDS). US Government.

[25] Blankenship, B. D., & Denison, B. (2019). Is America Prepared for Great-power Competition?. *Survival*, 61(5), 43–64.

Cold War exhibited a different pattern than the current situation and the responses that the United States can make to its opponents. The authors state that the strategic errors of wars have invalidated efforts to reduce the U.S. deficit. For "while tax cuts during a period of unipolarity" and American hegemony might make sense in the absence of any U.S. military operations, the supposed peace dividend stemming from a reduced need for military readiness after the Cold War ended did not go to domestic priorities. Nor did it go to keeping the deficit in check. Instead, since the launch of the war in Afghanistan in 2001, the United States has spent more than $6 trillion expanding its military footprint in the Middle East, Africa, and elsewhere as part of the "global war on terror"—spending that happened even as taxes were being cut and that now accounts for more than 25% of the national debt. The authors still criticize engagement in tariff wars with trade partners that have weakened domestic manufacturing and harmed the domestic economy.

The NDS (2018) document mentions China as a strategic competitor using predatory economics to intimidate its neighbors while militarizing features in the South China Sea (SCS) and leveraging military modernization, influence operations, and predatory economics to coerce neighboring countries to reorder the Indo-Pacific region to their advantage. As China continues its economic and military ascendance and maintains power through a long-term strategy for the entire nation, it will continue to pursue a military modernization plan and seek hegemony in the India-Pacific region in the near-term to replace the United States in global preeminence in the future. The most far-reaching goal of this defense strategy is to establish the military relations between our two countries on a path of transparency and non-aggression. The American intelligence approach to a "path of transparency and non-aggression" with China remains unclear. This pattern does not exist in American foreign policy under the Trump administration, much less in military intelligence agencies; that is, there is no contained measure of soft power.

Although the United States often takes unilateral diplomatic actions and attitudes involving the international, political, and military economy, NATO is still a powerful source of persuasion with regard to military strategic objectives. The frequent controversies and disagreements between Trump and NATO allies (mainly France and Canada) have prompted questions about the lack of greater financial participation by these countries. These disputes and disagreements have shown that although the United Stated is the country most involved in conflicts and wars, it still needs to take coordinated actions with NATO allies. The Trump administration has been severely criticized by military strategy experts both in the United States and overseas.

For François Heisbourg[26] (2020), Trump's election represented a radical change in American foreign policy and that of its allies. Among the severe criticisms put forward by the author, he characterizes Trump as an impulsive and vainglorious personality with an unorganized and nondetailed work style and retaliatory autocratic approach to the management of human resources. Trump believes he is a "very stable genius" and knows he is the boss, demonstrating a decision-making approach that combines streetwise cunning with recklessness and extreme short-termism, not to mention an emotional and childlike disregard for limits of any sort, including constitutional constraints or alliance commitments.

In addition to the difficulties and instabilities ("Trump has largely culled from his administration, to eliminate the possibility of an early-morning Twitter message serving notice that the United States is pulling its troops out of Europe or leaving NATO") that represents the Trump mandate, Heisbourg (2020) states that the priority in the current situation should be the creation of a NATO 4.0, a strategic change intended to contain the rise of China, the real danger to the "free world."

The author reports that

> the emergence and establishment of China as America's peer competitor, which will obtain over an unknowable but possibly decades-long period of time. This is leading the US to move its strategic focus from the European theater to Asia. Given the technological and commercial aspects of China's rise as well as its ideological, strategic and military dimensions, it will affect a broader range of issues than the Cold War rivalry with the Soviet Union did, which calls for innovative approaches in terms of statecraft.

He also signals that "the rise of China will also affect US and European interests in different, and sometimes even opposing, ways. These new

---

[26] Heisbourg, F. (2020). NATO 4.0: The Atlantic Alliance and the Rise of China. *Survival*, 62(2), 83–102.

realities call into question the future of NATO. Certainly, they will have a mutually reinforcing disruptive effect on the Alliance."

Heisbourg (2020), in his binary conception, still indicates concern for the European allies in NATO, who will have to choose to side with the United States or against the United States in the dispute with China, much as they did during the Cold War. The dispute between the United States and China concerning acquisition of 5G networks is the first major test of this proposition; handling the precedent-setting 5G confrontation is a first-order political issue. This view intersects with the NDS document (2018) that contends that Russia and China should be priorities for NATO, but there is no clarity regarding the most effective methods. If both Republicans and Democrats are able to consolidate around a concept called "Chinese Consensus," in the interests of national security, there is a real perception that the disputes between the United States and China will reach a much higher level than the trade wars.

In the United States, a number of institutes, foundations, think tanks, and study centers have launched a political and ideological battle in American society and government to shape China's image as a strategic competitor. The conservative Heritage Foundation adopts this approach in the document "Preparing the U.S. National Security Strategy for 2020 and Beyond[27] (2019)." One of the authors is Ambassador Terry Miller, a prominent representative of American anti-China foreign policy. The document points out that the next strategic steps for the United States would be to curb the influence of Russia and China on different continents. The United States began to worry about the presence of Russia and China in the Arctic, Latin America, and Africa and about their involvement in conflicts in Eastern Europe and about China's influence in the European countries of NATO.

Numerous quotes, claims, and recommendations call for the United States to act to curb China's influence in the United States and the rest of the world. In economic matters under the topic "Right the trajectory of the U.S.—China economic Relationship," critics recommend that the administration reach an agreement with China to address some of the

[27] Carafano, J. J., Coffey, L., Gardiner, N., Lohman, W., Miller, A. T., & Spoehr, T. Preparing the US National Security Strategy for 2020 and Beyond.

major structural impediments for American businesses trading with and operating in China, concerns over intellectual property rights, and the restraints on market access that both limit international engagement in the Chinese economy and enable the worst of its business environment. They highlight the need to fully unwind the tariffs it has imposed and shift attention to World Trade Organization (WTO)-compliant ways to enforce the rights of its businesses, placing an especially high priority on moving forward with a U.S.–Japan free-trade agreement and an agreement with Taiwan. They also cite China's push for fifth-generation (5G) wireless networking or its BRI, which pose legitimate risks to U.S. interests and national defense, stating that the United States must be careful not to constrain economic freedom beyond what is required for security. It is also suggested that the Committee on Foreign Investment in the United States (CFIUS) should have the power to block foreign companies in order to alleviate the challenge of China's investment in American start-ups, which might accept bad security measures in exchange for quick access to capital. The Heritage Foundation calls China's "corrosive" capitalism the main threat to global economic freedom. It has also launched a proposal aimed at delegitimizing the BRI in a global campaign to achieve the goals of the initiative and the Chinese government.

As mentioned by other experts and official documents from the U.S. government, the main concern is competition for the latest technology, and again, Huawei appears as a great villain that threatens U.S. national security. In this regard, "Prepare to operate in a global environment characterized by networks that are developed and run by hostile foreign actors—especially China" describes these "zero trust networks" as well as next-generation wireless networks and other telecommunications infrastructures, where Huawei could have as much as 50% of the global 5G market and is suspected of acting on behalf of Beijing's military and intelligence agencies. Experts suggest that is prudent for U.S. national security leaders to prepare for a digital domain that is crowded with, and sometimes controlled by, America's chief global challengers.

Implementing the Grand Strategy

For the historically long-standing U.S. think tank the Council on Foreign Relations, the strategic competition between the United States and China in the twenty-first century is clear. For Robert D. Blackwill, in the report "Implementing Grand Strategy Toward China,"[28] the Chinese grand strategy targets the following goals: (1) replace the United States as the primary power in Asia; (2) weaken and ultimately dissolve the American alliance system in Asia; (3) undermine Asian nations' confidence in U.S. credibility, reliability, and staying power; (4) use its economic power to pull Asian nations closer to PRC geopolitical policy preferences; (5) increase its military capability to strengthen deterrence against U.S. military intervention in the region and cast doubt on the U.S. economic, political, and societal model; (6) ensure that U.S. democratic values do not diminish the Chinese Communist Party's hold on domestic power; and (7) avoid a major confrontation with the United States in the next decade.

Given this scenario of expansion in China, the author points out the following central objectives of the U.S. grand strategy in the twenty-first century: (1) revitalize the U.S. economy to nurture those disruptive innovations that bestow on the U.S. asymmetric economic advantages over others and training a next-generation work force; (2) create new preferential trading arrangements among U.S. allies and partners to increase their mutual gains through instruments that consciously exclude China; (3) reestablish a technology-control regime that involves U.S. allies to prevent China from acquiring military and strategic assets that enable it to inflict "high-leverage strategic harm" on the United States and its partners; (4) build up the power capacities of U.S. allies and partners on China's periphery; (5) improve the means of U.S. military forces to effectively and promptly project power along the Asian rimlands and along vital sea lanes despite any Chinese opposition; and (6) promote American political, economic, and societal values in the international system.

[28] Blackwill, R. D. (2020). *Implementing Grand Strategy Toward China*: Twenty-Two U.S. Policy Prescriptions. Council on Foreign Relations. Council Special Report No. 85 January 2020.

In many documents, we identify that technology competition is at the core of disputes between the two countries. As mentioned by Wang and Zeng (2020), the NDS references the U.S. export ban against Huawei, a prominent example that America will mobilize multiple elements of national power—diplomacy, information, economics, and intelligence—to win the 5G technology race against China. The escalation of U.S.-China trade tensions from a tariff war to a technology war is fundamentally rooted in the strategic competition between the two countries. They have contributed to the growing competitive nature of U.S.-China economic relations; therefore, the trade friction has deep roots.

A whole government structure is preparing for a greater clash with China. In particular, the U.S. army recognized the People's Liberation Army (PLA) as its main rival. The "Annual Report to Congress: Military and Security Developments Involving the People's Republic of China 2019"[29] demonstrates U.S. concern about the military multicapabilities that China has developed. According to the report, China is experiencing a "period of strategic opportunity" during the first 20 years of the twenty-first century to facilitate domestic development and expand China's "comprehensive national power." Next, China seeks to implement security and military objectives characterized by economic and diplomatic measures: (1) implementation of long-term state-directed planning, such as "Made in China 2025" and other industrial development plans; (2) alignment of civil and defense technology development to achieve greater efficiency, innovation, and growth; (3) advancement of projects such as the One Belt One Road Initiative (OBOR), which probably drive military overseas based on a perceived need to provide security for OBOR projects; and (4) influential operations against media, cultural, business, academic, and policy communities in the United States, other countries, and international institutions to achieve outcomes favorable to China's security and military strategy objectives.

According to the U.S. army, China and Japan have conflicting, overlapping claims to both the continental shelves and the exclusive economic zones (EEZs) in the East China Sea (ECS). There are natural gas and oil

---

[29] US Secretary of Defense. (2019, May 2). Annual Report to Congress: Military and Security Developments Involving the People's Republic of China 2019. https://media.defense.gov/2019/May/02/2002127082/-1/-1/1/2019_CHINA_MILITARY_POWER_REPORT.pdf

in this area, although the hydrocarbon reserves are difficult to estimate. The South China Sea in particular plays an important role in security considerations across East Asia. Northeast Asia relies heavily on oil and commercial flows through South China Sea route, including more than 80% of the crude oil flowing to Japan, South Korea, and Taiwan. China claims sovereignty over the Spratly and Paracel Island groups and other land features within its self-proclaimed "nine-dash line." Brunei, the Philippines, Malaysia, and Vietnam have disputed all or parts of this claim. Taiwan, which occupies Itu Aba Island in the Spratly Islands, makes the same territorial assertions as China (Table 3.1).[30]

Table 3.1 Territorial disputes between China and its neighbors

Countries involved	Geographical advantage	Territorial disputes
The South China Sea		
China, Brunei, the Philippines, Malaysia, and Vietnam	A major shipping lane for the flow of oil and commerce in Northeast Asia	China claims that it has "indisputable sovereignty over the islands in the South China Sea and the adjacent waters, and enjoys sovereign rights and jurisdiction over the relevant waters as well as the seabed and subsoil thereof," while Brunei, the Philippines, Malaysia, and Vietnam disagree with China's nine-dash claim
The East China Sea		
China and Japan	A strategic spot containing rich offshore oil and gas deposits	China and Japan have overlapping claims to both the continental shelves and the exclusive economic zones (EEZs) and compete for natural resources in the East China Sea
Sino-Indian border		
China, India, Pakistan, and Bhutan	A strategic area connecting southern Tibet of China and the core plain area of India	Both China and India claim sovereignty over their shared border over Arunachal Pradesh, and tensions remain in the area

[30] Congressional Research Service. (2020, April 24). U.S.-China Strategic Competition in South and East China Seas: Background and Issues for Congress. https://crsreports.congress.gov 24 April/2020.

This document describes how China's bases in the South China Sea (SCS) could help China as follows: (1) controlling fishing operations and oil and gas exploration activities; (2) coercing, intimidating, or exerting political pressure on other countries; (3) declaring and implementing the Air Defense Identification Zone (ADIZ); (4) announcing and implementing a maritime exclusion zone in the waters around Taiwan; (5) promoting the further projection of China's military presence and political influence into the Western Pacific; and (6) helping achieve a broader goal of becoming a regional hegemon in its part of Eurasia.

The text qualifies China as "Major World Power," and the U.S. army needs to compete strategically with China in the SCS and ECS. The U.S. goals must include the following: (1) fulfilling U.S. security commitments in the Western Pacific, including treaty commitments to Japan and the Philippines; (2) maintaining and enhancing the U.S.-led security architecture in the Western Pacific, including U.S. security relationships with treaty allies and partner states; (3) maintaining a regional balance of power favorable to the United States and its allies and partners; (4) defending the principle of peaceful resolution of disputes, under which disputes between countries should be resolved peacefully, without coercion, intimidation, threats, or the use of force and in a manner consistent with international law, and resisting the emergence of an alternative "might-makes-right" approach to international affairs; (5) defending the principle of freedom of the seas, meaning the rights, freedoms, and uses of the sea and airspace guaranteed to all nations in international law, including the interpretation held by the United States and many other countries preventing China from becoming a regional hegemon in East Asia, and potentially as part of that, preventing China from controlling or dominating the ECS or SCS; and (6) pursuing these goals as part of a larger U.S. strategy for competing strategically and managing relations with China.

Another report, "Indo-Pacific Strategies of U.S. Allies and Partners: Issues for Congress,"[31] shows the contradictions in the Trump administration's posture in Asia based on the Department of Defense's report "Indo-Pacific Strategy Report: Preparedness, Partnerships, and Promoting

[31] Dolven, B., & Vaughn, B. (2020, January 30). Indo-Pacific Strategies of U.S. Allies and Partners: Issues for Congress. https://www.everycrsreport.com/files/20200130_R46217_770a61c4856a9a5aed99d6699f3423b6240ff1c3.pdf

a Networked Region"[32] of June 2019. It focuses mainly on the period after the United States withdrew from the proposed Trans-Pacific Partnership (TPP) trade agreement and canceled joint exercises with South Korea. In addition, President Trump has publicly questioned the value of many of the United States' alliance relationships, especially those with Japan and South Korea. The purpose of these documents is to outline strategic actions guiding the U.S. military operation in the region. In this case, the main U.S. instruments are the United States Southern Command[33] (USSOUTHCOM) and U.S. Indo-Pacific Command[34] (USINDOPACOM). We can identify that structuring within the military apparatus has already become a modus operandi.

For a national actor, the probability of an overwhelming victory over a superpower such as the United States in any military action is almost zero. No country in the world today is trying to fully challenge the military superiority of the United States, and China is no exception. Some countries are trying to weaken the ability of the United States to exercise a unilateral dominant position in a particular region. However, military means may not be the most appropriate way to solve today's security challenges. Although U.S. investment in the military and security fields has been increasing in the past decades, the cruel reality shows that military intervention has brought fewer marginal benefits to the United States over time. Accordingly, we understand that in today's competitive international community, the effectiveness of military means is greatly reduced, and state actors turn to other alternative military means to promote strategic and security objectives. In the environment of globalization and deepening interdependence, people are looking forward to geoeconomic means. The premise and methods of the effectiveness of contemporary geoeconomy are inseparable from traditional military and

[32] Department of Defense. (2019, June 1). *Indo-Pacific Strategy Report: Preparedness, Partnerships, and Promoting a Networked Region.*

[33] Posture Statement of Admiral Craig S. Faller Commander, United States Southern Command before the 116th Congress Senate Armed Services Committee, Feb. 7, 2019

[34] Posture Statement of Admiral Philip S. Davidson, U.S. Navy Commander, U.S. Indo Pacific Command before the Senate Armed Services Committee on U.S. Indo Pacific Command Posture, Feb. 12, 2019.

foreign policies. More radical economic sanctions may work, but they will not work when they are used only as a geoeconomic tool and have nothing to do with military and foreign policies.

Logically, the main reasons for China's argument are military power and China's influence in the region. For the commander of USINDOPACOM, who has 375,000 military personnel, there are many reasons to deploy a military presence in the region. He reports that for economic reasons, the United States conducted more than $1.8 trillion in two-way goods trade with Indo-Pacific nations in 2017 and more than $1.3 trillion by the third quarter of 2018. In 2017, U.S. foreign direct investment in the region reached $940 billion—more than doubling since 2007. The Indo-Pacific is home to half of the 20 fastest-growing economies. The Indo-Pacific currently contains over one-third of global GDP and 60% of global GDP growth. By 2030, 65% of the world's middle class will reside in the Indo-Pacific, representing an unrivaled amount of purchasing power. China thus represents the greatest long-term strategic threat to a free and open Indo-Pacific and to the United States, as it seeks to establish a new international order with "Chinese characteristics" led by China. According to the report, Beijing offers easy money in the short term, but these funds come with strings attached: unsustainable debt, decreased transparency, restrictions on market economies, and the potential loss of control of natural resources. For example, this is very similar to the consistent practice of the United States in Latin America.

For the U.S. army, the modernization of the People's Liberation Army (PLA) is the major threat to the U.S. interests, and it is rapidly increasing its ability to project power and influence beyond the First Island Chain. China continues to pursue the next-generation technologies and advanced weapons systems, including hypersonic glide vehicles, directed energy weapons, electromagnetic railguns, counterspace weapons, and unmanned and artificial intelligence-equipped weapons. China has also made significant technological, game-changing developments in its ability to defeat, or drastically reduce, the effectiveness of U.S. sensors and defensive weapons, and tested hypersonic missiles, hypersonic aircraft, and nuclear forces with the third-generation Type 096 nuclear-powered ballistic missile submarine (SSBN).

To contain China, it will be necessary to support countries that stand up to Beijing's coercive economic policies whenever possible and help those countries offset any economic blowback from Beijing through a whole-government undertaking in partnership with the private sector and civil society. In the territorial environment of the American continent, the United States should repeat China's political route. Under the responsibility of USSOUTHCOM (2019), command responsible for the continent where the United States has full political, economic, cultural and territorial hegemony, the United States is also disturbed by the possibility of China becoming a strategic presence on the continent.

China has accelerated expansion of its Belt and Road Initiative and supported the regimes in Venezuela, Cuba, and Nicaragua, which are counter to democracy and U.S. interests. The report provides poor data on the presence of China on the American continent, especially in Latin America. In summary, it is said that China uses the same predatory, non-transparent foreign lending practices it has implemented around the world to exert political and economic leverage in certain countries. Moreover, in the future, China could use its control over deep water ports in the western hemisphere to enhance its global operation. What is particularly concerning is that China is trying to control key infrastructure associated with the Panama Canal. The advancement of Chinese firms such as Huawei and ZTE in the region places intellectual property, private data, and government secrets at risk. To USSOUTHCOM, if the governments in Latin America and the Caribbean continue to gravitate toward using Chinese information systems, the ability and willingness to share information over compromised networks is likely to suffer.

The historic U.S. imperialist vision in Latin America applies in a new format when China is established as a strategic competitor. China represents the largest economic partner in Latin America, in exports and imports of goods, in foreign direct investments, and in partnerships with governments and companies, which extend far beyond Venezuela, Nicaragua, and Cuba. Countries such as Brazil, Argentina, Mexico, and Chile represent the largest recipients of Chinese investments, and China is among their main markets. The history of American insertion and meddling in the region has diminished in terms of economic role, but the United States still maintains ties with local elites, as they remain submissive. It remains for us to understand whether the conservative rise in Latin America, mirrored by Trump, will affect relations with China.

Another chapter that has opened in the trade war is how much developing countries can take advantage of trade opportunities with the aim of reducing dependence on the American market. For China, the global crisis and economic recession have brought about a new international environment in which developed countries are no longer benefiting to their export-driven growth strategies. As Japan recognized 30 years ago, export-oriented growth can be effective only if other countries are willing and able to adapt to this growth. In the late 1970s, just as in China before the crisis, developed countries tolerated Japan as a successful mercantilist country operating in a free world economy. However, once the world economy slowed down, the endurance of the United States and other countries was exhausted.[35] The United States was facing unemployment and huge foreign defense expenditures, whereas Japan had become the second-largest economy in the world. This led the United States to ignore its own problems and instead blame Japan's privileged position and the unfairness resulting from its rise. In response, the United States pressured Japan to restrict its exports, open up its own market, and increase domestic consumption. By 2010, China had replaced Japan as the world's most successful exporter and the second-largest economy, and the United States is now facing difficulties similar to those it faced during Japan's economic success. As a result of the global economic recession, the United States is facing a situation of slowing economic growth and high unemployment rate. Members of parliament are facing political pressure, and voters are demanding effective measures. At the same time, China insists on maintaining a relatively low RMB exchange rate, is unwilling to provide intellectual property protection, and is pursuing an independent innovation policy. This is seen as an unfair deal.[36] In addition, China faces greater uncertainty in its preferred export economic strategy and less ability to adapt to the political environment of the United States. China

[35] Dean, J. M., Lovely, M. E., & Mora, J. (2017). Decomposing China-Japan-US trade: Vertical specialization, ownership, and organizational form. *International Economic Integration and Domestic Performance* (pp. 119–132).

[36] Liu, T., & Woo, W. T. (2018). Understanding the US-China trade war. *China Economic Journal*, 11(3), 319–340.

is even more worried that the U.S. economy and its consumers cannot continue to serve as the last line of defense for the global market. Therefore, even if the United States reduces its political pressure on China, the financial crisis will force the U.S. economy to make fundamental adjustments and slow down the pace of consumption over time, which will directly affect the demand for Chinese imports.[37] Nevertheless, China will continue to become a major exporter in the world. Weak demand in the United States and Europe has led to China's increasing dependence on trade with developing countries. By 2012, China had become the largest trading partner of South Korea, India, and South Africa, and the second-largest partner of Indonesia, Mexico, and Brazil.[38]

This set of official documents led to the establishment of a very large lobbying group between the U.S. military and the Congress and Senate. The result was the creation of the Indo-Pacific Deterrence Initiative, or PDI. The initiative presented by U.S. Indo-Pacific Command head Adm. Phil Davidson and supported by the chairman of the House Armed Services Committee, Rep. Adam Smith, and the Pentagon proposes an investment[39] of $20 billion in a new Pacific-focused pot of money to deter Chinese military action in the region in the fiscal year 2021. The PDI was created as the Pacific version of the European Defense Initiative (EDI), a similar program that was undertaken after the Russian seizure of Crimea in 2014. The purpose of the bill[40] is to "enhance the United States deterrence and defense posture in the Indo-Pacific region, assuring allies and partners, and increasing capability and readiness to deter and defend against any aggression by an adversary." The funds target the following objectives: (1) presence and joint force lethality, (2) prepositioning and logistics, (3) infrastructure, (4) strengthening allies and partners in the Indo-Pacific region, (5) exercises and training, and (5) procurements.

[37] Lau, L. J., & Tang, J. (2018). The impact of US imports from China on US consumer prices and expenditures. *IGEF Working Paper* No.66.

[38] Morrison, W. M. (2018). *China's Economic Rise: History, Trends, Challenges, and Implications for the United States* (pp. 20–22). Washington, DC: Congressional Research Service.

[39] Mehta, A. (2020, April 2). Inside US Indo-Pacific Command's $20 billion wish list to deter China—and why Congress may approve it. Defense News. https://www.defensenews.com/global/asia-pacific/2020/04/02/inside-us-indo-pacific-commands-20-billion-wish-list-to-deter-china-and-why-congress-may-approve-it/.

[40] US House of Representants. H.R. 6613.

According to *The Diplomat*,[41] one option is utilizing the PDI to create a "deterrence by punishment" framework that not only focuses on strike missions on PLA military targets but also further threatens Chinese commercial shipping, imposes harsh economic sanctions, and undertakes other measures that aim to defeat the PLA's immediate military objectives and "punish" Chinese political and economic leadership.

The relationship between the United States and China, the world's largest and second-largest economies, respectively, affects the development of the world. Judging from the history of Sino-U.S. economic and trade cooperation, economic and trade cooperation has promoted the growth of the economies of the two countries and the world. The United States used the vast merchandise trade deficit as an excuse to stir up bilateral trade frictions between China and the United States. On this basis, the United States introduced a series of measures to suppress China in the fields of trade and investment. China responded immediately, and the trade frictions between China and the United States escalated into a trade war. However, is the trade deficit in goods between the United States and China truly the real reason for the Sino-U.S. trade war? Studies have shown that the large disparity in commodity trades is not the root of the Sino-U.S. trade war. The United States launched a trade war on the grounds that the trade deficit with China was huge, but the fundamental reason is that the United States is on guard against China's rapid rise and is carrying out strategic suppression of China's crucial high-tech industries. The formation of the Sino-U.S. trade deficit has a long history and is determined by a relatively fixed industrial structure, international division of labor, and comparative advantages. This cannot be resolved through tariff and non-tariff barriers. Trade friction will not help to reduce the trade deficit; it will only reduce the interests of China and the United States and the well-being of the world.

Although China agrees that increasing imports to the United States is a necessary adjustment of China's foreign trade policy in the new stage, the trade imbalance between China and the United States is structural, complex, long term and difficult to resolve in the short term. The

[41] Rimland, B., & Buchan, P. (2020, May 2). Getting the Pacific Deterrence Initiative Right. The Diplomat.

Sino-U.S. trade war is not only a conflict of economic interests between the two countries but also a confrontation between the Beijing model and the Washington model. At present, the world economy is just recovering from the financial crisis. The United States needs to cooperate with China to jointly start the engine of international trade and promote global economic growth. Only by supporting the main channels of WTO multilateral trade, pushing forward the reform and improvement of the WTO, opposing trade protectionism, and returning to WTO multilateral trade can China and the United States achieve win-win cooperation.

4

The G-2 (the United States-China)

The Impact on International Relations

Since opening its economy in the late 1970s, China's foreign policy has attempted to avoid imposing a hegemonic influence over other countries for many years and has reaffirmed the role of the United States as a world economic power, while China itself is playing an increasingly important role in resisting the unilateralism of the United States. In the 1970s, the idea spread that the trilateral liberal economies of the U.S. dollar, the Japanese yen, and the European common market, which would become the Eurozone, would consolidate and China was not yet prepared to dispute these large blocs. Yet, already in the first decades of the twenty-first century, that reality has changed, as has Chinese foreign policy, which is facing great challenges.

While Chinese diplomacy had aimed at maintaining lines of understanding with the United States based on mutual strategic trust, economic and trade-based cooperation, and person-to-person and cultural exchanges relations have soured with the rise of Trump. Since Trump was elected as president of the United States in 2016, he has considerably changed and subverted the tradition of American foreign policy, which

L. Sheng, D. Felix do Nascimento, *Love and Trade War*,
https://doi.org/10.1007/978-981-33-4897-4_4

has greatly impacted the United States and the international community. Yin[1] (2017) indicated that Trump's narcissistic, conceited, aggressive, unruly, and fickle character has made predicting the direction of American foreign policy difficult for the international community. Since Trump took office more than three years ago, he has made many unexpected adjustments to the domestic and international policies of the United States. Sino-U.S. relations will surely enter a new stage of strategic competition as competition between the large countries has become the primary strategic principle of the Trump administration. Sino-U.S. economic and trade relations, especially in high-tech commercial exchanges, bear the brunt of this strategy. Although China and the United States have signed the text of the first-stage agreement to resolve the trade war between the two countries, as Walters[2] (2019) and other scholars believe, the improvement in Sino-U.S. economic and trade negotiations may not resolve all the complaints of the United States against China, and friction between the two sides in the fields of high technology and social culture is inevitable.

Instead of maintaining "strategic mutual trust," the opposite occurred when China was portrayed as a strategic adversary. What should have been "economic and trade-based cooperation" eventually triggered a trade war on the part of the United States, where economic shocks and uncertainties in the markets continue because of the fragility of the Phase One Agreement and instabilities within American trade policy. It is impossible to believe that the trade dispute between the two countries will soon end with a treaty or agreement. What was dreamed of as closer ties with "person-to-person and cultural exchanges" has resulted in xenophobia, racism against Asians, the restriction of communication channels, and the expulsion of Chinese students and researchers in the United States. This was not what Beijing expected.

On the other hand, it should be noted that after 40 years of Sino--U.S. relations, the two countries have complementary interests in many fields. At the same time, many difficulties faced by the international

[1]Yin, J. (2017). An Analysis of Trump's Political Personality and Policy Preference. *Contemporary International Relations*. (2), 15–22.

[2]Walters, R. (2019). Is a U.S.-China Trade Deal Possible? *National Interest*, Sept. 29.

community cannot be separated from Sino-U.S. cooperation. Although there are increasingly few disagreements about recognizing China as America's largest potential competitor, the United States has not yet reached a decision on how to deal with it. Emphasizing the priority of the United States and adopting a comprehensively hostile strategy toward China is not the only choice, which is also the reason why the Trump administration suffered domestic criticism after launching the trade war with China.

The dynamics of the conflicts within the trade war reaffirmed a trend that many authors have long predicted: the consolidation of a G-2 (the United States and China) in the international panorama. The bipolar Cold War system between the capitalist groups and the communist groups had completely different characteristics, and this new global power structure has many more factors than what a simple dualistic logic can explain. The international insertion of Asian economies, as in the past with Japan or South Korea, has always been viewed skeptically by the Western hegemonic bloc. It could not have been different for the insertion of China, though the central economies, the United States and the European Union (EU), face an opponent much better prepared than the others. A G-2 is consolidating, arising from multiple actions, conflicts, agreements, disputes, and alliances, and an engagement with the main themes and issues in international relations. The global power and influence of the G-2 countries can be seen in their ability to influence the political behavior of other states in areas of international economics, global security, the environment, multilateral international organizations, energy, nuclear weapons, cyberspace, borders, and so on. Furthermore, as portrayed by Zeng and Breslin[3] (2016), the existence of a G-2 depends much more on how Chinese diplomacy thinks about itself and its insertion into the role of a great power than on outside approval: "This is a G-2 relationship defined by and for China on Chinese terms, rather than one established by outsiders primarily to serve the interests of others."

---

[3] Zeng, J. & Breslin, S. (2016). China's 'new type of Great Power relations': a G2 with Chinese characteristics?. *International Affairs*, 92(4), 773–794.

Trade Frictions of the G-2: The Trump Doctrine and Wealth Inequality

The economic policy options adopted by successive American administrations were consistent with the objectives of the commercial and financial sectors and investment funds, which led to increasing economic inequality, as well as changes in incomes and wealth distribution in the United States.

Chu[4] (2018) indicates that although the United States is a country ruled by law and has a perfect political system, its constitution and political system have given the president great decision-making power so that American diplomacy has always reflected the strong and obvious personal characteristics of the president. Especially when a leader with a personality like Trump takes office, the foreign policy of the United States is bound to undergo great changes, and a "doctrine" commensurate with Trump's personality will inevitably appear.

In fact, Jeffrey Goldberg[5] (2018), who once proposed the conception of the "Obama Doctrine," put forward the "Trump Doctrine" as early as June 2018. Goldberger believes that "no enemies, no friends" constitutes the basic overtones of the "Trump Doctrine." The Trump administration's first report of the *National Security Strategy*[6] in 2017 clearly stated that this is a priority strategy for the national security of the United States. Trump himself expressed similar views on many occasions. For example, in his speech at the 72nd UN General Assembly, Trump bluntly said that as the president of the United States of America, he would always put American interests in first place and vigorously promoted his vision of "America First." Michael Anton[7] (2019), a former U.S. State Department official, believes that if there is a "Trump Doctrine," it should be "America First." If Trump's actions since he took office are driven by a complete set

---

[4] Chu, S. & Zhou, L. (2018). Diplomatic Characteristics of Trump Administration and Its Influence. *Contemporary International Relations*, 8, 23.

[5] Goldberg, J. (2018). A Senior White House Official Defines the Trump Doctrine: We're America, Bitch. *The Atlantic*, June 11.

[6] The White House (2017), National Security Strategy, Washington, p. 3.

[7] Anton, M. (2019). The Trump Doctrine, *Foreign Policy*, April 20.

of ideas, "America First" is the core in this set of ideas, and it is also the key principle of Trump's foreign policy, which constitutes the central content of the emerging "Trump Doctrine."

Han[8] (2020) believes that the content of the "Trump Doctrine" includes great power competition, "America First," and unilateralism and compulsion, in which great power competition is the basic strategic goal, "America First" is the specific policy guideline, and unilateralism and compulsion are the actual behavior styles displayed under the policy guidelines of the "Trump Doctrine." The Trump administration's "America First" principle also embodies the concepts of "rust belt first" and "white people first." As is well known, the formulation and general style of a country's foreign policy are influenced not only by the external environment, such as the international pattern of authority, but also by the national- and individual-level variables, such as domestic politics and the leaders themselves. There is no doubt that the formation of the "Trump Doctrine" is also the result of various factors. The change in international standards and the consensus between the Republican Party and the Democratic Party on foreign policy helped to construct a national consensus seeing China as the principal competitor. The India-Pacific strategy, as a policy response to the basic strategic standard of great power competition, has led America to invest more resources than in the past and win over more countries' support to counter China's quick rise. The primary reason for promoting the introduction of this strategy is the remarkable change in the relative strengths of the emerging powers in relation to the United States.

If we look in general terms at the Trump Plan, which we mentioned in previous chapters, it contains a series of concrete measures to deregulate domestic markets, aimed at increasing employment, rather than a broader national plan such as the China 2025 Plan. The rise of Trump reflects this change in the social base and in the conception that part of the American population has about the role of the State and the role of free, private initiative in the context of international competition so encouraged by the American liberal model that its effects have reached sectors of its

[8] Han, Z. & Huang, Z. (2020). The Trump Doctrine: Connotation, Origin and Evaluation. *International Forum*, 4, 3–18.

domestic economy. Although the United States made large expenditures on wars (Afghanistan, Iraq, and Syria) and investment banks (Bank of America, JP Morgan, Merrill Lynch, Citibank, and others), other sectors lagged behind, especially those sectors that employed more unskilled labor. The civil and industrial construction sectors suffered a sharp decline after the 2008 financial crisis.

The changes that have taken place in the United States in recent years have attracted worldwide attention, at the same time that a series of chain reactions have occurred on a global scale. These changes come from profound historical and global realities and reflect the challenges facing the Western world in the era of globalization. To those who are familiar with American and world history of the early twentieth century, it seems that today, the United States is reexperiencing the tragedy of a century ago. After the ebullience brought on by rapid economic growth, the United States faces issues such as sharp social contradictions, the failure of elite governance, the spread of populism, the rise of trade protectionism, and disillusionment with the international order.

Han (2020) indicates that since the end of the Cold War, the power gap between China and the United States has undergone fundamental changes. China's economic and military investments have increased approximately ten-fold. If we look at the comprehensive national strength that is simply calculated as the average of economic and military strength, China's share of American strength has increased from 5% in 1993 to 50% when Trump took office in 2017, and the gap is still narrowing.

In addition to changes in the international standard of authority itself, the consensus in the United States has also been to strongly promote the formation of great power competition as the country's basic strategic goal and to promulgate the Indo-Pacific strategy. Lu[9] (2018) believes that the reason for this strategy is that there is no substantive difference between the two parties on whether the future of the twenty-first century belongs to the Asia-Pacific region or the Indo-Pacific region. In summary, the India-Pacific strategy is the product of structural contradictions in the changing international standard of authority, domestic factors in the

[9] Lu, H. & Sun, X. (2018). Structural Contradiction and Trump Doctrine: The Dual Motives of Trump Administration's Indo-Pacific Strategy. *Forum of World Economics & Politics*, 6, 1.

United States and Trump's personal interactions. In reality, America's new China policy, as the core of its Indo-Pacific strategy, reflects a common logic. At present, great changes are taking place in Sino-U.S. relations. Behind these changes are not only Trump's personality quirks but also trends in the evolution of America's policy toward China. At the same time, these changes are also influenced by the strong support of American business circles, social elites, ordinary people, and members of Congress for the Trump administration's China policy. Changes in public opinion, as well as Trump's own personality characteristics, business background, and other individual-level factors, are the bases for specific priority principles of the United States and the main reasons for its use of unilateralism and compulsion.

Regarding domestic factors in the United States, the Trump administration's pursuit of "America First" and unilateralism is influenced not only by electoral considerations but also by the change in mainstream opinion in the United States. Qian[10] (2017) believes that Trump's objective in promoting "America First" and unilateralism is obvious, that is, giving back to foundational voters of the Republican Party, especially middle-class and lower-class white people and the blue-collar workers in the Midwest. It can be seen that this is a tool of party politics in the United States and an important starting point for the Republican Party and Trump to seek an advantage over the Democratic Party and to win the presidential election. From the deeper perspective of mainstream opinion changes, the emergence of "America First" and unilateralism is due to a trend in thought in the United States that comprehensively questions globalization. The root cause is that the deterioration of the income distribution in the era of globalization has stimulated the populist views of those who have little or no benefit from globalization, making the liberal international view of generosity, tolerance, and collaboration no longer convincing.

From the above, it is the Trump administration's basic strategic goal that the United States return to the era of great power competition, and "America First" is a specific foreign policy guideline, in line with Trump's

[10] Qian, L. (2017). America under Trump: Characteristics and Prospects of Domestic and Foreign Policies. *Contemporary International Relations*, 12, 11.

personality, based on his strategic judgment. "America First" emphasizes that the primary and even the only goal of American foreign policy is to safeguard American interests. Instigating strategic competition among large countries, emphasizing only the priority of its own interests, and ignoring the interests and concerns of other countries are not the only strategic options. In this sense, "America First" has become a distinctive core concept of the "Trump Doctrine." "America First" is the specific policy of the Trump administration, while unilateralism and coercion are two behavioral characteristics of the Trump administration's foreign policy implementation under the guidance of this specific principle. In other words, unilateralism and coercion are not the guiding principles of American foreign policy but the concrete embodiment of the realization and practice of American priorities and principles.

Accordingly, after Trump took office, he began to completely deny and oppose globalization. The idea of globalism emphasized and pursued by the United States has now been replaced by the idea of "America First." Samuelson[11] (2017) believes that the United States in the Trump era has basically broken away from the narrative of globalization. Its policies have become conservative, and its strategy has turned to contraction. In fact, Trump's logic of "America First" contains the following interrelated basic concepts. First, "America First" is the gold standard for measuring whether all current and future policies of the United States are necessary, and there is no other standard. Second, regardless of how important the existing international agreements and rules are and whether they are recognized globally or not, once it has been determined that the United States has not benefited from its participation, it must withdraw. Third, American domestic policies should be abolished or reformulated based on whether they meet the criteria of "America First." Generally, it is the Trump administration's requirement for its core interests and values and the basic guide and standard for reshaping the framework of American economic policy to measure American domestic and foreign policies with the criterion of "America First" and to take whether something is beneficial to the United States as the logical starting point for most policy actions.

[11] Samuelson, R. (2020, January 1). The New World Order, 2017. *The Washington Post.*

Brzezinski[12] (2017), a famous American scholar in international relations, wrote an article in the *New York Times* to openly question Trump's idea of "America First."

> A vulnerable world needs an America characterized by clarity of thought and leadership that projects optimism and progress. 'Make America Great Again' and 'America First' are all very well as bumper stickers, but the foreign policy of the United States needs to be more than a campaign slogan … We would advise the president to give an address that offers a bold statement of his vision, including his determination to provide America's leadership in the effort to shape a more stable world.

It can be seen that Brzezinski, like many other scholars around the world, was puzzled by Trump's ruling idea of "America First."

In contrast to Brzezinski's circumlocution, many scholars and politicians have directly criticized Trump's idea of "America First." Ikenberry[13] (2017), a famous American scholar, believes that Trump's challenge to the free order is even more dangerous because it is arbitrarily defying the norms and values of freedom and democracy itself. John Kerry[14] (2019), the Secretary of State during Obama's administration, criticized Trump's "America first" mindset, saying that the incumbent president had taken self-destructive measures to make America the last one, which would damage the influence of the country and cause Americans to lose their jobs.

In the article "Trump's Foreign-Policy Revolution," Krauthammer[15] (2019) states that Trump's series of bold executive orders and provocative cabinet nominations are hints of American neo-isolationism. Trump did not realize that the slogan "America First," put forward by Charles Lindbergh, sent a new message of American isolationism to the international community. Trump even views diplomatic relations with a zero-sum perspective: his most inflammatory remark, "The wealth of our middle class has been ripped from their homes and then redistributed

[12] Brzezinski, Z. (2017, February 20). Why the World Needs a Trump Doctrine. *The New York Times*.

[13] Ikenberry, G. J. (2017). The plot against American foreign policy: Can the liberal order survive. *Foreign Affairs*. 96, 2.

[14] Kerry, J.F. (2019, November 5). Trump has formally pulled the U.S. out of the Paris agreement. This is a dark time for America. *The Washington Post*.

[15] Krauthammer, C. (2017, January 26). Trump's foreign policy revolution. *The Washington Post*.

across the entire world," defined his behavior as nationalistic. Krauthammer also pessimistically warned that the United States is becoming narrow-minded.

Bennett[16] (2017) emphasizes that "America First" can be traced back to antisemitism and isolationism before and during World War II. Although the Anti-Defamation League asked Trump to give up the slogan during the U.S. election, Trump insisted on it. Interestingly, when asked by a reporter from the *New York Times*, Trump denied that he was pursuing "America First" in an isolationist-oriented way. In addition, in the article "Save America First: What Is Responsible Nationalism," Bacevich[17] (2017) holds that the reflection of utopian liberal internationalism in American society and the public dissatisfaction caused by globalization are the logical backdrop for Trump's "America First" agenda. The "America First" policy is a manifestation of Trump's personal determination, which is random and impulsive, but Trump himself believes that everything is under his control. Giroux[18] (2017) believes Donald Trump is a first-class American nationalist. This conclusion can be drawn from his determination to resort to racism and anti-immigrant sentiments, to oppose free trade and to impose heavy taxes on imported goods.

While the vast majority of foreign scholars criticize Trump's political idea of "America First," there are a few scholars who affirm it. In the article "Why Americans Should Fight Donald Trump's Isolationism," Fishman[19] (2019) offered an opposing view, highly appreciating Trump's "America First" policy. The article mentions that Americans are tired of their current role in the world. After the Iraq War and the 2008 crisis, the rapid development of globalization and its accompanying complex problems have not been alleviated. Americans are worried about the dangers of ISIS, Russia's invasion of neighboring countries, the subversion of

---

[16] Bennett, B. (2017, January 20). 'America First,' a phrase with a loaded anti-Semitic and isolationist history. *The Angeles Times*.

[17] Bacevich, A. J. (2017). Saving America First: What Responsible Nationalism Looks Like. *Foreign Affairs.*, *96*, 57.

[18] Giroux, H. A. (2017). White nationalism, armed culture and state violence in the age of Donald Trump. *Philosophy & Social Criticism*, *43*(9), 887–910.

[19] Berengaut, A. & Fishman (2017, June 15). E. Why Americans Should Fight Donald Trump's Isolationism. *Time*.

American democracy, and the outbreak of war on the Korean Peninsula. He believes that Trump's refusal to save the world and his choice of "America First" would not upset most Americans.

What, then, do Americans think about the role of the U.S. government in promoting Trump's "America First" policy? Does this mean more interventions in foreign states or fewer interventions? Fewer taxes, more incentives and social investments? Why should China be responsible for the failure of the American economy? What is Trump's plan to solve the problem of stagnation in backward industries? Does this mean more liberalism or a certain type of national liberalism which will increase tariffs and impose barriers to survival? The answers, as well as the questions themselves, describe the reasons for the increasing inequality in the United States.

Out of all the difficult issues, economic inequality has become a core concern in American society, and nearly all the important phenomena in American politics today are related to it, such as political polarization, the populist movements, anti-free-trade sentiments, resistance to globalization, and the rejection of immigrants. The sudden rise of Trump and Sanders in the 2016 presidential election cannot be separated from the increasing economic inequality in the United States. Many scholars, such as Francis Fukuyama[20] (2016), even worry that the problems caused by inequality may lead to the decline of American democracy. Therefore, inequality reflects the complicated relationships among various stakeholders in American society and the special role of American political forces in dealing with these relationships, thus providing an extremely important window into the governance mechanisms of the United States.

Since the end of World War II, the United States has never faced challenges as large as it is facing today. Unlike the past, today's challenges basically arise from American society's difficulties in adjusting to the new globalized environment. That is, the ideological struggle that ran through the twentieth century has now given way to new social contradictions and changes in the governance of state relations. However, for the United States, its long-term prosperity and stability after the war and its superior

[20] Fukuyama, F. (2016). American Political Decay or Renewal: the Meaning of the 2016 Election. *Foreign Affairs*, *95*, 58.

position as the engine of globalization inevitably inhibited this society's ability to self-adjust and innovate, which led to increasing internal and external conflicts in the torrent of large global changes.

Among academics and scholars, there is some confusion in determining the American public's views on inequality and their desire to be involved in political choices. However, we can identify some studies and data that provide evidence on this topic. This will enable us to better understand Trump's questionable remarks on the trade war itself.

This disagreement among scholars is expressed in several works that try to ascribe a liberal ideological position to the behavior of the American public. For example, Graham Wright[21] (2018) believes that an increase in national concern regarding economic inequality does not lead to a subsequent increase in support for government intervention in the economy. Wright (2018) opposes the views of authors such as Page and Jacobs[22] (2009) and other scholars on the issues of inequality in the United States. Page and Jacobs (2009) argue that Americans were, by and large, tolerant of large-scale inequality or else profoundly ambivalent about what to do about it. However, we can see that after the financial crisis in 2008, Americans strongly supported concrete interventions taken by the government to promote greater equality in the American economy. While historically, Americans have had a "philosophically conservative" view of government, opposed to large government interventions, both authors realized that Americans' fear of inequality since 2008 has increased their desire for some form of government action.[23]

A. Rubin and D. Segal[24] (2015) follow the perspective of Piketty and Saez[25] (2006) and analyze the relation between growth and income inequality in the United States over the last six decades. Their analysis was

---

[21] Wright, G. (2018). The Political Implications of American Concerns About Economic Inequality. *Polit Behav*, 40, 321–343.

[22] Page, B. I., & Jacobs, L. R. (2009). *Class War: What Americans Really Think about Economic Inequality*. Chicago: University of Chicago Press.

[23] Sheng, L. (2011). Theorizing Free Capital Mobility: A Perspective on Developing Economies. *Review of International Studies* 37(5), 2519–2534.

[24] Rubin, A. & Segal, D. (2015). The Effects of Economic Growth on Income Inequality in the US. *Journal of Macroeconomics*, 45, 258–273.

[25] Piketty, T., & Saez, E. (2006). The evolution of top incomes: a historical and international perspective. *American economic review*, 96(2), 200–205.

based on the idea that wealth and labor income are affected by both current and expected future growth, yet different income groups react differently to these realities. Rubin and Segal (2015) showed that the growth process is multidimensional and that the concurrent growth rate is only one element that affects income distribution. They also showed that changes in expectations for future growth are just as important. They provided evidence that in the United States, during the postwar period (1953–2008), the growth process was accompanied by an increase in income inequality. In addition, they emphasized that "much of the increase in income inequality can be attributed to the increased importance of the stock market in the US economy together with the increased usage of pay-for-performance compensation, which makes labor income of top groups more closely align with future growth rates." The notorious inequality in the United States paints a picture of the social foundations and mode of economic operation in America. As much as a re-institution of the "New Deal" remains in the imagination of the American working middle classes, this is no longer an option that the political and financial elite will accept.

The economist M. Li[26] (2020) explains that beginning in 2006, the U.S. economy became heavily dependent on net private consumption, and the trade deficit reached 5.6% of GDP, which was mostly offset by net government expenditures (4.6% of GDP). Net private investment was 7.1%, net private consumption was 8.4%, and total domestic profit was 14.5% of GDP. Net private consumption accounted for 58% of U.S. domestic profit in 2006. The decline in the U.S. labor income share after the "Great Recession" (2008) was due to high unemployment in the post-recession years. By 2017, the U.S. labor income share had recovered to 58.6%.

Li (2020) concludes that

> long-term economic stagnation undermines the relative position of American capitalism in the capitalist world system. As the global economic center of gravity continues to shift away from the United States, it is a mat-

[26] Li, M. (2020). *Profit, Accumulation, and Crisis in Capitalism: Long-term Trends in the UK, US, Japan, and China, 1855–2018*. Routledge.

> ter of time before American capitalism loses its hegemonic status completely. In the modern American capitalist economy, only a small fraction of the capitalist profit is absorbed by productive investment. The rest is used for capitalist consumption and various forms of financial speculation. Such a development undermines the legitimacy of the capitalist economic system and may have already contributed to rising social tensions and political instabilities.

To reiterate this fact, we present some data on inequality in the United States. In 1990, the Gini coefficient measuring U.S. family income inequality was 0.4; between 2011 and 2018, the coefficient increased to 0.45. The 2008 crisis augmented the number of Americans with incomes at or below the poverty line from 39.83 million to 46.66 million in 2014, with a later decrease of 43.12 million (2015) to 38.15 million (2018). This is observed in the U.S. family poverty rate, which increased from 10.3% (2008) to 11.6% (2014) with a later decrease to 9% (2018). Another index that we can use to verify the country's inequality is the poverty rate among children: in 2010, 22% of American children were on the poverty line, decreasing to 16.2% by 2018. However, that still means 38.15 million children living at or below the poverty line. Rich states such as New York or California, or the District of Columbia have household inequality Gini coefficients above the national average: 0.51, 0.49, and 0.52, respectively.

According to a report[27] released by the Center on Budget and Policy Priorities in January 2020, the income growth rate of low-income and middle-income residents in the United States has dropped significantly since the 1970s, while the income of high-income residents has continued to grow steadily. In September 2019, the U.S. Census Bureau released the latest data from the American Community Survey. The data show that compared with 2017, income inequality in the United States has increased in 2018. Although the median household income of American residents reached a new high, the income gap widened to its highest level in the past 50 years, with the Gini coefficient rising from 0.397 in 1967 to 0.485 in 2018. This shows that in recent decades, the inequality in American income and wealth has become increasingly serious.

[27] Stone, C., Trisi, D., Sherman, A., & Debot, B. (2015). A guide to statistics on historical trends in income inequality. Center on Budget and Policy Priorities, 26.

Research by Lucas Chansell[28] (2018), codirector of the World Inequality Laboratory at the Paris School of Economics, shows that since the 1970s, rich countries, including the United States, have become richer, but their governments have become poorer. From 1970 to 2015, the total net wealth of the public and private sectors in the United States increased from 300% to 500% of GDP, but the net wealth of the public sector declined from over 50% to a negative value, which limited the government's ability to invest in public services. According to statistics from the Bureau of Economic Analysis in the U.S. Department of Commerce, in 2018, the U.S. federal government investment was approximately 1.4% of GDP, its lowest level since 1947. State and local government investments declined relatively little, but they also dropped from 3% of GDP in the late 1960s to less than 2% now. Investments in infrastructure and human resources are very important to economic prosperity, while the lack of public investment has a large impact on low-income groups, which leads to a vicious cycle of inequality.

According to a study by Edward Wolff[29] (2017), an economics professor at New York University, the richest 1% of Americans own 40% of American wealth. This calculation has been accepted by most economists, though the proportion found by some studies is slightly lower. Melissa Kearney[30] (2018), an economics professor at the University of Maryland in the United States, believes that no matter what the exact number is, there is plenty of evidence that the concentration of wealth in the United States is high and rising. This illustrates that the American economic system rewards highly educated and skilled workers, giving those at the highest level of society a winner-take-all reward while giving too little help to disadvantaged groups, including those who are facing long-term economic difficulties or living in despair.

Economic inequality may take various forms. If the distribution of income and wealth widens, the consequences are not necessarily

[28] Alvaredo, F., Chancel, L., Piketty, T., Saez, E., & Zucman, G. (Eds.). (2018). *World Inequality Report 2018*. Belknap Press.

[29] Wolff, E. N. (2017). *Household wealth trends in the United States, 1962 to 2016: has middle class wealth recovered?* (No. w24085). National Bureau of Economic Research.

[30] Abraham, K. G., & Kearney, M. S. (2018). *Explaining the decline in the US employment-to-population ratio: A review of the evidence* (No. w24333). National Bureau of Economic Research.

disastrous. With the continuous expansion of the aggregate economy, the income and wealth gap between different people will inevitably widen, but people with low income can still benefit from economic growth despite their lower income. This is the trickle-down effect that liberal economists asserted. Unfortunately, this is not exactly what economic inequality in the United States looks like. Although income and wealth are concentrated in the hands of very few people, most people not only lag far behind the income growth of the former, but some groups are actually being squeezed and marginalized gradually, with worrying consequences. This explains the disappearance of the middle class and the consequent polarization of the economy.

At a recent meeting of the Brookings Institution, Representative Jan Schakowsky[31] (2019) of Illinois said that the United States is one of the richest countries in the world and is experiencing its richest period in history, but its wealth is concentrated in the hands of a very small number of people who have not made enough contributions to society as a whole. Although the rich are richer than ever, the lives of other Americans are getting harder and harder. A lack of tax revenue leads to a lack of funds for key social projects and public services, such as Social Security, medical insurance, education, housing, infrastructure, and climate change mitigation projects. Schakowsky said that inequality not only distorts the American economy but also weakens the political power of non-wealthy people. During the 2012 general election, the richest 1% of Americans contributed 42% of the total donations. During the mid-term elections in 2014, just 32,000 wealthy donors provided nearly one-third of all donations.

Nathan J. Kelly[32] (2020), an associate professor in the Department of Political Science at the University of Tennessee, believes that the concentration of wealth has created a self-sustaining chaebol rule or an "inequality trap." Because they control most of the economic resources, a small number of people have more political power than they should have. These individuals launched a series of political activities aimed at

---

[31] Brookings (2019). Taxing Capital Income: Mark-to-Market and Other Approaches, Nov. 15, 2019.

[32] Kelly, N. J. (2020). *America's Inequality Trap*. University of Chicago Press.

convincing voters that it is unwise and not in the interest of ordinary Americans to reduce inequality. They also spent large sums of money to hire lobbying groups to influence Congress, the president, and the state governments to slow down or prevent reform.

There are four ways to increase economic inequality through the political system. The first strategy is to introduce policies that aggravate inequality, which is easier than introducing those that reduce it. The second strategy is to increase inequality through policy inaction. The third is to make it more difficult for political parties that support the redistribution of wealth, such as the Democratic Party in the United States, to win elections. The fourth is to lead voters to form more conservative policy preferences. Kelly found that when inequality in the United States was high, the Democratic Party performs poorly in elections, while the Republican Party does well. The 2016 presidential election was in line with this pattern. During the general election in 2016, the gap between the rich and the poor in the United States reached its highest point in history. Kelly also explains that when inequality is low, policy inaction has little effect on inequality, but when the level of inequality is very high, policy inaction aggravates inequality. However, there are many veto opportunities in the American political system. For example, the Senate, the House of Representatives, and the president all have veto power, which would allow them to change the status quo, but instead they often maintain the status quo and seek consensus, making it difficult to introduce new policies. In addition, policy discussions in the United States are often chaotic, and those who oppose income and wealth redistribution have time to cover up the negative implications of their claims.

In view of the fact that inequality in the United States is unlikely to be alleviated in a short time, Trump could add yet another reason for the trade war, blaming China for the social inequality in the United States. However, this would not be true. One of the main measures that demonstrate the gap between the poor and the rich is the *mean household income of the lowest quintile and the top 5%*. In 2010, the lowest quintile and the top 5% earned US$12,600 and US$331,400 per year, respectively. In 2018, mean income for the top 5% increased to US$416,500, while the lowest quintile reached US$13,700, a large gap that illustrates the brutal concentration of income in the United States. At both ends of the *household income distribution*, 10.2% receive less than US$15,000 and 8.5% receive over US$200,000 per year (2018). As of June 2019, the top 10% held 69.4% of total U.S. net worth with the top 1% holding about half of that wealth (32.4%), while the next 9% held approximately the other half, at 37%. The bottom 50% of U.S. residents held only 2% of all U.S. wealth. As recently as 2011, that number was as low as 0.2%, caused by the downturn of the Great Recession[33] (Buchholz, 2019). We can see the concentration of wealth in the incomes of the leading billionaires worldwide. Of the top ten richest individuals in the world, eight are Americans: Jeff Bezos (US$113 billions), Bill Gates (US$98 billions), Warren Buffet (US$67.5 billions), Larry Allison (US$59 billions), and Mark Zuckerberg (US$54.7 billions). The dynamics of the U.S. economy produce more richness than real wealth.

But what does American society think about social inequality and its related issues? According to the General Social Survey[34] (GSS), in 2018, 51% of respondents answered "No" when asked whether their income is enough to pay their bills (among those who have jobs). However, if divided into classes, 61% of the lower classes answered "no" in 2018, and 80% gave the same answer in 2014. Additionally, 64% (2014) and 59% (2018) of the working class also responded that their wages were not enough to pay their bills. From 2016 to 2018, 71% of the respondents thought that the state spent too little on helping poor people. However, among the lower class, 83% (2018) thought expenditures were "too low"; among the working class, 73% (2018); and among the middle class, 65% (2018). In addition, 80% (2018) of the unemployed thought the state spent too little helping poor people.

Another measure presents us with a portion of the American population's perceptions of the government's role in *reducing wage differences*. In total, 22% of respondents "strongly supported" the government having a role in 2014, while 21% did so in 2018. However, by class strata, 38% (in 2014) and 36% (in 2018) of the lower-class respondents "supported"

---

[33] Buchholz, K. (2019). The Top 10 Percent Own 70 Percent of U.S. Wealth. https://www.statista.com/chart/19635/wealth-distribution-percentiles-in-the-us/.

[34] The General Social Survey (GSS) is a project of NORC at the University of Chicago, with principal funding from the National Science Foundation. Since 1972, the GSS has been monitoring societal change and studying the growing complexity of American society.

the government's role, and 23% (in 2014) and 22% (in 2018) of the working class "supported." Among the wealthy classes, 21% (2018) said there should be "no government interference."

The measures taken by Trump are in line with this logic, such as the tax cuts for large companies, pushed through Congress in January 2017, that reduces the corporate tax rate from 35% to 21%, a change that favors the richest 1%, decreasing their overall tax rate by 2.3 percentage points. According to the Joint Congressional Taxation Committee (JOC), workers earning between $20,000 and $30,000 annually will pay more in taxes as of 2021.

According to the Tax Policy Center[35] (TPC), the impact of this proposal (*Tax Cuts and Jobs Act*) on individual taxpayers varies according to their income sources, demographic, family status, and other characteristics that affect tax deductions and credits. TPC estimates that compared with the current law, the number of taxpayers who pay more or less in taxes is determined by some minor clauses of the law, so it is difficult to estimate tax changes for specific taxpayers.

Trump's tax-policy reform has been the largest tax-policy reform in the United States since Ronald Reagan's tax reform, which will not only have a large impact on the American economy but will also have spillover effects in other countries. Gale and Gelfond[36] (2019) analyze how the *Tax Cuts and Jobs Act*, signed by President Trump in January 2018, could potentially encourage bank to loan more, mainly studying the reasons why enterprises suspect that profits will increase after the implementation of the tax cuts, warning bank investors and analysts not to expect the tax cuts to lead to an increase in loan volume, and warning that the demand for commercial loans may remain moderate. President Trump adopted the slogan "Make America Great Again" during his election campaign, and solving historic problems such as the loss of manufacturing industry, unemployment among residents, and the complexity of the U.S. tax system was the policy objective of Trump when he took office. The complexity of the tax system before the Trump reforms increased administrative

[35] Tax Policy Center (2017). Distributional Analysis of the Conference Agreement for *The Tax Cuts and Jobs Act*. December.

[36] Gale, W. G., Gelfond, H., Krupkin, A., Mazur, M. J., & Toder, E. J. (2019). Effects of the Tax Cuts and Jobs Act: A preliminary analysis. *National Tax Journal, 71*(4), 589–612.

costs and placed demands on taxpayers' time. There were many overlapping clauses in the previous tax system, so taxpayers needed to spend much time calculating their taxes and determining their own tax standards. For example, the previous system included an alternative minimum tax, and taxpayers were expected to calculate the alternative minimum tax and standard tax based on their actual tax situation, thus determining the corresponding tax amounts.

On the other hand, due to changes in the global division of labor, the shrinking American middle class has recently losing income year by year, and the unemployment rate has also been increasing. The current tax system is more beneficial to high-income earners while workers' wages have declined, thus widening the gap between the rich and the poor, another result of Trump's tax-policy reform. In the past, the higher corporate tax rate stipulated in U.S. tax laws led to an increase in the tax burden on domestic enterprises in the United States, which in turn led corporations to transfer their profits overseas. In the past 20 years, the proportion of overseas investment from the United States has increased from 38% to 70%, and the combination of overseas tax policies and policies which incentivize deferred tax payments has reduced the proportion of American enterprises investing in their local areas. Therefore, the former tax system in the United States had not adapted to the current economic situation and the actual conditions within the American economy.

Despite the internal contradictions of the American economy, for economists Joseph Stiglitz and Bruce Greenwald[37] (2014) in *Creating a Learning Society (2014)*, what separates developed countries from developing countries is not just a gap in resources but a gap in knowledge (Stiglitz 1999b; World Bank 1999). For the authors, "much of the difference in per capita income between these countries and the more advanced is attributable to differences in knowledge, the development strategies should be centered on promoting learning, closing the knowledge gap between more- and less-developed countries. Policies that transformed their economies and societies into 'learning societies' would enable them to close the gap more rapidly, with marked increases in incomes."

[37] Stiglitz, J. and Greenwald B. (2014). Creating a Learning Society: A New Paradigm for Development and Social Progress. New York: Columbia University Press.

To Stiglitz and Greenwald (2014), that trade liberalization by itself does not ensure growth is obvious from the huge gap within developed countries with the United States as an example. Before the federal government took action (including providing aid), the United States had narrowed (but far from eliminated) the income gap between the North and the South. The authors develop three specific conclusions: (1) countries cannot simply look to what other countries have done at similar stages of development. History matters. (2) Given the difficulties of determining a country's (static or dynamic) comparative advantage, Lin's argument (2012, 2014) that countries should be careful about pursuing industrial policies that "defy" comparative advantage may not be of much help. (3) Countries have to be strategic—because history matters, they have to take into account how enhancing capabilities today (through trade policies) will affect their potential for capability enhancement in the future.

The G-2 in the United Nations

Even at the level of the United Nations, we can see high levels of disagreements and divergences within the developed countries' bloc, whether expressed in the General Assembly, the Commissions, or the Security Council. However, it is obvious that developing countries are limited in their main decision-making spaces. In this way, we were also able to identify the disagreements that the United States and China have in the UN. We want to demonstrate that the divergences and conflicts in the economic agendas between these countries can also be found in the UN Commissions, years before the beginning of the trade war.

Yan Xuetong[38] (2010) already noted destabilizing factors between the two countries in his article "The Instability of China-US Relations." One of the factors put forward by then-U.S. President Barack Obama was the rise of Chinese nationalism, which would lead to conflicts with neighboring countries and regions allied to the United States, mainly Taiwan.

[38] Yan, X. (2010). The Instability of China–US Relations. *The Chinese Journal of International Politics*, Vol. 3, 263–292.

U.S. sales of sophisticated weapons to Taiwan have become the basis for increasing conflicts between the two countries, which have worsened with the rise of Trump. Yan (2010) defined Sino-U.S. relations with a typology divided into economic, political, security, and culture, as well as common, complementary, conflicting, and confrontational interests. What is interesting about this typology is that the factors that were causing conflict 10 years ago (2010–2020) still exist during the trade war. The author pointed out that there were common and complementary economic interests 10 years ago, including joint investment, the growth of the global market, bilateral trade, the purchase of U.S. bonds and tourism. We can attest that Trump's trade policy has disregarded this common ground. Although the main points of the Phase One Agreement obliged China to purchase goods worth 200 billion U.S. dollars, which led to an unforeseen increase in bilateral trade, Trump's policy is to withdraw U.S. investments from China to give priority to American producers.

The time was ripe for the economies to come into conflict, and those conflicts deepened, resulting in an economic war. Issues such as intellectual property rights, exchange rates and the trade surplus, the transfer of high-tech research and development, and the control of strategic economic resources and materials have become the focus of disputes between the countries. Due to the Trump administration's contempt for multilateral entities and environmental agendas, other topics, such as global financial reform and carbon dioxide emission reduction standards, have actually disappeared from its agenda.

In addition to the security issues, any issue in which there were points of frequent divergence between the countries remains highly conflicted after Trump. Issues such as arms sales to Taiwan, the arms embargo on China, the Uygur terrorists, the Iranian nuclear problem, U.S. deployment of the National Missile Defense (NMD) in East Asia, maritime control of the South China and Yellow Seas, military modernization, space research and development, and arms exports have become exponentially worse problems that could lead to an arms race, damaging economic interdependence and bringing instability to East Asia. Ten years ago, the author stated that because "the extent of mutually favorable interests varies among different sectors, clarifying strategic relations according to different sectors would better serve both China and the United States." However, this recommendation has not been carried out.

The work of Michael A. Bailey, Anton Strezhnev, and Erik Voeten,[39] which analyzes the preferences of each country in each UN session, compared to existing measures, allows for better intertemporal comparisons, is less sensitive to shifts in the UN's agenda, and is strongly correlated with measures of liberalism. We also compare the performances of China and the United States from this perspective.[40] Major themes of their work include (1) politics and security (disarmament and weapons in general), nuclear weapons, territorial integrity—sovereignty, internal policy/civil rights, peace operations, and others—politics and security (Israel-Palestine); (2) economics (industrial and economic development, food and agriculture, assistance, trade, and natural resources); (3) social, technical, and cultural; (4) colonial tutelage; (5) administration and finance—UN; and (6) legal (International Court of Justice, treaties, legal instruments, investigations, and reports).

From 2001, with China's accession to the World Trade Organization (WTO), to 2015, we have been able to verify the degree of difference between U.S. and Chinese foreign policy in the UN. When we consider voting in the UN sessions on economic issues, we realize how opposed the countries already were, whether during the George W. Bush (2001–2009) or Barack Obama (2009–2017) administrations. Between 2001 and 2015, a total of 76 economic issues were voted on, with the United States and China divided on 65 issues. Approximately 85% of the votes were on economic issues, and the two countries had different voting positions. The only areas with common ground were international aid and agricultural development. Other topics included the right to develop, unilateral economic measures as a means of political and economic coercion against developing countries, international trade and development, economic and other activities affecting the interests of people in non-self-governing territories, globalization and its impact on human rights, the

[39] Bailey, M.A., Strezhnev, A. & Voeten, E. (2010). Estimating Dynamic State Preferences from United Nations Voting Data. *Journal of Conflict Resolution*. jcr.sagepub.com. pp. 1–27.

[40] According to studies and the database organized and provided by Prof. Octávio Amorim (Fundação Getúlio Vargas-Brasil), he was able to correlate the levels of interaction/conflict between countries according to the votes in the assemblies.

promotion of multilateral disarmament and nonproliferation, sustainability, and the development of external debt. In the discussion of these issues, there have been constant differences between the two countries. China often sided with the developing countries while the United States maintained its position of its own interests and those of its allies.

Analysis by the United Nations University Center for Policy Research[41] entitled "The G2 at the UN (2020)" and based on the perspectives of ambassadors and diplomats at the UN showed that a certain number of analysts and international relations experts already identified that disputes between the United States and China were increasingly present in multilateral entities. According to the analysis, "under the Trump Administration, the global outlook of the U.S. has become more transactional, mercantile, nationalist and unpredictable—with a greater emphasis on sovereignty and a reduced focus on alliances." On the issue of alliances, China, which does not deny the principle of sovereignty, has "to an extent, a consistent commitment to upholding an effective multilateral system in general, and in the UN in particular." In the same document, it is clear that the United States' alienation from and rejection of the multilateral principle of strengthening international institutions has created a power vacuum, which provides a space for China's growing influence. This analysis identified three scenarios for the relationship between China and the United States over the next five years through to 2025: (1) competition and confrontation; (2) increasing utilization of the UN by the great powers; and (3) international recognitions of China as a global power. What this survey of UN diplomats actually demonstrates is that the great powers will seek confrontation at all levels of international politics as a means of measuring strength.

Trump's attitude in despising multilateral entities and removing the United States from entities such as the WHO and WTO can be understood as an attitude of "where I do not hegemonize, I withdraw." While Chinese diplomacy makes an effort to be present and influence policies at global levels, American diplomacy demonstrates total arrogance and indifference to the entities that, for many years, it indisputably dominated.

[41] Whineray, D. (2020) *The G2 at the UN: United States and the People's Republic of China at the United Nations Before COVID-19*. New York: United Nations University.

For Samuel Guimarães,[42] China has so far directed its foreign policy from a tactical perspective, focusing on avoiding military confrontations with the United States, ensuring diversified sources of raw materials for the Chinese economy, opening markets for Chinese exports and investments, not interfering in the political or economic affairs of other countries nor imposing undesired political or economic conditions, strengthening their ties with their neighboring countries, particularly Russia, and having relative success until the worsening of relations with the trade war. The author emphasizes that in the eyes of the American people, this title of "enemy" is necessary to prove that the expenditures paid to the companies and military structures of the industrial-military complex for weapons are beneficial, as are the subsidies for scientific and technological research and development projects of those companies, which sometimes cause deep losses but are justified and legal because of "national security."

The changing role of Europe in U.S.-China disputes poses a dilemma in relations between the European Union and the Trump administration. Trump's separation from German leader Angela Merkel and French President Emmanuel Macron aggravated the weakening of the Western bloc, as the current administration also adopted tariff measures against the EU and supported Britain's withdrawal from the EU.

In the struggle against China, Trump ensured that the "Five Eyes" countries (the UK, Canada, New Zealand, and Australia) as well as other states in Asia such as India, Japan, the Philippines, and Indonesia would be principal allies. Contrary to what happened during the Cold War, the American tactic of isolation from China has tended to fail, precisely because of increasingly complex and interdependent global markets containing a large share of integrated Chinese investments and value chains.

For Charis M. Vlados,[43] to understand the first stage of the trade war, it is necessary to understand the restructuring of globalization in the age of the fourth industrial revolution and to focus on certain aspects: (1) the search for a "new globalization"; (2) the establishment of a new, more

---

[42] Guimarães S.P. (2020). El Sistema Internacional y el Imperio. Alba Movimientos.

[43] Vlados, C.M. (2020). The Dynamics of the Current Global Restructuring and Contemporary Framework of the US–China Trade War. *Global Journal of Emerging Market Economies*.

balanced, and sustainable model of development on a global scale; (3) the structural integration and further deepening of the "revolutionary process" in global socio-economic terms; (4) the acceleration of creative destruction and innovation processes on a global scale; and (5) the progressive consolidation of new and more effective change management mechanisms throughout all spatial and functional levels of the global reality.

Vlados (2020) sees the current U.S.-China trade war as a new challenge: (1) if it leads to a trajectory of limiting the innovative potential and performance of actors on a global scale, it will be a hindrance and a factor that reproduces and perpetuates the current crisis. (2) Should this trade war give rise to a repositioning of change management mechanisms in the relationship of global socio-economic partners, it will be a factor in accelerating the exit from the current crisis, as well as a structural component of a "new globalization" capable of providing a relatively stable new long-term equilibrium and growth framework for the world. In his book, published after he left the Trump administration, John Bolton,[44] a former National Security Advisor, reaffirms the vision that we developed in previous chapters: China and Russia as strategic opponents of the United States.

There is no good news in the rhetoric of Bolton and Trump, especially when China is mentioned on the North Korean nuclear issue. Their rhetoric raises the possibilities of war, but its main purpose is to test China's position, the "real strategic game," in disputes over the South China Sea and the use of bases in the Philippines.

On issues of economics and trade wars, Trump repeats what already exists in the official documents of business representatives, that China had played with this system, implemented mercantilist policies of trade in the World Trade Organization (WTO), stolen the intellectual property rights of the United States, and devoted itself to forced technology transfer, which deprived the United States of countless dollars' worth of capital and trade for decades.

---

[44] Bolton, J. R. (2020). The Room Where It Happened: A White House Memoir. (La habitación donde ocurrió Una memoria de la Casa Blanca—Spanish version).

Bolton believes that Trump's intention to strengthen the powerful national economy of the United States is the key to effectively demonstrate the political and military strength of the United States. Quotes like "The Chinese don't give a shit; they are cold-blooded killers [in trade]" and "the EU is worse than China, only smaller" are tweets typical of Trump and prove this argument.

Mike Lofgren[45] (2016), former Republican Congressional assistant, and author of the book *The Deep State: The Fall of the Constitution and the Rise of a Shadow Government*, thinks that on the one hand, there is a paradox of poverty and dysfunction in the United States; on the other hand, infinite wealth and seemingly omnipotent people and corporations are outside the control of government, which is a sign that a shadow government rules the United States, and it pays little attention to the Constitution.

For the author, the United States is facing a difficult future after experiencing two failed wars, a precarious economy, and accumulated debts of 17 trillion U.S. dollars (2014). There are two opposite interpretations: (1) those who see a fragmented, dysfunctional political system which is impossible to reform, and an economy that will soon be overtaken by China. (2) Other "reformers" offer a profusion of panaceas to transform the nation: public financing of the elections to cut the artery of money between corporations and politicians dependent on financing to be elected, reverse the tide of outsourcing of government functions and the conflicts of interest it creates, a fiscal policy that values human labor more than financial transactions, and a trade policy that favors the export of manufactured goods rather than capital investment.

[45] Mike Lofgren (2016). *The Deep State: The Fall of the Constitution and the Rise of a Shadow Government*. Paperback.

5

Conclusion

"Focus on China"

After the start of the trade war, the deterioration of Sino-American relations put the world in a situation of shocks between the two main economies. As stated in the first chapter, it is too early to look for definitive results in the data and reliance should never be placed on short-term outcomes, though the trade war has already caused damage to both sides and even the world. We also warn that contemporary history shows that trade barriers are easy to impose and hard to remove, but afterward, any damage done can take decades to repair.

The conflicting views about what kind of globalization project the world should follow remain, generating reactions in different directions. Contrary to civil society movements that question globalization for not combating social inequalities, what we see today is that the right and extreme right populism, which so much identifies with Trump, has invested its efforts with a strong ideological trend against China, and the trade war was a justification for this initiative.

As much as experts could predict that a future clash between the United States and China would be inevitable, it was not clear how intense

L. Sheng, D. Felix do Nascimento, *Love and Trade War*,
https://doi.org/10.1007/978-981-33-4897-4_5

the aggressiveness of American foreign policy would be, let alone what we witnessed after the end of the first phase of the agreement. There has been nothing similar to this type of dispute between great powers, whether in Eric Hobsbawm's[1] historiographical perspective in the *Age of Empires* or in the *Age of Extremes*,[2] although the elements of war can be thoroughly identified. What we have witnessed in practice in this trade war is that protectionist policies and other unilateralist mechanisms are once again triggered by Western European and U.S. countries when they feel they are losing markets.

With some measure of reason, American trade policy turned against China in order to reverse what experts call "market distortion." After decades of American investments in companies in China, the Trump administration has decided that American industry and, consequently, American jobs are suffering declines because of the displacement of U.S. factories and investments to China. Thus, attempting to reallocate U.S. private investment into the United States itself as well as reducing the trade deficit with China, forcing it to buy more American products.

Although we also believe that this is a dispute in the field of technological hegemony, market restrictions against China target the most advanced technology platforms and companies in the world, in the case of Huawei and ZTE. These trade protection measures that sought to revise points of the agreements signed by the United States has not only affected China. As we have shown, this has also occurred in the case of NAFTA (North American Free Trade Agreement) agreements with Canada and Mexico, with the European Union and in attempts to discredit the World Trade Organization (WTO), thereby affecting its operations.

The question remains whether the policies adopted by the United States for commercial protection will be, in the eyes of history, a government policy, in the case of the Trump administration, or a state policy, with a view to the continuity or not of these policies in accordance with changes in American domestic politics, between Republicans and

[1] Hobsbawm, E. (1987). *Age of empire: 1875–1914*. Hachette UK.

[2] Hobsbawm, E. J., & Cumming, M. (1995). Age of extremes: the short twentieth century, 1914–1991 (p. 111). London: Abacus.

Democrats. We try to demonstrate that the meanings of the trade war go far beyond market disputes, import/export transactions, or tariff issues, even if they are clear signs of tensions, which, in another context, could perhaps be resolved within multilateral institutions such as the WTO. But they were not.

There are specifics to this trade war. The speed of events after the first agreement makes it difficult to predict scenarios, other than the outbreak of geopolitical conflicts between the two nations. We seek to affirm that the rise of Trump and his advisers has built a speech of victimization of the weakening of the American economy. The causes would be the excessive opening to foreign markets and the absence of defensive actions to contain the advance of China in the United States and in the world. The most ideological, conservative, and military sectors, mainly intelligence services, took on the task of creating a vision that China was an adversary and an enemy of U.S. strategic pretensions and its influence in the world. They produced a narrative that in this competition between countries, multilateral institutions would not be prepared to favor American power, since Chinese influence had "distorted" these institutions.

In Trump's administration there was an impulse of anti-China sentiment on different fronts of disputes in both domestic and international fields; however, we show that even during the Obama administration there was a strategic shift in military priorities toward the Indian and South China Seas, toward investments in capacity for the U.S. Indo-Pacific Command and American allies such as Japan, Taiwan, the Philippines, and NATO allies. In trying to blame China for structural problems of the American economy, Trump failed to come up with a government plan for growing social inequality in the United States, making it the most unequal country in the developed world.

Changes in the world economy have made China one of the principal international players in the twenty-first century. Economic diversity in the industrial sector of technology, a policy of expansion of the productive sector focused on exports, insertion in global value chains, the modeling of a financial sector connected to the state and private companies/join ventures, the interaction of state, private national, and foreign capital in the constitution of companies, the establishment of the Shanghai Cooperation Organization (SCO) in 2010 added to the strategic vision of the Chinese Communist Party are just a few elements that have solidified the country's foundations.

China's economic policy has been preparing for and adapting to the turbulence of world markets. The 2008 global crisis, which had domestic effects, meant that the country increased its foreign direct investments inside and outside the country, diversified markets to depend less on the United States, and planned to modernize its domestic market. In the 2015 market disruptions caused by the drop in oil prices, caused by the increase in shale production by the United States, and by the devaluation of the dollar, China implemented measures to protect its currency, advance in education and science and technology, and reaffirm the role of the Belt and Road Initiative. The current phase of the trade war initiated by Trump has become yet another test for the Chinese economy and foreign policy, as in this situation, China is the main target of the United States.

The outbreak of the trade war weakened hegemonic views in international relations about interdependence. These were no longer sufficient to explain the scale of these disputes. We demonstrate that there is a dialectic perspective in pointing out the contradictions between the economic and political spheres, because in a given historical period the actors do not move and interact in a homogeneous way, with periods of greater cooperation and imminent conflicts.

In terms of the International Political Economy, the trade war has produced a new dilemma that we try to expose. Thinkers who defend a (neo) liberal view found themselves without arguments after the American government's anti-market protectionist measures. The old liberal view based on the idea that greater opening of markets would bring harmony between states was again invalidated. While China proposes more liberalization of markets, the United States closes when they find themselves threatened by the loss of hegemony.

The Trade War Post COVID-19

Shortly after the signing of Phase One of the Trade Agreement, on January 15, 2020, the Trump administration sent a message of strength to the world. This was a message that the tariff pressure on China had provided concrete results. Despite considering the agreement with many weak points of difficult compliance, the Trump administration used it as propaganda for its electoral base and supporters. The United States used stick diplomacy in the economic sense to get China to accept or impose taxes. But the storms were just beginning.

Beginning in the city of Wuhan, the coronavirus spread (COVID-19) on a global scale turning into a serious pandemic that hit all continents. The Chinese state acted quickly to slow the spread by decreasing production in several sectors, closing trade, diminishing the circulation and transportation of people, and closing schools and universities. In addition, a series of measures were taken in the face of an extreme emergency caused by an unknown disease. The priority was to strengthen the country's public health structure in conjunction with regional sectors, provinces, towns, cities, and society, in an effort to establish a collective quarantine to combat the epidemic. At the time of writing (07/31/2020), Mainland China had reached 84,292 confirmed cases, 78,974 recovered and 4643 deaths while the world reached 17,297,296 cases, 10,132,579 recovered and 673,223 killed. The United States has become the country with the highest number of cases and deaths in the world with 4,577,862 cases and 154,249 dead.

At the beginning of the epidemic in the United States in March 2020, Trump repeatedly said that everything was under control and that the United States was prepared to fight the virus. Yet Trump was a systematic opponent of Obamacare, a project of the then Obama administration to facilitate access to healthcare for the poorest Americans. For Trump, the idea of public health was similar to the implementation of socialism in the United States. Even with the accelerated spread of the virus and growing fatalities, Trump maintained a denialist stance, attacking opposing governors who tried to follow World Health Organization (WHO) recommendations with measures of social isolation, such as the closure of commercial establishments and factories, the use of masks, and other measures of protection. While denying the scope and dangers of the epidemic, Trump was advertising hydroxychloroquine, a drug used for malaria and without scientific proof to fight the virus, as a way of curing COVID-19.

Since the beginning of the epidemic, Chinese authorities worked together with the World Health Organization (WHO) to establish preventative actions and send information to different laboratories and research institutes in order to unveil the genetic structure and spread of the virus. The political solution that Trump found due to his government's inability to control the epidemic was to blame China and the World Health Organization (WHO). In calling COVID-19 the "Chinese virus," Trump brought the same logic he had done with regard to economic affairs and the trade war, to attack China as the entity most responsible for the pandemic.

The impacts of the epidemic on world economies will still be the subject of studies for many years to come; however, initial data on its effects on the American economy in the second quarter of 2020 are staggering. There was a 32.9% decline in Gross Domestic Product, the sharpest drop in production since the government started recording data in 1947, according to the Department of Commerce. Data from the Department of Labor show that unemployment increased by 12,000, to 1.434 million in the week ended on July 25. About 30.2 million Americans received aid in the week of July 11, while the unemployment rate reached 14.7% (May 8, 2020), the highest in 70 years, with a loss of 20.5 million jobs (May 8, 2020).

After tough measures to combat the epidemic, China may return to production in several regions of the country. China's economy grew 3.2% in the second quarter compared to 2019, after a 6.8% contraction in the first half of 2020, even though the economy fell by 1.6% in the first six months compared to 2019. China's industrial production rose 4.8% in June (2020) compared to the previous year. Exports rose 3.5% in April compared to the same month of March 2019. The increase in exports came mainly from the medical sector in the amount of 71.2 billion yuan (10 billion dollars) in April, up 300% from the previous month.

In the midst of an epidemic, the propaganda machine of aggressive speeches against China became the focus of American foreign policy. Not only speeches pressuring China to comply with the Phase One Agreement by buying more American products, but also a policy of restraining technology companies (like Huawei) and increasing U.S. and allied military presence in the South China Sea.

Secretary of Defense Mark Esper used[3] the term quite precisely in describing the main purpose of the National Defense Strategy (NDS): "Focus the Department on China." To reaffirm the U.S. position in considering the importance of prioritizing the implementation, the NDS and then China, then Russia constitute on top strategic competitors. To Esper the focus on China is necessary for "our future leaders must understand how China thinks about war, how the People's Liberation Army (PLA) is organized, what kind of weapons and equipment they use, and how they fight." He said that he personally "directed the National Defense University to refocus its curriculum by dedicating 50 percent of the coursework to China, and I tasked the Military Departments and Services to make China the pacing threat in all of our schools, programs, and training." For him the problem is that "as China and Russia continue to modernize their militaries and pursue advantages in emerging technologies like artificial intelligence (AI) and 5G."

Mark Esper's speech follows the same political line as Mike Pompeo, one of the most aggressive representatives of Trumpism. In a tough speech in front of the Richard Nixon Presidential Library and Museum, Pompeo [4] reproduced all the ideological baggage that make up the anti-China sentiment of the Trump administration, in the same logic of We against Them, of the values of the free world against tyranny, similar to Reagan referring to the USSR as the Evil Empire. In questioning the results of the past 50 years of U.S.-China relations, Pompeo describes the United States as a victim who has been misled. And that "the Trump administration's long-standing trade war with a fight for human rights and U.S. national security."

---

[3] Staff, R. (2020, October 29). Chinese, U.S. military chief hold crisis communication. *Reuters*.

[4] U.S. Department of State. (2020, July 23). Communist China and the free world's future. https://www.state.gov/communist-china-and-the-free-worlds-future/.

Pompeo strives to compare the current moment with the logic of the Cold War, such as "the U.S. must be more cautious in its approach to China than its handling of the Soviet Union"; "The hegemony communist in the world based on a 'bankrupt, totalitarian ideology,'" and, "The U.S. and China cannot ignore the fundamental ideological differences between them." Finally, Pompeo calls for other international entities, which Trump has despised, such as the United Nations, NATO, the G7 countries, the G20, to "our combined economic, diplomatic, and military power is surely enough to meet this challenge if we direct it clearly and with great courage." The U.S. trade representative Robert Lighthizer was a principal architect and negotiator of the trade war. In this book we sought to identify his influence within the Trump administration, the possible reasons for triggering the trade war against China, as part of the strategy to contain the rise of the Chinese economy. Surprisingly, Lighthizer declares at an event in London that "I don't know what the end goal is" in a trade war with China. And added that, "we have to figure out new rules—what phase one is, is an attempt to find those kinds of rules—and these are setting aside all the aggression in India and in Hong Kong." It is increasingly proven in the Lighthizer statements that geopolitical considerations are the true intention of the trade war with economic impacts being secondary. The logic of the conflict is summarized in the political line adopted by Mike Pompeo and Mark Esper.

As much as Lighthizer has tried to justify the trade war with China in the article "Trump's Trade Policy Is Making America Stronger,"[5] stating that there is a new consensus in the case of the Trump administration's trade policy. As much as Lighthizer tried to justify the trade war with China, in the article Trump's trade policy is strengthening America, he argues that there is a new consensus in the case of trade policy. China's dependence on access to the American market has produced the consensus that it is necessary to contain China at home and abroad.

Lighthizer denies that the use of a Section 301 investigation on forced technology transfer was a justification for the trade war and that trade policy with both China and NAFTA had support from workers' unions

[5] Lighthizer, R. E. (2020). Trump's Trade Policy Is Making America Stronger. *Retrieved May*, 5, 2020.

and business associations. Lighthizer contradicts himself by saying that geopolitical reasons hinder the conduct of American trade policy, as was the case with the Trans-Pacific Partnership (TPP). What then would justify the continued militarization of the South China Sea and Huawei's boycott?

In any case, the trade war leaves some questions unresolved: however, the role of the state in the global economy and the changes in the domestic policy of the United States remain important considerations for the analysis of its international relations. The trade war may have represented the end of the period of cooperation and the beginning of conflicts that are mutually economic or geopolitical. These responses, however, are not the breaking of relations, but the growth of technological competition and value chains, by other laws than that of international institutions.

Bibliography

Abraham, K. G., & Kearney, M. S. (2018). *Explaining the Decline in the US. Employment-to-Population Ratio: A Review of the Evidence*. No. w24333. National Bureau of Economic Research.

Alvaredo, F., Chancel, L., Piketty, T., Saez, E., & Zucman, G. (Eds.). (2018). *World Inequality Report 2018*. Berkeley, CA: Belknap Press.

Anton, M. (2019, April 20). The Trump Doctrine. *Foreign Policy*.

Archibald, R. B., & Feldman, D. H. (1998). Investment During the Great Depression: Uncertainty and the Role of the Smoot-Hawley Tariff. *Southern Economic Journal, 64*(4), 857–879.

Bacevich, A. J. (2017). Saving America First: What Responsible Nationalism Looks Like. *Foreign Affairs, 96*, 57.

Bailey, M. A., Strezhnev, A., & Voeten, E. (2010). Estimating Dynamic State Preferences from United Nations Voting Data. *Journal of Conflict Resolution*. jcr.sagepub.com. pp. 1–27.

Barber, P. G., & Lem, W. (2004). Commodities, Capitalism and Globalization: Introduction. *Anthropologica, 46*(2), 123–129.

Baru, S. (2012). Geo-Economics and Strategy. *Survival, 54*(3), 47–58.

Beaudreau, B. C. (2017). Reexamining the Origins of the Smoot–Hawley Tariff Act. In *Research in Economic History*. Bingley: Emerald Publishing Limited.

L. Sheng, D. Felix do Nascimento, *Love and Trade War*,
https://doi.org/10.1007/978-981-33-4897-4

Bennett, B. (2017, January 20). 'America First,' a Phrase with a Loaded Anti-Semitic and Isolationist History. *The Angeles Times*.

Berengaut, A., & Fishman (2017, June 15). E. Why Americans Should Fight Donald Trump's Isolationism. *Time*.

Bidwell, P. W. (1930). The New American Tariff: Europe's Answer. *Foreign Affairs, 9*(1), 13–26.

Bingxi, Z. (2007). Rethinking Economic Globalization. *China International Studies, 8*, 86.

Blackwill, R. D. (2020, January). *Implementing Grand Strategy Toward China: Twenty-Two. U.S. Policy Prescriptions*. Council on Foreign Relations. Council Special Report No. 85.

Blankenship, B. D., & Denison, B. (2019). Is America Prepared for Great-Power Competition? *Survival, 61*(5), 43–64.

Blendon, R. J., Casey, L. S., & Benson, J. M. (2017). Public Opinion and Trump's Jobs and Trade Policies. *Challenge, 60*(3), 228–244.

Bolton, J. R. (2020). The Room Where It Happened: A White House Memoir [La. habitación donde ocurrió Una memoria de la Casa Blanca—Spanish version].

Bottelier, P. (2018). *Economic Policy Making in China (1949–2016): The Role of Economists*. New York: Taylor & Francis Group.

Bown, C. P. (2019). The 2018 US-China Trade Conflict After Forty Years of Special Protection. *China Economic Journal, 12*(2), 109–136.

Brennan, J. (2016). United States income Inequality: The Concept of Countervailing Power Revisited. *Journal of Post Keynesian Economics, 39*(1), 72–92.

Brennan, D. (2019, May 15). Jimmy Carter Took Call About China from a Concerned Donald Trump: 'China Has Not Wasted a Single Penny on War'. *Newsweek*.

Brzezinski, Z. (2017, February 20). Why the World Needs a Trump Doctrine. *The New York Times*.

Buchholz, K. (2019). The Top 10 Percent Own 70 Percent of U.S. Wealth. Retrieved from https://www.statista.com/chart/19635/wealth-distribution-percentiles-in-the-us/.

Capri, A. (2020a, August). Techno-Nationalism: The US-China Tech Innovation Race. *Hinrich Foundation*. Retrieved from https://technode.com/2020/04/24/export-controls-and-the-rise-of-us-china-techno-nationalism/.

Capri, A. (2020b). Semiconductors at the Heart of the US-China Tech War. *Hinrich. Foundation*. Retrieved from https://hinrichfoundation.com/trade-research/global-trade-research/thought-leadership/semiconductors-at-the-heart-of-the-us-china-tech-war/.

Carafano, J. J., Coffey, L., Gardiner, N., Lohman, W., Miller, A. T., & Spoehr, T. Preparing the US National Security Strategy for 2020 and Beyond.

Carbaugh, B. (2019). Trump's America First Program: A Flawed Approach. *Challenge, 62*(2), 144–162.

Castle, S. (2019, May 8). Pompeo Attacks China and Warns Britain Over Huawei Security Risks. *The New York Times*.

Chong, T. T. L., & Li, X. (2019). Understanding the China–US Trade War: Causes, Economic Impact, and the Worst-Case Scenario. *Economic and Political Studies, 7*(2), 185–202.

Chu, S., & Zhou, L. (2018). Diplomatic Characteristics of Trump Administration and Its Influence. *Contemporary International Relations, 8*, 23.

Chunmei, Y., & Wenyi, M. (2016). The US High Technology Export Control Towards China. *Journal of Business, 1*(2), 13–16.

Cohen, A. (2019, August, 6). Trump's China Trade War Hamming Oil Markets. *Forbes*.

Dean, J. M., Lovely, M. E., & Mora, J. (2017). Decomposing China-Japan-US Trade: Vertical Specialization, Ownership, and Organizational Form. *International Economic Integration and Domestic Performance*, pp. 119 132.

Di, D., Luft, G., & Zhong, D. (2019). Why Did Trump Launch a Trade War? A Political Economy Explanation from the Perspective of Financial Constraints. *Economic and Political Studies, 7*(2), 203–216.

Dobbins, J., Solomon, R. H., Chase, M. S., Henry, R., Larrabee, F. S., Lempert, R. J., et al. (2015). *Choices for America in a Turbulent World: Strategic Rethink*. Santa Monica, CA: Rand Corporation.

Dolven, B., & Vaughn, B. (2020, January 30). *Indo-Pacific Strategies of U.S. Allies and Partners: Issues for Congress*. Retrieved from https://www.everycrsreport.com/files/20200130_R46217_770a61c4856a9a5aed99d6699f3423b6240ff1c3.pdf.

Du, X., & Xie, Z. (2020). Occurrence of Turning Point on Environmental Kuznets Curve in the Process of (De) industrialization. *Structural Change and Economic Dynamics, 53*, 359–369.

Eaton, J., & Kortum, S. (2012). Putting Ricardo to Work. *Journal of Economic Perspectives, 26*(2), 65–90.

Edwards, J. A. (2018). Make America Great Again: Donald Trump and Redefining the US Role in the World. *Communication Quarterly, 66*(2), 176–195.

Federico, G. (2005). Not Guilty? Agriculture in the 1920s and the Great Depression. *Journal of Economic History, 65*(4), 949–976.

Feldstein, M. (2010). America's Saving Surprise. *Project Syndicate*.

Fengru, C., & Guitang, L. (2019). *Global Value Chains and Production Networks: Case Studies of Siemens and Huawei*. London: Academic Press. ISBN: 978–0–12-814,847-1.

Ferguson, N. (2005). Sinking Globalization. *Foreign Affairs, 84*(2), 64–77.

Findlay, R., & O'rourke, K. H. (2009). *Power and Plenty: Trade, War, and the World Economy in the Second Millennium* (p. 450). Princeton, NJ: Princeton University Press.

Fleming, D. (1936). How the Smoot-Hawley Tariff Was Made. *Proceedings of the. Annual Session (Southern Political Science Association), 9*, 14–19. The University of Chicago Press on Behalf of the Southern Political Science Association.

Foreman-Peck, J., Hughes Hallett, A., & Ma, Y. (2007). Trade Wars and the Slump. *European Review of Economic History, 11*(1), 73–98.

Francois, J., & Baughman, L. M. (2003). *The Unintended Consequences of US Steel Import Tariffs: A Quantification of the Impact During 2002*. Washington, DC: CITAC Foundation.

Frankel, J. (2015). *The Plaza Accord, 30 Years Later* (No. w21813). National Bureau of Economic Research.

Fukuyama, F. (2016). American Political Decay or Renewal: the Meaning of the 2016 Election. *Foreign Affairs, 95*, 58.

Gale, W. G., Gelfond, H., Krupkin, A., Mazur, M. J., & Toder, E. J. (2019). Effects. of the Tax Cuts and Jobs Act: A Preliminary Analysis. *National Tax Journal, 71*(4), 589–612.

Galloway, L. T. (1972). Star Industries, Inc. v. United States: Sequel to The Chicken War. *The International Lawyer, 6*(1), 48–63.

Gao, Y., Cheng, W., & Yuan, Q. (2018). Understanding the Global Imbalance from the Perspective of Processing Trade Value Added of China. *Journal of Chinese Economic and Business Studies, 16*(4), 337–356.

Gartzke, E., & Li, Q. (2003). War, Peace, and the Invisible Hand: Positive Political Externalities of Economic Globalization. *International Studies Quarterly, 47*(4), 561–586.

Gerasimov, V. (2013, February 26). The Value of Science Is in the Foresight: New Challenges Demand Rethinking the Forms and Methods of Carrying out Combat Operations. *Voyenno-Promyshlennyy Kurier*. Online. Retrieved from http://vpk-news.ru/articles/14632.

Gerasimov, V. (2017). Contemporary Warfare and Current Issues for the Defense of the Country. *Military Review, 97*(6), 22.

Giroux, H. A. (2017). White Nationalism, Armed Culture and State Violence in the Age of Donald Trump. *Philosophy & Social Criticism, 43*(9), 887–910.
Goldberg, J. (2018, June 11). A Senior White House Official Defines the Trump Doctrine: We're America, Bitch. *The Atlantic*.
Gomez-Ibanez, J. A., & Harrison, D. (1982). Imports and the Future of the US Automobile Industry. *The American Economic Review, 72*(2), 319–323.
Grinols, E. L., & Perrelli, R. (2006). The WTO Impact on International Trade Disputes: An Event History Analysis. *The Review of Economics and Statistics, 88*(4), 613–624.
Gu, X., & Sheng, L. (2010). Sensible Policy Tool for Pareto Improvement: Capital Controls. *Journal of World Trade, 44*(3), 567–589.
Guillén, A. (2019). USA's Trade Policy in the Context of Global Crisis and the Decline of North American Hegemony. *Brazilian Journal of Political Economy, 39*(3), 387–407.
Guimarães, S. P. (2020). El Sistema Internacional y el Imperio. *Alba Movimientos*.
Guo, K. (2018). Sino-US Trade War: Motivation Analysis and Scenario Deduction. *Journal of International Economic Cooperation., 2018*(05), 14–24.
Hall, T. (2020, February 15). *Trump's "Blue Collar Boom": Myth vs Reality*. Retrieved from https://www.wsws.org/en/articles/2020/02/15/boom-f15.html.
Hallin, D. C. (2019). Mediatisation, Neoliberalism and Populisms: The Case of Trump. *Contemporary Social Science, 14*(1), 14–25.
Han, Z., & Huang, Z. (2020). The Trump Doctrine: Connotation, Origin and. Evaluation. *International Forum, 4*, 3–18.
Hanemann, T., Rosen, D. H., & Gao, C. (2016). Two-Way Street: 25 Years of US-China Direct Investment. *National Committee on United States-China Relations*. Retrieved from www.us-china-fdi.com.
Heisbourg, F. (2020). NATO 4.0: The Atlantic Alliance and the Rise of China. *Survival, 62*(2), 83–102.
Held, D., McGrew, A., Goldblatt, D., & Perraton, J. (1999). Globalization. *Global Governance, 5*(4), 483–496.
Hobsbawm, E. (1987). *Age of Empire: 1875–1914*. London: Hachette UK.
Hobsbawm, E. J., & Cumming, M. (1995). *Age of Extremes: The Short Twentieth Century, 1914–1991* (p. 111). London: Abacus.
Hoffman, F. G. (2007). *Conflict in the 21st Century: The Rise of Hybrid Wars* (p. 51). Arlington: Potomac Institute for Policy Studies.
Holton, K. (2019). *UK Tells Telecom Firms to be Cautious Over Huawei After U.S. Warnings*. London: Reuters.

Hong, Y. (2019). The Logic of Four Decades of Economic Reform and Major Breakthroughs in Political Economy in China. *China Political Economy, 2*(1), 2–13.

Hu, F., & Spence, M. (2017). Why Globalization Stalled: An How to Restart It. *Foreign Affairs, 96*, 54.

Huotari, M., & Heep, S. (2016). Learning Geoeconomics: China's Experimental. Financial and Monetary Initiatives. *Asia Europe Journal, 14*(2), 153–171.

Ikenberry, G. J. (2017). The Plot Against American Foreign Policy: Can the Liberal. Order Survive. *Foreign Affairs, 96*, 2.

Iqbal, B. A., Rahman, N., & Elimimian, J. (2019). The Future of Global Trade in the Presence of the Sino-US Trade War. *Economic and Political Studies, 7*(2), 217–231.

Irwin, D. A. (2015). *Free Trade Under Fire*. Princeton, NJ: Princeton University Press.

Irwin, D. A. (2017a). *Peddling Protectionism: Smoot-Hawley and the Great Depression*. Princeton, NJ: Princeton University Press.

Irwin, D. A. (2017b). The False Promise of Protectionism: Why Trump's Trade Policy Could Backfire. *Foreign Affairs, 96*(3), 45–56.

Irwin, D. A., Mavroidis, P. C., & Sykes, A. O. (2008). *The Genesis of the GATT*.

Jackson, J. K. (2018). The Economic Effects of Trade: Overview and Policy Challenges. *Congressional Research Service*, 7–5700.

Jwala, K. (2009). Globalization and the Dalits. *The Indian Journal of Political Science, 70*(3), 919–924.

Kahn, J. (2018) Comparing the Bush and Trump Tariffs. *Dartmouth Business Journal*. Retrieved from http://dartmouthbusinessjournal.com/2018/09/04/comparing-bush-trump-tariffs/.

Kellner, D. (2002). Theorizing Globalization. *Sociological Theory, 20*(3), 285–305.

Kelly, N. J. (2020). *America's Inequality Trap*. Chicago, IL: University of Chicago Press.

Kerry, J. F. (2019, November 5). Trump Has Formally Pulled the U.S. Out of the Paris Agreement. This is a Dark Time for America. *The Washington Post*.

Kimberly, A. (2019, December). Trade Wars and their Effect on the Economy and You: Why Trade Wars Are Bad and Nobody Wins. *The Balance*.

Koopman, R., Wang, Z., & Wei, S. J. (2012). Estimating Domestic Content in Exports When Processing Trade is Pervasive. *Journal of Development Economics, 99*(1), 178–189.

Krauthammer, C. (2017, January 26). Trump's Foreign Policy Revolution. *The Washington Post*.

Kuang, Y. (2010). Economic Interdependence and Sino-US Trade Friction: A Study Based on Multi-Stage Trade Model. *Journal of International Trade, 2010*(11), 36–43.

Lai, E. L. C. (2019). The US–China Trade War, the American Public Opinions and Its Effects on China. *Economic and Political Studies, 7*(2), 169–184.

Lake, D. A. (1988). Protection, Retaliation, and Response, 1930–1939. In D. A. Lake (Ed.), *Power, Protection, and Free Trade: International Sources of US Commercial Strategy, 1887–1939*. Ithaca, NY: Cornell University Press.

Lake, D. A., & Weiss, J. C. (2018, September 24). The Trump Administration Wrongly Assumed China Would Capitulate in a Trade War. What Happens Now? *The Washington Post.*

Langdon, F. (1983). Japan–United States Trade Friction: The Reciprocity Issue. *Asian Survey, 23*(5), 653–666.

Lau, L. J., & Tang, J. (2018). *The Impact of US Imports from China on US. Consumer Prices and Expenditures*. IGEF Working PaperNo.66.

Lawder, D. (2018). *IMF Cuts World Economic Growth Forecasts on Tariff War, Emerging Market Strains*. London: Reuters.

Lawrence, S. V. (2013, August). US-China Relations: An overview of policy. In *Congressional Research Service: CRS Report for Congress-Prepared for Members and Committees of Congress* (Vol. 1).

Lawrence, R. Z. (2018). *Five Reasons Why the Focus on Trade Deficits Is Misleading* (No. PB18-6).

Lee, B. A. (1982). The New Deal Reconsidered. *The Wilson Quarterly (1976–), 6*(2), 62–76.

Lee, Y. (2018). Economic Interdependence and Peace: a Case Comparison Between. the US-China and US-Japan Trade Disputes. *East Asia, 35*(3), 215–232.

LeRoy, W. (2019, August, 12). New Figures Show U.S.-China Trade War is Hurting Germany—Europe Economic Motor. *Global News.*

Li, M. (2020). *Profit, Accumulation, and Crisis in Capitalism: Long-term Trends in the UK, US, Japan, and China, 1855–2018*. New York: Routledge.

Li, Q., & Reuveny, R. (2003). Economic Globalization and Democracy: An Empirical Analysis. *British Journal of Political Science, 33*(1), 29–54.

Li, C., He, C., & Lin, C. (2018). Economic Impacts of the Possible China–US Trade War. *Emerging Markets Finance and Trade, 54*(7), 1557–1577.

Liangyu. (2019, June 6). Joint Statement Between China and Russia on the Development of a Comprehensive Strategic and Cooperative Partnership in the New Era. *Xinhua News Agency.*

Lighthizer, R. E. (2020). Trump's Trade Policy Is Making America Stronger. Retrieved May 5, 2020.

Lin, Y. (2019). China's New Era and Sino-US Trade Disputes. *Wuhan University Journal of Social Science, 72*(02), 159–165.

Lind, M. (1994). The Op-Ed History of America. *The National Interest, 37*, 16–28.

Liu, T., & Woo, W. T. (2018). Understanding the US-China Trade War. *China Economic Journal, 11*(3), 319–340.

Lu, H., & Sun, X. (2018). Structural Contradiction and Trump Doctrine: The Dual Motives of Trump Administration's Indo-Pacific Strategy. *Forum of World Economics & Politics, 6*, 1.

Lukin, A. (2019). The US–China Trade War and China's Strategic Future. *Survival, 61*(1), 23–50.

Mandle, J. (2001). Reforming Globalization. *Challenge, 44*(2), 24–38.

Matsushita, M. (1987). A Japanese View of United States Trade Laws. *Northwestern Journal of International Law & Business, 8*, 29.

McDonald, J. A., O'Brien, A. P., & Callahan, C. M. (1997). Trade Wars: Canada's. Reaction to the Smoot-Hawley Tariff. *The Journal of Economic History, 57*(4), 802–826.

McKeown, A. (2007). Periodizing Globalization. *History Workshop Journal, 63*(1), 218–230. Oxford University Press.

Mehta, A. (2020, April 2). Inside US Indo-Pacific Command's $20 Billion Wish List. To Deter China—And Why Congress May Approve It. *Defense News*. Retrieved from https://www.defensenews.com/global/asia-pacific/2020/04/02/inside-us-indo-pacific-commands-20-billion-wish-list-to-deter-china-and-why-congress-may-approve-it/.

Mendes, N. (2017). As relações dos EUA com a China: Uma perspectiva geo-econômica. In *A economia política do governo Obama*. João Pessoa: Editora UFPB.

Mendonça, F., Thomaz, L. F., Lima, T., & Vigevan, T. (2019). *"America first but not alone": uma (nem tão) nova política comercial dos Estados Unidos com Donald Trump, Tempo do mundo/Instituto de Pesquisa Econômica Aplicada*. Brasília, pp. 107–142.

Metzger, S. D. (1962). Trade Expansion Act of 1962. *The Georgetown Law Journal, 51*(3), 425.

Mike, L. (2016). The Deep State: The Fall of the Constitution and the Rise of Shadow Government. *Paperback*.

Moeller, J. O. (2018). *U.S.–China Trade War: Opportunities & Risks for Southeast Asia*. © ISEAS Yusof Ishak Institute. Retrieved from http://hdl.handle.net/11540/8906.

Moisés, N. (2009). Globalization. *Foreign Policy, 171*, 28–30, 32, 34.

Moon, B. E. (2010). *Dilemmas of International Trade* (2nd ed.). New York: Routledge.

Morrison, W. M. (2014). *China-US Trade Issues* (CRS Report for Congress RL33536). Washington, DC: Congressional Research Service.

Morrison, W. M. (2018). *China's Economic Rise: History, Trends, Challenges, and Implications for the United States* (pp. 20–22). Washington, DC: Congressional Research Service.

Morrissey, J. (2017). Geoeconomics in the Long War. *Antipode, 49*, 94–113.

Naggar, T. (1977). Adam Smith's Laissez Faire. *The American Economist, 21*(2), 35–39.

Nascimento, D. F. (2017). TISA/TTIP/TPP and the Exclusion of the BRICS: The Possible Impacts in Brazil. *Revista Contexto Internacional*, 17, 13–22. Rosário, Argentina.

Navarro and Ross (2016). *Scoring the Trump Economic Plan: Trade, Regulatory, & Energy Policy Impacts*. Peterson Institute for International Economics (PIIE), Washington, DC, Disponível em. Retrieved from https://bit.ly/2daD7H3.

Navarro, P., & Autry, G. (2011). *Death by China: Confronting the Dragon—A Global Call to Action*. New York: Pearson Prentice Hall.

Noack, R. (2019, August 7). Germany was Europe's Economic Growth Engine, Trade War Could Drive It To Recession. *The Washington Post*.

Nolan, M. (2011). Gender and Utopian Visions in a Post-Utopian Era: Americanism, Human Rights, Market Fundamentalism. *Central European History, 44*(1), 13–36.

Page, B. I., & Jacobs, L. R. (2009). *Class War: What Americans Really Think About Economic Inequality*. Chicago: University of Chicago Press.

Papagianni, K. (2010). Mediation, Political Engagement, and Peacebuilding. *Global Governance: A Review of Multilateralism and International Organizations, 16*(2), 243–263.

Pashentsev, E. (2020). Coronavirus Pandemics, Huawei 5G Technologies. *Artificial Intelligence and Psychological Operations*. Retrieved from http://www.eurocontinent.eu/2020/04/coronavirus-pandemics-huawei-5g-technologies-artificial-intelligence-and-psychological-operations-evgeny-pashentsev/.

Pham, H. N. A., Ramiah, V., Moosa, N., Huynh, T., & Pham, N. (2018). The Financial Effects of Trumpism. *Economic Modelling, 74*, 264–274.

Piketty, T., & Saez, E. (2006). The Evolution of Top Incomes: A Historical and International Perspective. *American Economic Review, 96*(2), 200–205.

Pooch, M. U. (2016). *DiverCity–Global Cities as a Literary Phenomenon: Toronto, New York, and Los Angeles in a Globalizing Age.* transcript Verlag.

Qian, L. (2017). America Under Trump: Characteristics and Prospects of Domestic. and Foreign Policies. *Contemporary International Relations, 12,* 11.

Qiu, L. D., & Wei, X. (2019). China–US Trade: Implications on Conflicts. *China Economic Journal, 12*(2), 175–194.

Qiu, H., & Zhao, M. (2019). The US Dollar and New Imperialism Under the Logic of Capital Accumulation. *China Political Economy, 2*(1), 98–107.

Redding, S., Amiti, M., & Weinstein, D. (2019). *The Impact of the 2018 Trade War on US Prices and Welfare.* CEP Discussion Papers (1603). Centre for Economic Performance, LSE, London. Retrieved from http://eprints.lse.ac.uk/102619/.

Rimland, B., & Buchan, P. (2020, May 2). Getting the Pacific Deterrence Initiative Right. *The Diplomat.*

Roach, S., & Roach, S. S. (2014). *Unbalanced: The Codependency of America and China.* New Haven, CT: Yale University Press.

Robinson, S., & Thierfelder, K. (2019). Global Adjustment to US Disengagement from the World Trading System. *Journal of Policy Modeling, 41*(3), 522–536.

Rostow, W. W. (1970). The Past Quarter-Century as Economic History and the Tasks of International Economic Organization. *The Journal of Economic History, 30*(1), 150–187.

Rowthorn, R., & Wells, J. (1987). *De-Industrialization Foreign Trade.* Cambridge: Cambridge University Press.

Rubin, A., & Segal, D. (2015). The Effects of Economic Growth on Income. Inequality in the US. *Journal of Macroeconomics, 45,* 258–273.

Rudolph, T. (2019). Populist Anger, Donald Trump, and the 2016 Election. *Journal of Elections, Public Opinion and Parties,* 1–26.

Ruggie, J. G. (1982). International Regimes, Transactions, and Change: Embedded Liberalism in the Postwar Economic Order. *International organization, 36*(2), 379–415.

Ruggie, J. (1994). Trade, Protectionism and the Future of Welfare Capitalism. *Journal of International Affairs, 48*(1), 1–11.

Samuelson, R. (2020, January 1). The New World Order, 2017. *The Washington Post.*

Satapathy, C. (1998). US-EU Trade War Over Bananas. *Economic and Political Weekly, 33*(52), 3303–3304.

Schmucker, C. (2018). *US-China Trade War: Why Germany Should Support EU?* Milan: Itituto Per Gli Studi Di Politica internazionale.

Schulze, D. L. (1985). US-Japan Trade Relations. *Economic and Political Weekly, 20*(28), 1176.

Schwob, C. (2009). Did the Reciprocal Trade Agreements Act of 1934 Initiate a Revolution in the American Trade Policy? *Historical Social Research/Historische Sozialforschung, 34*(4), 130. In Halling, T., Fehlemann, S., & Voegele, J. (2009). *Premature Death and Patterns of Identity and Meaning from a Historical Perspective*, 377–379.

Semin, A. N., Kostyaev, A. I., Truba, A. S., Ponkratov, V. V., & Gagarina, M. V. (2019). Economic Ramifications of China–United States Trade War for the Russian Federation. *China Economic Journal, 12*(3), 316–335. https://doi.org/10.1080/17538963.2019.1591573.

Shank, G. (1994). Japan—US Trade War? *Social Justice, 21*(2 (56)), 20–23.

Sheng, L. (2010). Growth–Volatility Tradeoff in the Face of Financial Openness: A Perspective of Developing Economies. *Cambridge Review of International Affairs, 23*(4), 609–622.

Sheng, L. (2011a). A Political Economy Approach to Foreign Investment and Local Welfare. *The Social Sciences Journal, 48*(1), 52–71.

Sheng, L. (2011b). Theorising Free Capital Mobility: The Perspective of Developing Countries. *Review of International Studies*, 2519–2534.

Sheng, L. (2012). Dealing with Financial Risks of International Capital Flows: A Theoretical Framework. *Cambridge Review of International Affairs, 25*(3), 463–474.

Sheng, L. (2013). Free Capital Mobility and Sustainable Community Development: A Theoretical Framework. *Habitat International, 40*(4), 278–284.

Sheng, L. (2014a). Economic Structure, Cost Outsourcing and Global Imbalances. *The Journal of Australian Political Economy, 74*, 81.

Sheng, L. (2014b). Income Inequality, Financial Systems, and Global Imbalances: A Theoretical Consideration. *Global Policy, 5*(3), 311–320.

Sheng, L. (2015a). Theorizing Global Imbalances: A Perspective on Savings and Inequality. *Cambridge Review of International Affairs, 28*(2), 191–204.

Sheng, L. (2015b). Theorizing Income Inequality in the Face of Financial Globalization. *The Social Science Journal, 52*(3), 415–424.

Sheng, L. (2016). Explaining US-China Economic Imbalances: A Social Perspective. *Cambridge Review of International Affairs, 29*(3), 1097–1111.

Sheng, L., & Gao, J. (2018). Foreign Investors Versus Host Communities: An Urban Political Economy Model for Tourist Cities. *Argumenta Oeconomica, 41*(2), 257–275.

Sheng, L., Zhao, H., & Zhao, J. (2019). Why Will Trump Lose the Trade War? *China Economic Journal, 12*(2), 137–159.

Spence, M., Katz, R., & Lawrence, R. Z. (2011). Manufacturing Globalization: The Real Sources of US Inequality and Unemployment. *Foreign Affairs, 90*(6), 166–171.

Staff, R. (2020). *Chinese, U.S. Military Chief Hold Crisis Communication.* London: Reuters.

Stallings, B. (2007). The Globalization of Capital Flows: Who Benefits? *The Annals of the American Academy of Political and Social Science, 610*(1), 201–216.

Stiglitz, J., & Greenwald, B. (2014). *Creating a Learning Society: A New Paradigm. for Development and Social Progress.* New York: Columbia University Press.

Stone, C., Trisi, D., Sherman, A., & Debot, B. (2015). *A Guide to Statistics on Historical Trends in Income Inequality.* Center on Budget and Policy Priorities, 26.

Sukar, A., & Ahmed, S. (2019). Rise of Trade Protectionism: The Case of US-Sino Trade War. *Transnational Corporations Review, 11*(4), 279–289.

Tan, H. (2019, August 9). US Soybean Farmers are Working New Markets Now that Exports to China Have Tanked. *CNBC.*

Van Neuss, L. (2018). Globalization and Deindustrialization in Advanced Countries. *Structural Change and Economic Dynamics, 45*, 49–63.

Vlados, C. M. (2020). The Dynamics of the Current Global Restructuring and. Contemporary Framework of the US–China Trade War. *Global Journal of Emerging Market Economies, 10*(1–3), 11–24.

Walker, H. (1964). Dispute Settlement: The Chicken War. *The American Journal of International Law, 58*(3), 671–685.

Walling, K. F. (2018). The United States, China, and Thucydides's Many, Many Traps. *Naval War College Review, 17*(1), 152–158. Reviewed Naval War College Review Allison, G. (2017). *Destined for War: Can America and China Escape Thucydides's Trap?.* Houghton Mifflin Harcourt.

Walters, R. (2019, September 29). Is a U.S.-China Trade Deal Possible? *National Interest.*

Wang, Z., & Zeng, J. (2020). From Economic Cooperation to Strategic Competition: Understanding the US-China Trade Disputes through the Transformed Relations. *Journal of Chinese Political Science, 25*(1), 49–69.

Whineray, D. (2020). *The G2 at the UN: United States and the People's Republic of China at the United Nations Before COVID-19*. New York: United Nations University.

Wigell, M. (2016). Conceptualizing Regional Powers' Geoeconomic Strategies: Neo-Imperialism, Neo-Mercantilism, Hegemony, and Liberal Institutionalism. *Asia Europe Journal, 14*(2), 135–151.

Wolff, E. N. (2017). *Household Wealth Trends in the United States, 1962 to 2016: Has Middle Class Wealth Recovered?* (No. w24085). National Bureau of Economic Research.

Wong, D, & Koty, A. C. (2020, August 25). The US-China Trade War: A Timeline, China Briefing. Retrieved from https://www.china-briefing.com/news/the-us-china-trade-war-a-timeline/.

Wright, G. (2018). The Political Implications of American Concerns About Economic Inequality. *Political Behavior, 40*, 321–343.

Xia, Y., Kong, Y., Ji, Q., & Zhang, D. (2019). Impacts of China-US Trade Conflicts on the Energy Sector. *China Economic Review, 58*, 101360.

Yan, X. (2010). The Instability of China–US Relations. *The Chinese Journal of International Politics, 3*, 263–292.

Yin, J. (2017). An Analysis of Trump's Political Personality and Policy. Preference. *Contemporary International Relations, 2*, 15–22.

Yu, T. (2004). Reasons for Sino-US Trade Friction and Countermeasures. *Management World, 2004*(09), 67–72.

Yu, M., & Zhang, R. (2019). Understanding the Recent Sino-US Trade Conflict. *China Economic Journal, 12*(2), 160–174.

Zeng, J., & Breslin, S. (2016). China's 'New Type of Great Power Relations': A G2 with Chinese Characteristics? *International Affairs, 92*(4), 773–794.

Zhang, Y. (2018). Trump Administration's Foreign Trade Policy and Sino-US Trade Game. *Foreign Affairs Review, 35*(03), 12–36.

Zheng, Z. (2018). Sino-US Trade Friction Seen from Sino-US Trade Structure. *China Business and Market, 32*(10), 80–92.

Documents and News Reports

2018 National Defense Strategy (NDS). US Government.

Brookings. (2019, November 15). *Taxing Capital Income: Mark-to-Market and Other Approaches*.

Canada Claims to Have a Third Rapeseed Exportter's Chinese Business in Trouble. (2019, April 3). Reuters.

Canada Suspends All Meat Expoerts to China at China's Request. (2019, June 27). *Street Journal.*

Canola is Banned by China, Canada Has Limited Options, Voice of America. (2019, April 3).

Center for China & Globalization Report. (2018*). Understanding the US-China Trade War: Analyses and CCG Recommendations.* Retrieved from http://en.ccg.org.cn/html/publications/2362.html.

Congressional Research Service. (2020, April 24). *U.S.-China Strategic Competition in South and East China Seas: Background and Issues for Congress.* Retrieved from https://crsreports.congress.gov.

Department of Defense. (2019, June 1). *Indo-Pacific Strategy Report: Preparedness, Partnerships, and Promoting a Networked Region.*

Financial Times. (2019, November). Why US Farmers Are Falling Out of Love with Trump.

Industrial Analytics Platform. (2019). What Are Global Value Chains and Why Do They. Matter? Retrieved from https://iap.unido.org/articles/what-are-global-value-chains-and-why-do-they-matter.

OECD. Quarterly International Trade Statistics, Volume 2018 Issue 4.

Posture Statement of Admiral Craig S. (2019, February 7). Faller Commander, United States Southern Command Before the 116th Congress Senate Armed Services Committee.

Posture Statement of Admiral Philip S. (2019, February 12). Davidson, U.S. Navy Commander, U.S. Indo-Pacific Command Before the Senate Armed Services Committee on U.S. Indo-Pacific Command Posture.

President Hoover on the Hawley-Smoot Tariff Act of 1930, Advocate of Peace Through Justice, 191–193, Sage Publications, Inc.

Russian Trade with China in 2018, Russian Foreign Trade. (2019, February 10).

Tax Policy Center. (2017, December). Distributional Analysis of the Conference Agreement. For. *The Tax Cuts and Jobs Act.*

The Strenghening of China-Russia Comprehensive Strategic Cooperation Arouses Concern in the United States. (2019, April 1). Voice of America.

The White House. (2017). National Security Strategy, Washington, p. 3.

U.S. Department of State. (2020, July 23). Communist China and the Free World's Future. Retrieved from https://www.state.gov/communist-china-and-the-free-worlds-future/.

US Secretary of Defense. (2019, May 2). Annual Report to Congress: Military and. Security Developments Involving the People's Republic of China. Retrieved from https://media.defense.gov/2019/May/02/2002127082/-1/-1/1/2019_CHINA_MILITARY_POWER_REPORT.pdf.

USTR. (2019). Trade Policy Agenda and 2018 Annual Report of the President of the United States on the Trade Agreements Program.Xinhua Português. (2020, March 3). Fatos e dados: Progressos econômicos e sociais. da China em 2019. Retrieved from http://portuguese.xinhuanet.com/2020-03/02/c_138835771.htm.

The manufacturer's authorised representative in the EU is Springer Nature Customer Service Centre GmbH, Europaplatz 3, 69115 Heidelberg, Germany. If you have any concerns regarding our products, please contact ProductSafety@springernature.com

Printed and bound by CPI Group (UK) Ltd, Croydon, CR0 4YY
30/09/2026
02225325-0001